Praise for *Nowhere to Go*

Also by the author

Ethical Issues in Medicine
The Death of Psychiatry
Why Did You Do That?
Schizophrenia and Civilization
Witchdoctors and Psychiatrists
The Roots of Treason: Ezra Pound and the Secret of St. Elizabeths
Care of the Seriously Mentally Ill: A Rating of State Programs
Surviving Schizophrenia: A Family Manual

NOWHERE TO GO

The Tragic Odyssey

of the Homeless

Mentally Ill

E. FULLER TORREY, M.D.

PERENNIAL LIBRARY

HARPER & ROW, PUBLISHERS, New York
Grand Rapids, Philadelphia, St. Louis, San Francisco
London, Singapore, Sydney, Tokyo

A hardcover edition of this book is published by Harper & Row, Publishers, Inc.

Permissions acknowledgments appear on pages xv–xvi.

First PERENNIAL LIBRARY edition published 1989

Designed by Helen L. Granger/Levavi & Levavi

Library of Congress Cataloging-in-Publication Data

Torrey, E. Fuller (Edwin Fuller), 1937–
  Nowhere to go.

  "Perennial Library."
  Bibliography: p.
  Includes index.
  1. Mentally ill—Care—United States. 2. Homelessness—United States. I. Title.
RA790.6.T67 1988   362.2′08806942   88-45065
ISBN 0-06-091597-8 (pbk.)

89 90 91 92 93 CC/FG 10 9 8 7 6 5 4 3 2 1

For Robert L. Taylor and Sidney M. Wolfe,
valued colleagues and esteemed friends

"The dead, they got all the eyes."
                    —WILLIAM KENNEDY, *IRONWEED*

Between the conception
And the creation
Between the emotion
And the response
Falls the Shadow

Life is very long

—T. S. ELIOT, "THE HOLLOW MEN"

About the Author

A clinical and research psychiatrist in Washington, D.C., Dr. Torrey specializes in schizophrenia. He was from 1970 to 1975 a special assistant to the director of the National Institute of Mental Health and from 1976 to 1984 a staff psychiatrist at St. Elizabeths Hospital. For five years he has also run a clinic for mentally ill homeless women. He has written extensively about mental illness, contributing to both professional journals and lay publications and appearing on such programs as "Donahue" and "60 Minutes." His more recent books include *Witchdoctors and Psychiatrists, Schizophrenia and Civilization, Surviving Schizophrenia: A Family Manual,* and *The Roots of Treason: Ezra Pound and the Secret of St. Elizabeths,* which was nominated by the National Book Critics Circle as one of the five best biographies of 1983. He was twice awarded Commendation Medals by the United States Public Health Service and was given the Special Friends Award in 1984 by the National Alliance for the Mentally Ill.

Contents

Illustrations

Preface

For many afternoons I sat in the Library of Congress reading the congressional hearings out of which came the National Institute of Mental Health, the Joint Commission on Mental Illness and Health, and community mental health centers. The hearings were filled with promises of better services for the mentally ill—humane, close to home, high-quality services. No longer would unfortunate individuals have to spend cruel years in state mental hospitals—the era of "mental health" had arrived. Sound of trumpets!

Then I would go downstairs to the Library's coffee room. It was usually half filled with mentally ill individuals who had been deinstitutionalized. They were seeking shelter, warmth, company. Over in the corner sat a man whom I remembered as an inpatient at St. Elizabeths Hospital; on medication he had functioned well, but now, living in the community, he had not had medication for months and he sat talking to invisible voices. A family touring Washington from the Midwest was trying to avoid the friendly importunities of an obviously psychotic, bizarrely dressed man surrounded by bulging plastic bags. The mother and father looked embarrassed, the older children looked confused, but the youngest child just kept staring at the man. She did not know enough not to; he probably looked like the clown in her picture books. I wondered how the parents would explain this man to their children.

I thought of what Mike Gorman, that dedicated advocate for the mentally ill, had told me: "No matter how bad it is for those people on the streets, it's better than it was in the hospital." Are these really the only choices we have for individuals who cannot care for themselves—the brutality of hospitals or the brutality of the streets? Is this the best we can do in the wealthiest nation in the world? I felt both anger and sadness to be living in such a nation.

Writing this book has taken me on wild swings between anger and sadness. It has brought back memories of visits to Lincoln Hospital Mental Health Services when it was thought to be the hope for the future, of seminars with my colleagues on community psychiatry when it promised to change the world, of five years working at the National Institute of Mental Health when it was claimed that all things were possible. How could things have gone so wrong? What combination of chutzpah and hubris unraveled our skein of good intent? And, above all, how can we explain our mistakes to the people who have paid such a terrible price for them?

Dr. Donald Langsley, one of the early advocates of the mental health movement, captured the essence of the lost era cogently when he wrote: "Those of us who were once so enthusiastic now weep a little as we look backwards at what has happened to the promising child of the 1960s and early 1970s."

Acknowledgments

I am indebted to many for their kind assistance in writing this book. The librarians at St. Elizabeths Hospital and the Library of Congress were unfailingly helpful. James Stockdill, Charles Windle, and Harry Schnibbe offered useful comments on earlier drafts. Ted Lutterman and Ron Manderscheid reviewed the fiscal data in Appendix B. Camille Callahan and Judy Miller typed the manuscript. Carol Cohen provided editorial assistance. And my wife, Barbara, contributed her usual constructive criticism and encouragement.

I am also grateful to the following:

The American Psychological Association for permission to reprint excerpts from the *American Psychologist.*

The American Psychiatric Association for permission to reprint excerpts from the *American Journal of Psychiatry* and *Hospital and Community Psychiatry.*

The American Sociological Association for permission to reprint excerpts from the *Journal of Health and Social Behavior.*

Human Sciences Press for permission to reprint excerpts from the *Community Mental Health Journal.*

The American Medical Association for permission to reprint excerpts from *Archives of General Psychiatry* 18:257–66, 1968, copyright 1968, American Medical Association.

Williams and Wilkins Inc. for permission to reprint excerpts from the *Journal of Nervous and Mental Diseases* 40:753–57, 1913, copyright 1913, Williams and Wilkins.

Harcourt Brace Jovanovich, Inc., for permission to reprint from "The Hollow Men" in *Collected Poems 1909–1962* by T. S. Eliot, copyright 1936 by Harcourt Brace Jovanovich, Inc.; copyright 1963, 1964 by T. S. Eliot. Reprinted by permission of the publisher.

Mike Gorman for permission to quote from his book *Every Other Bed.*

Dimensions of a Disaster

ife magazine told it all in two issues exactly thirty-five years
apart.

May 6, 1946. "Bedlam 1946: Most U.S. Mental Hospitals Are a
Shame and a Disgrace." The author, Albert Q. Maisel, shocked
America with an indictment of the nation's mental hospitals
more graphic and damning than anything previously published.
The states, he said, had allowed their institutions for the mentally
ill "to degenerate into little more than concentration camps on
the Belsen pattern." Conditions in the hospitals were said to be
atrocious, with the quality of food being "what is usually found
in most garbage cans" and food sometimes simply thrown on the
table with "the patients expected to grab it as animals would."
Hospitals were described with *no* trained nurses at all and in
which attendants, who had had no training, regularly gave medication to patients without orders from a physician.

The *Life* article contained excerpts from reports of conscientious objectors who had worked as attendants in the hospitals in
place of doing military service; such reports and court records,
it said, documented "scores of deaths of patients following beat-

ings by attendants." Descriptions of such beatings were included from the reports of the conscientious objectors, including one in which a handcuffed patient had been kicked by the attendants in the back of the neck as well as "in the genitals which caused the victim to scream and roll in agony."

What was most shocking, however, was the pictures that accompanied the article—pictures of wards of completely naked patients, pictures of wards with beds so tightly packed that the floor was not visible, and especially a large, haunting, three-quarter-page picture that looked like a drawing done by William Blake to illustrate Dante's *Inferno*. The picture was captioned: "These Byberry [Philadelphia State Hospital] male patients are left to live day after day sitting naked on refuse-covered floors without exercise or diversion." It was the kind of picture that stayed with the reader long after that issue of *Life* had been discarded. It was the type of picture that would fundamentally change the venue, but not the manner, in which the seriously mentally ill are treated in America.

May 1981. "Emptying the Madhouse: The Mentally Ill Have Become Our Cities' Lost Souls." Without referring to the article of thirty-five years earlier, *Life* described in words and pictures the fate of patients who had been deinstitutionalized from state mental hospitals. There was William Hopkins, shown walking down a street in Springfield, Massachusetts, "hallucinating between fleeting moments of clarity, butting his head against store windows, pounding his forehead until it bleeds." He had been admitted to and discharged from Northampton State Hospital ten separate times.

Then there were pictures of Neal and Rita DeLuck, both discharged from the same mental hospital. Neal, diagnosed with schizophrenia, had been in and out of hospitals twenty-nine times, a classic revolving-door case. Neal and Rita were pictured living in an unheated attic of a halfway house run by another ex-patient. According to the article, both Neal and Rita had body lice and neither had changed clothes in two months. They described themselves as "two happenstance nuts who cling together." Neal occasionally became violent because of his untreated illness and had once broken Rita's jaw. Despite this Rita claimed that "all I have in the world is to look after him [and] empty his piss bottle . . . If he dies, I'll kill myself." The article asserted that two-thirds of similar individuals living in Springfield who needed psychiatric care were receiving none. The fate of such individuals was summarized by a psychiatrist who observed: "The majority get dumped amid the broken promises."

"Broken promises" is in fact the motto of America's psychiatric establishment for the past forty years. The professionals promised to improve the lot of the seriously mentally ill, abused and neglected in the nation's asylums. Deinstitutionalization it would

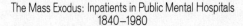

The Mass Exodus: Inpatients in Public Mental Hospitals
1840–1980

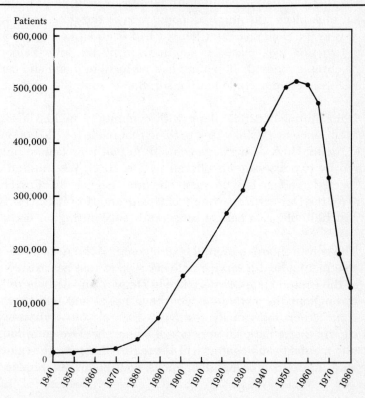

be called, officially defined by the Director of the National Institute of Mental Health as "(1) the prevention of inappropriate mental hospital admissions through the provision of community alternatives for treatment, (2) the release to the community of all institutionalized patients who have been given adequate preparation for such a change, and (3) the establishment and maintenance of community support systems for noninstitutionalized people receiving mental health services in the community."

So what happened? Certainly nothing remotely resembling the definition of deinstitutionalization given above. Instead, the seriously mentally ill were dumped out of mental hospitals into communities with few facilities and little aftercare. And as soon as they were gone, the hospitals were closed down so that they could not return. Rather than deinstitutionalization, which implied that alternative community facilities would be provided, what took place was simply depopulation of the state hospitals. It was as if a policy of resettlement had been agreed upon but only eviction took place. As summarized by Dr. John Talbott, "the chronic mentally ill patient had his locus of living and care transferred from a single lousy institution to multiple wretched ones."

Deinstitutionalization, along with community mental health centers, once had a shiny ring to them that made people hopeful and proud. How far we have come from that time can be measured by two assessments offered by Dr. H. G. Whittington, a respected psychiatrist who was at one time the director of psychiatry for the Denver Department of Health and Hospitals. Testifying in 1969 before a Senate subcommittee Whittington said:

The comprehensive mental health center is the most effective mental health service delivery system that has existed in the United States. Experience in Denver, and elsewhere, throughout the nation—as you have heard and will hear from other individuals testifying before you—indicates clearly that a national network of comprehensive community mental health centers will assure care that is more available, more comprehensive, more continuous, of higher quality, and genuinely of more usefulness to our citizens than that provided by any preexisting system.

Fourteen years later Dr. Whittington assessed the community mental health center movement as he had seen it evolve:

> I was already beginning to feel very much like a parent must feel who has a badly handicapped child. Should I smother it in its sleep, or should I help the poor little deformed bastard grow up to do the best it can in life? The deformed creature that has developed from the original community mental health center movement does not arouse much enthusiasm in any of us, I am sure, who had some more grandiose visions.

Deinstitutionalization has become, in the words of a *New York Times* editorial, "a cruel embarrassment, a reform gone terribly wrong."

How bad are the effects of the policy of deinstitutionalization— a policy that affects an estimated two million seriously mentally ill people in the United States? Here are eight aspects of the problem.

1. There are at least twice as many seriously mentally ill individuals living on streets and in shelters as there are in public mental hospitals.

2. There are increasing numbers of seriously mentally ill individuals in the nation's jails and prisons.

3. Seriously mentally ill individuals are regularly released from hospitals with little or no provision for aftercare or follow-up treatment.

4. Violent acts perpetrated by untreated mentally ill individuals are increasing in number.

5. Housing and living conditions for mentally ill individuals in the community are grossly inadequate.

6. Community mental health centers, originally funded to provide community care for the mentally ill so these individuals

would no longer have to go to state mental hospitals, are almost complete failures.

7. Laws designed to protect the rights of the seriously mentally ill primarily protect their right to remain mentally ill.

8. The majority of mentally ill individuals discharged from hospitals have been officially lost. Nobody knows where they are.

1. *There are at least twice as many seriously mentally ill individuals living on streets and in shelters as there are in public mental hospitals.*

The problem of the homeless floated slowly into the nation's consciousness in the early 1980s. Isolated editorials progressed to news stories of fasts, sleep-ins on grates, the involvement of Hollywood stars, and bag-lady-chic clothing styles. Cornell University began offering a course on how to manage public shelters for the homeless. Lily Tomlin added a bag lady skit to her comedy routine. Bhagwan Shree Rajneesh courted homeless persons for his ranch in Oregon so he could register them to vote in local elections. The homeless had truly arrived.

From the beginning there has been a spirited debate about who the homeless are. There is no question that large numbers of them became homeless because of gentrification of inner cities and the concomitant decrease in numbers of rental units for low-income families. Nor is there any doubt that some of the homeless are recently released denizens of jails who need a place to stay, newly arrived immigrants with no resources, alcoholics and drug addicts who spend their rent money getting high, and simply lazy individuals who will do anything to avoid working.

Nor is there any question that many of them are mentally ill. Defenders of public mental health programs have minimized this number, while critics of the programs have maximized it.

Ms. S., living in a shelter in Washington, D.C., was hospitalized in 1984 at St. Elizabeths Hospital because of her clearly psychotic behavior (crawling on the street on her hands and knees, running in front of cars, eating eggs shell and all). She was diagnosed with schizophrenia and her condition improved modestly with antipsychotic medication over the next eight months. Either because of her illness or her personality traits she was not fully cooperative with hospital routines, often refusing to attend scheduled activities. One day she was told by the staff that if she refused to go to occupational therapy she would be discharged. She did refuse, and was discharged the same day. She was escorted from the ward wearing a cotton dress, thin sweater, and sneakers, but no underclothing or socks; the temperature was projected to go below freezing that night. She was given a list of shelters, a week's supply of medicine, and told to make her own appointment for aftercare. The next day, when I evaluated her in a shelter, she was still markedly psychotic.

There is now a reasonably good consensus that approximately one-third of homeless individuals are seriously mentally ill. (The definition of "serious mental illness" usually used in such assessments includes schizophrenia and manic-depressive psychosis, also known as bipolar disorder, but does not include alcoholism or drug addiction.) Estimates, however, vary depending on the city. In a 1986 survey of cities done by the United States Conference of Mayors, the percentage of the homeless population estimated to have "chronic mental illness" (excluding alcohol and drug abuses) varied from 60 percent in Louisville to 45 percent in San Francisco and Salt Lake City; 40 percent in Minneapolis, Charleston, and Seattle; 25 percent in New York City and Phoenix; 20 percent in Cleveland; and 15 percent in Philadelphia, Los Angeles, and New Orleans. Direct psychiatric assessment of individuals living in shelters for the homeless has been more consistent; for example, studies in Washington, Boston, and Philadelphia all found that between 36 and 39 percent of the homeless suffered from schizophrenia. A 1988 study of homeless individuals in Los Angeles reported that 44 percent of them had had a psychiatric hospitalization.

When one moves out of the shelters and looks exclusively at individuals living on the streets, those with serious mental illnesses make up more than one-third. A study of individuals living on heating grates and in doorways, alleys, and abandoned buildings in New York City found "that 60 percent exhibit evidence of schizophrenia as manifested by disorganized behavior and chronic delusional thinking." Prior to deinstitutionalization, these people would have been treated in public mental hospitals.

> I first saw Ms. Z. in a women's shelter in Washington. She was extremely paranoid and delusional but acknowledged that she had been married to a professional man and had raised several children. She refused to take medication. She left the shelter, and I next heard that she had been living on the mezzanine of National Airport for several months; it was apparently the only place she felt safe from Israeli secret agents who she believed were injecting her in her sleep and were responsible for her voices. One of her daughters, on her way back from college, accidentally discovered her mother at the airport.

If a minimum of one-third of the homeless in the United States are seriously mentally ill—mostly with schizophrenia—then what is their total number? The answer to this depends on the total number of homeless in the United States, a number that has been widely debated. A well-publicized estimate by the United States Department of Housing and Urban Development was 350,000 individuals, although many experts think this estimate is too low. In New York City alone there are said to be at least 40,000 homeless individuals, including several hundred living in subway tunnels beneath the city. A 1988 survey of the homeless by the Urban Institute in Washington estimated the total homeless population at between 567,000 and 600,000. Some advocates for the homeless have claimed that the total number is over one million, but there are no data to support such a figure. If a relatively conservative estimate of 450,000 homeless individuals is used, and this is multiplied by the one-third who have serious mental illnesses (excluding alcohol and drug problems), then there are approximately 150,000 seriously mentally ill individuals in the United States living on streets and in shelters. The *total* patient population of all public mental hospitals in the United States was 116,136 in 1984; this included all diagnoses, from alcohol and drug problems to 59,582 individuals diagnosed with schizophrenia. In view of the above it seems likely that there are now at least twice as many seriously mentally ill individuals living on streets and in shelters as there are in public mental hospitals.

When I saw Mr. A. I hardly recognized him. He had been sleeping in fields and abandoned barns for several months. His clothing and hygiene betrayed his chronic psychotic state. He agreed to meet me outside the District of Columbia line, saying that he could not go into the District because the FBI might pick him up. He believed they had implanted electrodes in his brain, which he heard as voices, so he had to be careful. He refused all offers of medication. I remembered him as one of the leaders of my graduating class at Princeton University, a young man with an obviously bright future.

There is also evidence that the segment of the homeless population with serious mental illnesses is continuing to increase. A study from Ohio published in 1988 showed that 36 percent of patients discharged from state mental hospitals had become homeless within six months. In Massachusetts a study of discharged psychiatric patients published in 1989 revealed that 27 percent were occasionally or predominantly homeless within a six-month period. The numbers continue to grow daily. The vast hordes of mentally ill homeless persons are tragic by any measure. Crowded into public shelters they look like displaced persons or refugees from a war, which in fact they are. The generals in the war were mental health professionals and administrators who convinced the nation that deinstitutionalization would work. It did not, and the psychiatric refugees bear mute testimony to its outcome.

It is useful to compare the present situation to that which

existed in the early years of the nineteenth century. At that time there was a public outcry about the large number of obviously mentally ill and retarded individuals who were residing untreated in poorhouses, as they were called, and jails. The humane thing was to build hospitals for them, it was said. Our current public shelters are the equivalent of the poorhouses of nineteenth century America; we have returned to the point of our departure. As summarized by one psychiatrist: "The shame of the states in the first part of this century [has become] the shame of the streets in the last part of the century."

The ultimate irony for the homeless mentally ill can be found in New York City. During the 1960s and '70s, many buildings at Manhattan State Hospital were closed as patients were deinstitutionalized. As the number of homeless individuals in the city climbed rapidly, however, one of these buildings was reopened as a men's shelter, operated on a city contract by the Volunteers of America. Some of the same mentally ill individuals who once used that building as hospitalized patients now use it as shelter residents. The difference is that now there are no nurses, no doctors, no medication, and no treatment.

> The man called himself Joe No Name and was living in a doorway in Philadelphia. He admitted that he had been in a psychiatric hospital many times. An observer visited him regularly over six months, trying to gain his trust and persuade him to accept help. On one occasion Joe "reached out and asked if I would touch the tip of his finger so he could see if I was real or 'just part of the electric current in the wires above.'" He refused to go to a shelter because "to go inside would mean instant death." One night he suddenly disappeared and was not seen again.

Living on the streets or in shelters as a rational, sane person with a normally functioning brain must be a difficult task. To attempt to do so with a brain which is not functioning normally—with illogical thought processes, delusional ideas, and intermittent auditory hallucinations—must be a circle of Hell unimagined even in medieval times.

2. *There are increasing numbers of seriously mentally ill individuals in the nation's jails and prisons.*

In 1985 there were about 750,000 individuals in the jails and prisons of the United States. Evidence has accumulated in recent years that an increasing proportion of these prisoners is seriously mentally ill and prior to deinstitutionalization would have been treated in mental hospitals. It is likely, in fact, that there are now more seriously mentally ill persons in jails and prisons than at any time since the early nineteenth century. It was in part a reaction to such inhumane conditions that led to the building of state mental hospitals, as we have noted.

> In 1987 a 29-year-old woman, arrested for breaking an antenna off a car, gave birth to a baby in a cell of the Erie County Holding Center, a county jail in Buffalo. Nobody, including the woman, was aware that she had been eight months pregnant. She was known to be seriously psychotic, and at the time of the birth screamed loudly to the guards to get the "animal" out of her clothing. By the time the guards retrieved the baby it was dead. At the time the jail was estimated to be holding more seriously mentally ill persons, approximately ninety, than was the psychiatric unit of the Erie County Medical Center.

How many prisoners are seriously mentally ill? Reports vary from 5 percent to 20 percent. In Denver, 5 percent of newly arrived county jail inmates were found to be psychotic; in another study in the same jail, 14 percent of the inmates were said to have had prior psychiatric inpatient care. A study of five county jails in California found that 6.7 percent of the prisoners were psychotic; a similar study in the Los Angeles County Jail reported a figure of 7.8 percent. Another study, of convicted federal prisoners, concluded that 8 percent were psychotic, and this same percentage of "severe psychiatric or functional disabili-

11

ties" was reported for New York State prison inmates. In Oklahoma, 10 percent of prisoners were found to be severely disturbed, while a 1987 study of inmates in Michigan prisons reported that "20 percent of the state's 19,000 convicts suffered from severe mental impairment, meaning delusions, hallucinations, and loss of contact with reality." If overall 9 percent of the nation's 750,000 prisoners suffer from serious mental illnesses (not including alcohol and drug problems) then that number, 67,500, would approximately equal the number of people with serious mental illnesses in the nation's public mental hospitals.

> Timothy Waldrop, 24 years old and who had been
> voted the friendliest boy in his high school graduating
> class, had been treated for schizophrenia for several
> years. He was arrested for armed robbery and
> sentenced to five years in the Georgia state prison. In
> prison his antipsychotic medication was stopped; "a
> few days later Waldrop gouged out his left eye with his
> fingers." Despite resuming his medication he then cut
> his scrotum with a razor and, while in restraints,
> "punctured his right eye with a fingernail leaving
> himself totally blind."

Jail and prison officials throughout the United States report that the number of seriously mentally ill prisoners has increased sharply as the nation's mental hospitals have been emptied. In Fairfax County, Virginia, "Sheriff Wayne Huggins estimates that between 35 and 40 percent of those in jail need treatment for mental disorders and between 15 and 17 percent need it immediately." In his eight years in office, Sheriff Huggins observed, "the situation has become worse because it's becoming increasingly difficult to get a person institutionalized." In neighboring Arlington County, Sheriff James A. Gondles noted that "the number of mentally ill persons in the Arlington jail has been increasing each year—the result of . . . laws that prohibit the courts from committing a person for treatment unless he is judged a danger to himself or others." Across the Potomac River, in the District of Columbia jail, it is estimated that 20 percent of the inmates are mentally ill. Most of them have previously been hospitalized at St. Elizabeths Hospital.

> Wayne B., a 31-year-old man who has been afflicted with paranoid schizophrenia since age 17, responds well to antipsychotic medication. He was under my care for four years and, on medication, was able to share an apartment with three other released patients and hold a half-time job. Then his outpatient care was transferred to a local community mental health center, which simply dropped him from its rolls when Mr. B. did not keep an appointment. He ran out of medication and was lost to follow-up until three months later when he was arrested for stabbing a neighbor who he thought was trying to hurt him. Mr. B. is now serving a long sentence in the District of Columbia jail.

In addition to the increased number of mentally ill prisoners who have been charged or convicted of serious crimes as a direct consequence of grossly inadequate outpatient psychiatric care, there has also been a sharp increase in mentally ill prisoners charged with petty crimes just to get them off the streets. This has been referred to as the criminalization of psychosis. In extreme examples, patients may be arrested by police officers on the grounds of mental hospitals. In Erie County, New York, a total of seventy-two psychiatric patients (two-thirds with psychoses) were arrested during 1982 on the grounds of Buffalo State Psychiatric Center and three general hospitals with psychiatric units; 61 percent of the patients were charged with trespassing. Such arrests, which overload the criminal justice system, are often used by authorities because restrictive commitment laws make it impossible to control difficult patients any other way. Like a hydraulic pump, the reduction in state mental hospital beds has triggered an increase in jail and prison beds.

> George Wooten, age 32, was booked into the Denver County Jail in 1984 for his one hundredth time. He had been diagnosed with schizophrenia at age 17 and

developed a fondness for sniffing paint, after which he creates "a disturbance" and the police arrest him. According to a newspaper account: "Eight years ago the officers might have taken Wooten to a community mental health center, a place that was supposed to help the chronically mentally ill. But now they don't bother . . . Police have become cynical about the whole approach. They have learned that 'two hours later [those arrested] are back on the street . . . the circle of sending the person to a mental health center doesn't work.' "

The vast majority of mentally ill prisoners would not be in jail or prison if a rational system of psychiatric care existed for them. For example, one study in San Francisco's courts of "almost 500 defendants in need of psychiatric treatment" found that they averaged three prior psychiatric hospitalizations. At the time of their arrest, "94 percent were not involved in any outpatient program." In a plaintive if understated conclusion, the author of the study asks: "If continued outpatient treatment could prevent this behavior and prevent its costly and tragic consequences, it is important to ask why community mental health programs cannot keep these patients under their umbrella of services."

3. *Seriously mentally ill individuals are regularly released from hospitals with little or no provision for aftercare or follow-up treatment.*

The revolving door has become the symbol of care for the seriously mentally ill in the 1980s. A 1982 survey of psychiatric inpatients in New York City found that 24 percent of them had ten or more previous psychiatric admissions.

Probably the best description of what happens to many mentally ill individuals once they leave the hospital was written by Susan Sheehan in her award-winning book, *Is There No Place on Earth for Me?* Sheehan follows the saga of Sylvia Frumkin (a pseudonym) as she migrates through a total of forty-five "treatment settings" over eighteen years, including twenty-seven readmissions to eight different hospitals. It is like a medieval pilgrimage, which goes on year after year, with hardships endured in order to attain grace. Unfortunately for the mentally ill, the best they can hope for from their involuntary pilgrimage is survival.

> Alan P. was admitted to St. Elizabeths Hospital for the twenty-seventh time in twelve years with a diagnosis of chronic schizophrenia. He invariably responded well to antipsychotic medication and improved markedly on medication within three weeks. He was then discharged to live in the community, given medication for two weeks and strong admonitions to keep his outpatient appointment at a local community mental health center. He had no insight into his illness or his need for medication, however, and usually discarded the pills in a trash can en route to his boarding house. Slowly over the ensuing weeks his behavior would become increasingly bizarre as his psychosis returned. The community mental health center simply crossed his name off its list when he failed to come for his scheduled appointment. His most recent admission was precipitated by an arrest for disorderly conduct; he had alarmed tourists by standing in the pool next to the Lincoln Memorial and picking apart dead pigeons.

A small number of seriously mentally ill individuals may become dangerous to other people when they are not treated. A 1983 study in Los Angeles County of individuals found mentally incompetent to stand trial showed that of the eighty-five individuals studied, 92 percent had been arrested on felony charges (the majority for murder, attempted murder, armed robbery, rape, or assault with a deadly weapon), 68 percent had prior felony arrests, and 86 percent had previous psychiatric hospitalizations. Yet when these individuals were located by a psychiatric researcher two years later to ascertain what had become of them, only 36 percent were still in prison or in a hospital. The remaining 64 percent had been released, in over half the cases (thirty-four individuals) with *no plans whatsoever* for follow-up or after-care. In only two cases had the court ordered mandatory outpatient treatment, while another fourteen individuals continued on probation. The following is one of the cases:

> A 31-year-old, single man had a long criminal history including numerous arrests for burglary, grand theft, grand theft auto, and petty theft. He was first hospitalized at age 20 and had a total of fourteen psychiatric hospitalizations, on which he had been diagnosed as having schizophrenia, paranoid type. He consistently refused follow-up outpatient treatment, and there was no attempt to provide outreach psychiatric treatment to this patient or to establish conservatorship. The current arrest was for assault and battery with a golf club on his roommate, who was reported to have sustained serious injuries. On examination in jail, the patient exhibited a marked thought disorder and was responding to internal stimuli. He was found incompetent to stand trial and sent to a forensic mental hospital. He was returned to court a year later and found competent. Two weeks later the case was dismissed when the victim did not appear in court. At this point the patient was released. No arrangements were made for either psychiatric treatment or supportive living arrangements.

If the public ever becomes fully aware of how often mentally ill individuals with a history of violent behavior are released from jails and hospitals with no mandatory continuing treatment, there will be a mass outcry directed toward the lawyers, judges, and psychiatrists who are responsible for this state of affairs.

4. *Violent acts perpetrated by untreated mentally ill individuals are increasing in number.*

In 1961, the Joint Commission on Mental Illness and Health

16

discussed the public stereotype of the "berserk madman," the psychiatric patient who senselessly commits acts of violence. Such persons exist, the Commission said, but they are rare. They are, it claimed, "in a somewhat similar proportion as airplanes that crash in relation to airplanes that land safely."

Since 1961 it has become evident that the number of violent acts committed by mental patients has increased dramatically. The mental patients responsible for these acts have usually been diagnosed with schizophrenia. The acts of violence sometimes include homicide. In most such instances the individuals have been successfully treated for their illnesses with medication but then released and allowed to live in the community without taking medication. To return to the 1961 metaphor, it might be said that airplanes are now crashing more frequently.

Public discussion of this problem is avoided by psychiatric professionals because it implies—correctly—that they have not been doing their jobs. Such discussion is avoided by families of the mentally ill and advocacy groups such as the National Alliance for the Mentally Ill because it inevitably increases stigmatization of the mentally ill. Families and advocacy groups correctly argue that most mentally ill individuals are not violent and that most acts of violence are not perpetrated by mentally ill individuals. Despite the truth of both these assertions, the fact remains that mentally ill individuals, dumped from mental hospitals and left to wander in society without treatment or aftercare, are responsible for an increasing number of violent acts.

What is the evidence for this? For the nonscientist, the evidence consists of an increasing number of news stories, describing senseless violent acts by individuals identified as former mental patients.

Herbert Mullin, a young Californian diagnosed with paranoid schizophrenia, was admitted to facilities for the mentally ill five times. At least twice he was labeled as potentially dangerous because of his illness, yet he was released without continuing treatment or aftercare. In a period of four months he randomly

17

murdered thirteen individuals in order to avert, in his delusional thinking, an earthquake along the San Andreas Fault.

Following his conviction the foreman of the jury wrote a letter to then-Governor Ronald Reagan saying that "I hold the state executive and state legislative offices as responsible for these . . . lives as I do the defendant himself—none of this need ever have happened."

On December 31, 1987, a single page of the *Washington Post* contained these three separate stories: a Michigan man with a history of schizophrenia and refusal to take medication had murdered his two young sons; an Iowa man with "a history of mental problems" had killed six members of his family; and an Arkansas man "was moved to the state hospital in Little Rock for psychiatric evaluation" after murdering sixteen people.

For the scientist, the evidence consists of studies. Studies of arrest rates and violent acts by mentally ill persons prior to 1950 (in 1922, 1930, 1938, and 1945) unanimously showed "that mentally ill persons had lower arrest rates than the general population." After deinstitutionalization got underway, the results of these studies changed dramatically. Since 1965 at least eight surveys of arrest rates and violent acts by mentally ill individuals found the rates to be considerably higher than rates for the general population. For example, Zitrin and his colleagues in New York studied the arrest rates of 867 patients discharged from the psychiatric division of Bellevue Hospital in the early 1970s. Over 23 percent of the patients were "arrested at least once during the two years before and the two years after their admission to the study." Comparing their rates to rates for the population of American cities generally, the researchers reported that the mental patients were twice as likely to commit murder, five times as likely to commit aggravated assault, seven times as likely to commit rape, and eight times as likely to commit robbery. In a classic understatement, the researchers concluded that "the discharge of patients from mental hospitals without provision for decent housing and humane follow-up care for those who require it is regressive. It is not the great social and psychiatric advance that it has been claimed to be."

Sylvia Seegrist, age 25, walked into a shopping center near Philadelphia in 1985 and randomly shot ten people, killing two. She had been hospitalized for schizophrenia twelve times in the previous ten years, clearly labeled as potentially dangerous (she had tried to strangle her mother and had stabbed a psychologist), and had told psychiatric professionals repeatedly that "she felt like getting a gun and killing people." Yet she had been released with no follow-up or assurance that she would take the medicine which controlled the symptoms of her illness.

Steadman *et al.* compared the arrest rate of patients released from New York State mental hospitals in 1968 and 1973. The arrest rate of the 1968 group was 6.9 percent and for the 1973 group, 9.4 percent. For the crimes of murder, manslaughter, and assault, the arrest rate increased from 0.9 percent to 1.9 percent. More recently, Karras and Otis compared psychiatric patients in a New York City hospital in 1975 with those in 1982; the latter group had had significantly more encounters with the criminal justice system and almost twice as many episodes of violence toward persons. As one outraged observer asked: "Where do you think the . . . patients who were in these hospitals went after their release? Do you suppose they went to private, costly mental hospitals? Or do you suppose they went to the ghettos of our large cities . . . ?"

Mary Ventura, a young woman with a history of severe mental disorder, walked into a subway station in New York City in October 1985 and pushed a stranger into the path of an oncoming train. A month previously she had been released from a mental hospital despite evidence that she was still sick and needed ongoing

19

care. As she was being led away from the subway
station by police she cried out: "I'm sick, I'm sick, and
I have no one."

Individuals diagnosed with paranoid schizophrenia appear to
be especially likely to commit acts of violence if released from
hospitals without aftercare. In a recent study by Dr. Heinz
Hafner in Germany of 248 "mentally disordered offenders" who
committed crimes after being discharged from psychiatric hospitals, "39 percent committed their act of violence during the first
six months after discharge. Paranoid schizophrenics were over-
represented in this group." A review of studies concerning the
risk of violence in psychotics by Dr. Pamela J. Taylor in London
similarly found that "recent estimates of rates of schizophrenia
among those convicted of unlawful homicide are remarkably
consistent: between 8 percent and 11 percent. Schizophrenics
appear also to be over-represented in all other kinds of violent
crimes." Another noteworthy aspect of the English studies:
three-quarters of individuals with psychoses who committed violent crimes were homeless at the time of the crime.

Lois E. Lang, 44 years old, walked into the corporate
headquarters of a financial firm in New York City in
November 1985 and shot to death the elderly
president of the firm and a receptionist. Three months
previously Ms. Lang had been arrested for at least the
fifth time, diagnosed with paranoid schizophrenia, and
released from the hospital after fourteen days. At the
time of the killings Ms. Lang was homeless and said to
have a delusion that she was part-owner of the firm
and was owed money.

People with schizophrenia are *not* more dangerous than other
people *if* their symptoms are being treated. Delusions and hallucinations are among the symptoms of this disease that respond
most completely to the antipsychotic medications commonly
used to treat it. However, if such individuals are released from

the hospital without ongoing treatment, a small number of them will act upon their delusional beliefs. If a person with paranoid schizophrenia believes that others are trying to kill him, for example, he may reason that it is necessary to strike first to save his own life. In Hafner's study in Germany, 71 percent of the offenses committed by patients with schizophrenia were "motivated by delusion or hallucination." Similarly in Taylor's study of mentally disordered offenders in London, 43 percent of those with psychosis "were delusionally driven" to their act.

> Juan Gonzalez, age 43, took a sword with him in July 1986 aboard the Staten Island ferry where he proceeded to randomly kill two and wound nine other passengers. He had been staying in a public shelter and had been observed saying repeatedly: "I'm going to kill. God told me so. Jesus wants me to kill." He was taken to a university hospital, diagnosed with paranoid schizophrenia, and released after two days of observation. Two days later he committed the crime.

Every professional who works with the seriously mentally ill can testify to the relationship between inadequate treatment of such patients and their likelihood of becoming violent. A research study at Stanford University showed that when patients with schizophrenia are not adequately treated (as measured by their blood level of antipsychotic medication) they "may become violent because of undercontrol of their core schizophrenic symptoms." Other studies have demonstrated the same thing. Most individuals with schizophrenia who commit acts of violence are not under treatment at all. As Taylor concluded in her English study: "Almost all psychotics who go on to commit serious violence have been psychiatric patients, but few have been in receipt of any treatment in the six months leading up to their offense."

> In early 1986 I was asked to see a woman in a public shelter in Washington, D.C. She was blatantly

psychotic with symptoms of paranoid schizophrenia.
On checking her hospital records I found that eight
years previously she had been found not guilty by
reason of insanity for having killed one of her children
because of delusions. She had been hospitalized at St.
Elizabeths Hospital, responded well to medications,
and four years later was released on condition that she
continue to take medication. She did so for two more
years, at which time the hospital discharged her with
no further follow-up. She apparently stopped taking
medication shortly thereafter and relapsed. One week
after I saw her she disappeared.

Given the virtual absence of follow-up and aftercare for seriously ill mental patients released from the hospital, it should not
be surprising that some of them commit acts of violence as a
result of their illness. The only surprise is that more of them do
not.

5. *Housing and living conditions for mentally ill individu-*
als in the community are grossly inadequate.

Over 430,000 beds in state mental hospitals have been elimi-
nated over the past thirty years. In the early years of deinstitutionalization, many of the individuals who had been sleeping in
those beds left the hospitals and went to live in low-income housing such as boarding houses and single-room-occupancy hotels.
During the 1970s, however, there was progressive gentrification
of this low-income housing and conversion of many of the units
to condominiums. One wonders where the builders, public officials, and psychiatric professionals thought the people living
there were going to go. One wonders whether the builders, public officials, and psychiatric professionals even thought to ask the
question.

In California in 1987, officials became concerned about
where to put homeless individuals in the affluent city of Irvine,
where the average home sold for $125,000. A proposal was
made and passed by the City Council to convert an unused ani-

mal shelter to living units for homeless families. Many objections were raised, including some by neighbors who feared that the facility would act as a magnet and attract other homeless individuals. "Good point," a columnist in the *San Francisco Examiner* responded sarcastically, "half the population wants to live in a dog pound."

Housing for homeless individuals has evoked an extraordinary array of responses from public officials in recent years. In New York City, one of the more widely praised suggestions was to create "floating shelters for homeless adults" by converting "surplus troop ships, ocean liners, oil rigs, or barges . . . moored at waterfront piers." One advantage of such a plan, it was said, was "that if the floating shelters proved unpalatable to neighborhoods they could be moved from site to site." This is remarkably reminiscent of the "ships of fools" filled with mentally ill individuals in the Middle Ages that sailed endlessly from port to port. It also has echoes of the garbage scow from Long Island that wandered to Mexico and back looking for a place to dump unwanted rubbish. New York's proposals appear remarkably humane, however, compared to those of other cities, such as Los Angeles, with its temporary "tent city" or Washington, D.C., which closed subway stations to the homeless without creating additional beds in the already over-filled public shelters.

Housing for mentally ill individuals who are not homeless is often not much better. Consider the following:

New York Times, Aug. 5, 1979. "21 Ex-Mental Patients Taken from 4 Private Homes."

[Detectives removed residents from four homes in Queens where] dozens of other former mental patients have lived for years amid broken plumbing, rotting food and roaches . . . The former patients in the homes were often poorly clothed, had at times gone without winter heat, and lived as virtual prisoners in the homes . . . Last May the police found the decaying corpse of a former patient lying undisturbed in one home inhabited by six other residents.

New York Times, Oct. 21, 1982. "9 Ex-Patients Kept in Primitive Shed in Mississippi."

Nine ragged, emaciated adults have been found living in primitive conditions in a tiny outbuilding at an unlicensed boarding home for former mental patients . . . They were taken Tuesday from a 10-by-10-foot building which was guarded by two vicious dogs . . . The room had no toilet or running water, only a plastic bucket to collect body wastes . . . There were two mattresses on the concrete floor and a single cot in the room.

New York Times, Mar. 25, 1984. "Fire Raises Questions about Mental Patients."

A state investigation of a rooming house [in Worcester, Massachusetts] in which seven former mental patients died has raised questions about the methods used by the State Department of Mental Health to discharge patients from institutions to community residences . . . The report released this week said officials at Worcester State Hospital who referred the former patients to the rooming house had been warned by community health workers that the privately owned house was not safe.

Such substandard living conditions for the mentally ill are not confined to rural communities or urban ghettos. I have personally visited a home for discharged patients that was a rat- and roach-infested firetrap only five blocks from the White House. In addition to substandard housing, there is a problem in obtaining food for many mentally ill homeless persons. In theory mentally ill individuals living in the community obtain food with an SSI check, food stamps, or from soup kitchens. For many this system works, but for a few who are too mentally ill it does not. One patient I saw in a shelter, for example, believed that food in soup kitchens was being poisoned by Russian spies so she, like many others, obtained food by foraging in garbage cans and dumpsters. Such individuals are sufficiently common for the *New England*

Journal of Medicine in 1986 to publish a letter describing three cases of "dumpster-diving injuries" in Minneapolis within a three-month period. In one of them a man "fell backwards into a dumpster that contained broken glass . . . on examination he was observed to be hypotensive and two large shards of glass were found to be protruding from his back." In a fourth case alluded to in the letter "a 30-year-old man apparently fell asleep in a dumpster and was killed when it was emptied into the back of a trash truck." Such deaths are not rare occurrences; in June 1987 when a 20-year-old homeless man was crushed to death in a dumpster in Pompano Beach, Florida, a spokeswoman for the city told the local newspaper, "It is not uncommon for people to sleep in the dumpsters."

Given the living conditions available for many mentally ill individuals in the community, a return to the mental hospital, bad as it is, may be preferable. The rehospitalization rate for individuals released from mental hospitals is approximately 50 percent within one year. What such figures do not tell, however, is that many of these individuals purposefully do such things as stopping their medicine or acting bizarre in public in order to get themselves rehospitalized. This fact may be the ultimate commentary on the quality of life for many mentally ill persons who have been deinstitutionalized.

6. *Community mental health centers, originally funded to provide care for the mentally ill so these individuals would no longer have to go to state mental hospitals, are almost complete failures.*

As will be discussed in chapters 4 and 5, community mental health centers were originally conceived and funded for the explicit purpose of providing psychiatric care in the community as an alternative to state mental hospitals. As such, their primary responsibility was to individuals with serious mental illnesses who were being released from hospitals and to mentally ill individuals who were potential candidates for such hospitals. To date 789 centers have been funded with federal money, and the vast majority of their funds continues to come from federal, state, and local government subsidies. Twenty-five years ago one would have predicted that areas better covered by community mental health centers would deliver better services for the seriously mentally ill persons living there. With only a few exceptions, such a prediction would have been dead wrong. There appears to be virtually no relationship between community mental health centers and community services for the mentally ill. In fact, as will be discussed in chapter 7, community mental health centers have ignored the seriously mentally ill in favor of individuals with relatively minor problems. This is not only true in areas of the United States that are traditionally thought to provide deficient human services—rural West Virginia, Mississippi, or Alabama, for example. It is even *more* true in urban areas where psychiatrists and psychologists are abundant and where one would expect services to be better.

Take Washington, D.C., for example, which has more psychiatrists and psychologists than anywhere else in the United States. Area C Community Mental Health Center (CMHC) in southeast Washington was given over $2.5 million in 1965; it was one of the first CMHCs in the nation to receive federal funds. The National Institute of Mental Health proclaimed it a model for the nation and gave it special consideration and exemptions from federal rules. What did it look like in late 1987 when the District of Columbia's mental health services were finally reorganized? Like a run-down warehouse. There was so little activity that it was difficult to ascertain what the building was being used for. On most of the five floors was virtually no staff or patients, and the standard joke in the local psychiatric community was that Area C CMHC specializes in "phantom therapy." When I last examined some random patients' charts in 1986 I found patients whose medications had been renewed routinely for as long as *eight years* without being seen by a psychiatrist.

Or take San Francisco, another urban mecca for mental health professionals, where being "in therapy" is as accepted as driving an automobile or getting a haircut. San Francisco distinguished itself early in the community-mental-health-center era by becoming the first major American city to be geographically covered by its five CMHCs. Furthermore, it claimed to have dramatically reduced the number of the city's mentally ill residents committed to state mental hospitals, from 2,882 in 1964 to 129 in 1968. By 1973 San Francisco was being cited in congressional hearings as a model for psychiatric services.

And then what happened? Today San Francisco vies with Los Angeles County for the distinction of having the worst public psychiatric services in the state. The vaunted CMHCs became counseling centers for the worried well, and the deinstitutionalized mentally ill can now be seen on the streets everywhere, overtly psychotic and without care. According to city officials, "the city's police department reported 20,000 calls for psychiatric problems in 1986" and "roughly one in five prisoners at San Francisco's Hall of Justice requires psychiatric treatment . . . those not qualified for care elsewhere are often brought in to overcrowded jails via so-called mercy bookings—trumped up charges that at least serve to get a troubled person off the street and into a shelter." In 1987 Mayor Dianne Feinstein claimed that approximately thirty mentally ill individuals "so disturbed that they threaten others" must be forcibly removed from the streets each month.

Or take Hawaii, another area once praised for the services it promised to provide for the seriously mentally ill. In 1964 NIMH Director Robert Felix visited Hawaii and designated it a special federal-state demonstration project to develop alternatives to hospitalization. By 1975 Hawaii's 800,000 population was completely covered by five federally funded CMHCs and another three funded by the state. The mentally ill were therefore emptied out of the state hospital, which reduced its population from 1,232 in 1958 to 232 in 1982.

As summarized in 1975 by a pair of researchers who studied the system, those deinstitutionalized patients who were lucky ended up in third-class unlicensed boarding houses in Honolulu's Filipino ghetto; finding better housing was impossible because Hawaii's "public welfare officials were reluctant to accept these patients and the lists of [licensed] available boarding homes would not even be shared with the hospital . . . Initially at least, aftercare planning for the mentally ill did not consist of rehabilitation planning but merely of insuring that ex-patients would not have to sleep in the streets." Even that modest goal was not achieved, for on any given night seventy-five to one hundred seriously mentally ill individuals ended up in Honolulu's public shelter.

In Honolulu, emergency psychiatric services, one of the five services all CMHCs are supposed to provide, are nonexistent in the CMHCs; instead, patients with psychiatric emergencies must go to the emergency room of a private hospital where they are not wanted. None of the four federally funded CMHCs that cover the Honolulu area have inpatient services, another one of the five essential services; instead, patients needing hospitalization are shunted through private hospitals to the state hospital, an institution of unrestrained bleakness whose admission ward, euphemistically called "the patio," looked like a prison in a Third World country when I visited it in 1987. Praised by the director of NIMH in 1964, Hawaii was ranked last in a 1986 survey of state programs for the seriously mentally ill by Public Citizen's Health Research Group.

Another aspect of the failure of community mental health centers is their abandonment by the psychiatric professionals who are essential for providing services to the seriously mentally ill. This will be discussed in detail in chapter 8, but two news stories in October 1987 illustrated the problem. In Chambersburg, Pennsylvania, the Cumberland Valley Community Mental Health Center announced that it "will be forced to close its doors in January if it cannot find a psychiatrist." Two psychiatrists who had been providing part-time services had announced that they were leaving to go into full-time private practice, and despite a salary of $85,000 and six months of recruiting, none of the 1,628 psychiatrists living in Pennsylvania was interested in the job. Another CMHC in nearby Carlisle, Pennsylvania, was also unable to recruit a full-time psychiatrist despite salary and benefits totaling $100,000. Virtually all psychiatrists in Pennsylvania, as well as other states, receive part of their training with public funds (either federal or state) but elect to work in the private rather than the public sector.

Also in October 1987, Dr. James L. McKee, director of Park Center in Fort Wayne, Indiana, was in the news. McKee, a psychologist, was receiving a salary of $84,000, an annual incentive bonus, a pension plan, and a 1987 car (his third car in five years). However, this was apparently not enough to keep him on the job, so the board of directors of the Park Center voted McKee an *extra* $200,000 bonus if he would remain with the Park Center for ten years. Park Center is a CMHC that received $12.7 million in federal funds between 1977 and 1981 and still operates with predominantly state and federal funds. It was originally called the Fort Wayne Community Mental Health Center, but in 1983, under Dr. McKee, it changed its name to the Park Center. According to the Center's newsletter, the new name "would enable Park Center to better reach those persons who need counseling services for life adjustment problems such as marital, family, and personal problems." Like most community mental health centers in Indiana, the Park Center has a reputation for focusing on the worried well and having little interest in seriously mentally ill patients, and it was specifically cited for this deficiency in the 1986 national survey mentioned above.

Given the failure of community mental health centers to provide services for the seriously mentally ill, then, community psychiatric services in most areas remain merely an idea from the past or an ideal for the future. When such patients get into the system at all it is as case folders filled with official forms entitled "Progress Notes" for individuals for whom there will be no progress. Eventually a final notation—"Deceased" or "Whereabouts Unknown"—is entered and the case folder is sent to a distant archive.

7. *Laws designed to protect the rights of the seriously mentally ill primarily protect their right to remain mentally ill.*

Apparently drafted by the law firm of Franz Kafka and Lewis Carroll, the laws on the mentally ill that have emanated from the

29

deinstitutionalization era are both absurd and tragic. They have had consequences merely dire for some but disastrous for many. Most disturbing, despite overwhelming evidence that the laws are not working as they were intended to, legislators and lawyers have been slow to redress the situation. The current laws, it is often said, are more thought-disordered than the mentally ill they were designed to serve.

> Mark X lived under a subway platform in downtown Philadelphia. "He smeared his feces and picked constantly at large open sores, stopping only to respond briefly to voices . . . He was truly regressed, and often survived only by reaching out to the tracks a few feet from his hiding place to pick crumbs or crusts discarded by passengers on the platform above. Many times large rats would outrace Mark for the food . . . There were many days when he seemed almost catatonic. His occasional attempts to respond [to a volunteer trying to make contact] were usually interrupted by the deafening rumble of the steel wheels of subway cars . . . He was removed from under the subway platform when private subway police were hired to "clear the bums out." Attempts to get Mark X committed for treatment to a psychiatric hospital failed.

The laws governing involuntary commitment of the mentally ill in most states require that persons be demonstrably dangerous to themselves or to others. "Dangerous" is, of course, a relative term, and its interpretation is left up to local police and judges. In the District of Columbia, I have personally asked police to commit an overtly psychotic woman who was walking the streets carrying an axe; they refused, saying that she had not done anything with her axe. In Wisconsin, "a man barricaded himself in his house and sat with a rifle in his lap muttering 'kill, kill, kill.' A judge ruled that the man was not demonstrably violent enough to qualify for involuntary commitment." The criteria for dangerousness to self are even more subjective, with some police unwilling to get involved until they see the person perched on a bridge ready to jump—if then.

In Washington, D.C., an attractive young woman was observed by a newspaper reporter panhandling in the city's train station. On talking to her he learned that she was a college graduate and had been recently released from a psychiatric hospital. Her conversation did not make sense and she was hallucinating. A policeman was persuaded to take her to St. Elizabeths Hospital for possible commitment. The admitting psychiatrist, however, refused to commit her saying that she had not demonstrated dangerousness to self or others. A few days later she was found raped and murdered in an alley near the train station.

The changes in state commitment laws that took place in the 1960s and '70s, making involuntary commitment much more difficult, were created with the best of intentions. Well-meaning civil liberties lawyers, often working with the American Civil Liberties Union or the Mental Health Law Project, believed they were protecting individuals from unnecessary and sometimes endless incarceration, and many lawyers advocated the complete abolition of involuntary commitment. But serious mental illnesses like schizophrenia are brain diseases in which parts of the brain are not functioning normally. The brain is the organ we depend upon to think about ourselves and to appreciate our need for help. Since the organ is impaired, it makes little sense to insist that only those persons should be treated who want help and ask for it. As one observer phrased it, "we are protecting the civil liberties [of the mentally ill] much more adequately than we are protecting their minds and their lives."

At a commitment hearing in Wisconsin a man with schizophrenia, being held in jail, was said to be mute and refusing all food. He was also said to be eating feces, a fact which his public defender did not dispute. The question, rather, was whether eating feces qualified as dangerousness to self:

PUBLIC DEFENDER: Doctor, would the eating of fecal material on one occasion by an individual pose a serious risk of harm to that person?

DOCTOR: It is certainly not edible material . . . It contains elements that are considered harmful or unnecessary.

PUBLIC DEFENDER: But, Doctor, you cannot state whether the consumption of such material on one occasion would invariably harm a person?

DOCTOR: Certainly not on one occasion.

The public defender then moved to dismiss the action on the grounds that the patient was in no imminent danger of physical injury or dying. The judge ruled that the man was not a danger to himself and released him.

Absurd and tragic outcomes for the mentally ill are also coming from laws other than those governing commitment. In 1979, a federal judge in Massachusetts ruled that patients in state mental hospitals could refuse to take medication unless "there is a substantial likelihood of extreme violence, personal injury, or attempted suicide." Similar rulings have been handed down in Oklahoma, Colorado, New Jersey, and New York, raising the specter of psychiatric hospitals full of individuals who cannot be treated without a specific court order for each case. This would be like a return to the 1930s when all that was available for the seriously mentally ill was incarceration.

Other laws mandate placing hospitalized mental patients in the community as the "least restrictive setting." In Washington, D.C., for example, lawyers representing the Mental Health Law Project continue to go to court insisting that more hospitalized patients be released into the community despite evidence that nursing homes are full and many run-down boarding houses are in ghettos where terrified ex-patients are afraid to go outside. Such living conditions, often far inferior to the hospital, clearly do not qualify as the "least restrictive setting." Yet lawyers continue to press for release, acting on ideals of earlier years. If mentally ill patients perseverated in their behavior as lawyers do with so little attention to the consequences of their behavior, we would cite it as evidence that they were in need of further treatment. As Dr. Loren Roth summarized it: "A large number of patients have been kidnaped by a small number of lawyers in order to make a philosophical point on their own behalf."

Victimization of the homeless mentally ill is their daily fare, sometimes just having a purse snatched or disability check taken but too often including rape or murder. According to *U.S. News and World Report* one can buy T-shirts in California reading "troll buster," honoring young men who beat up homeless individuals living beneath bridges.

Most assaults against the homeless mentally ill are of course never reported, and those that are rarely make the news. Occasionally one does. In New York City "a homeless man, attacked by seven teenagers, was thrown over a wall and dropped about 50 feet into Riverside Park early yesterday leaving him with a fractured leg and back injuries." In Quincy, Massachusetts, three teenagers were charged with beating a homeless man to death. In Hyannis, Massachusetts, a homeless man and woman were beaten to death: "The attackers had pounded his head against the wall . . . The woman was savagely beaten and raped . . . Last Monday's assault is unique only in its savagery. The street people, among the most helpless of adult human beings, are the natural prey of anyone looking for some loose change, a pack of cigarettes, a bottle. They are rabbits forced to live in company with dogs."

> Phyllis Iannotta, age 67, had been diagnosed with paranoid schizophrenia and hospitalized. Following her discharge no follow-up or aftercare took place and she became a shopping bag lady on the streets of New York. In 1981 she was raped and stabbed to death in a parking lot on West 40th Street. In her bag was found two sweaters, a ball of yarn, an empty box of Sloan's liniment, a vial of perfume, a can of Friskies turkey-and-giblet cat food, and a plastic spoon.

How did callousness become disguised as civil rights? Why don't the mentally ill have the right to be protected from disease, from physical harm, and from victimization on streets where they are unable to protect themselves? Freedom to be insane is an illusory freedom, a cruel hoax perpetrated on those who cannot think clearly by those who will not think clearly.

8. *The majority of mentally ill persons discharged from hospitals have been officially lost. Nobody knows where they are.*

A walk through the parks of any large city will tell an observer that the deinstitutionalized mentally ill are personally lost. Large numbers of them sit anonymously on benches talking to unseen voices. Later, they shuffle through food lines in soup kitchens, where they may be known only by names such as "Graycoat" or "Redcap," and sleep in public shelters where they may not have to register. They can go for weeks or months at a time never having to identify themselves or being identified. As noted by one observer, such persons have not merely fallen between the cracks, "they are lost in ravines."

What is more disturbing for those of us accustomed to thinking of government as competent, however, is that the majority of these mentally ill persons are officially lost as well. This became clear in November 1986, when the director of the National Institute of Mental Health testified before Senator Lowell P. Weicker's subcommittee of the Committee on Appropriations regarding neglect of the seriously mentally ill. In response to a question regarding how much was known about the distribution of persons with schizophrenia in the United States, NIMH staff had prepared the chart on the next page, which was presented as part of the NIMH testimony.

What is extraordinary about this chart is not only that 58 percent of all individuals with schizophrenia had been officially lost but that nobody at the Senate hearings seemed shocked by the revelation. The NIMH, with an annual budget of over $250 million, did not even appear to be embarrassed about it. One would not expect federal officials to know where every single released patient was living or receiving care; it would seem reasonable,

---

Distribution of Adult Schizophrenics
in the United States

1986 NIMH data illustrating how little is known about their care

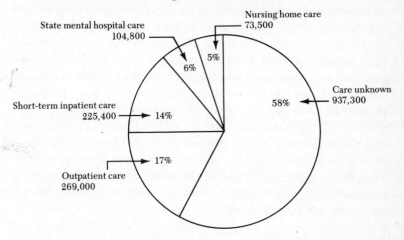

Nursing home care
73,500

State mental hospital care
104,800

5%

6%

Care unknown
937,300

58%

Short-term inpatient care
225,400 ➤ 14%

➤ 17%

Outpatient care
269,000

however, to expect officials to have carried out studies to ascertain more precisely the outcome of the massive shift in population that had taken place with deinstitutionalization. When 937,300 individuals with serious mental illnesses have been lost to follow-up care, then something is gravely wrong.

The present situation should be contrasted with that of a hundred years ago. In 1880 the United States, as part of its ten-year census, carried out a special project to locate all individuals who were "defective, dependent, and delinquent." In order to do this, each institution where they might be found was surveyed. Census takers going door to door were specially trained to inquire about them, and letters were sent to each of the 100,000 physicians in the United States urging them "to report to the Census Office all idiots and lunatics within the sphere of their personal knowledge." The census information from these three sources was then cross-tabulated *by hand* "to purge the list of duplicates, and great pains were taken with this branch of the work." The result was a detailed enumeration of the numbers of "idiots and lunatics" by age, sex, and county in which they resided, which could be used to plan services for them.

This, then, is our progress in federal information on the seriously mentally ill. In 1880 there was detailed information available on where they were; in 1980 there was very little information available. In 1880 it was known that most individuals with serious mental illnesses were not receiving care, but their whereabouts were known; in 1980 it was known that most such individuals were not receiving care, and their whereabouts were unknown.

In short, the policy of deinstitutionalization has been a disaster whose dimensions are apparent everywhere. The disaster is not, in the words of psychiatrist and columnist Charles Krauthammer, "the result of society's mean-spiritedness . . . [or] of mysterious determining forces, but of a failed though well-intentioned social policy. And social policy can be changed." But in order to do so it is necessary to understand how the mistakes were made that led to the present situation.

2

The Making of the "Mental Health" Myth

The origins of the homeless mentally ill in America are inextricably entwined with concepts of mental illness and mental health that date to the nineteenth century. The homeless mentally ill at present lining the sidewalks of America are mileposts marking the years of failed policies, their piled bags and belongings cairns to departed psychiatric shibboleths.

It was the existence of large numbers of mentally ill homeless people that led to the building of insane asylums in the last century. In 1830 there were just four public mental hospitals in the United States, with together less than two hundred residents. Most individuals with serious mental illnesses were kept at home or in jails or wandered about begging their meals. Because of the large number of homeless people—mentally ill and otherwise—cities and large towns began building almshouses to shelter them. As soon as they were built, however, the almshouses—or poorhouses as they were more widely known—became filled.

The mentally ill comprised a substantial percentage of the inhabitants of almshouses, and this was duly noted by elected officials. In Massachusetts, for example, an 1833 report to the legislature decried the large number of mentally ill filling a Boston almshouse that had been opened ten years earlier:

> Instead of being a House of Industry, the institution [almshouse] has become at once a general Infirmary—an Asylum for the insane, and refuse for the deserted and most destitute children of the city. So great is the proportion of the aged and infirm, of the sick insane, idiots, and helpless children in it, that nearly all the effective labor of the females, and much of that of the males, is required for the care of those who cannot take care of themselves.

Partly because of such reports, Massachusetts opened its first public asylum for the insane that same year. Other states followed suit, and by 1880 there were seventy-five public mental hospitals in the United States with 36,780 inhabitants. The era of the insane asylum had fully arrived, in sprawling rural estates punctuated with stone or brick buildings, "monasteries for the mad" as they were called.

The increasing number of individuals in public mental hospitals had become an important public issue by 1880. An 1871 report of the United States Commissioner of Education had declared that "the successive reports, upon whatever source or means of information procured, all tend to show an increasing of the insane . . . There has been a great increase of provision for the insane within forty years and a very rapid increase within twenty years." Because of such concerns the United States Census Office, as mentioned in chapter 1, was ordered in 1880 to do a special investigation of the problem and subsequently reported:

> The most striking result of the investigations made in 1880 respecting the insane, the idiotic, the blind, and the deaf in the United States is the apparent increase in their number relative to the total population . . . In thirty years the population has little more than doubled, but the number of insane,

idiots, blind, and deaf-mutes appears to be nearly five times as great as it was thirty years ago.

The number of hospitalized insane continued climbing precipitously during the following years, reaching 150,151 by 1904.

Psychiatrists and neurologists debated how to stem the increasing tide of mental patients in the closing years of the nineteenth century. Interest in the "moral therapy" of the 1830s and '40s, in which efforts were made to rehabilitate the patients, had been forgotten. Efforts to reform the asylums, spearheaded by Dorothea Dix in the 1840s and '50s, had similarly slipped quietly into history. Instead, biological thinking about the causes of mental illness had become predominant.

As described by one historian: "The late nineteenth century was an era of extreme somaticism in psychiatric thought . . . psychiatrists and neurologists agreed that insanity was a disease of the brain or a symptom of such disorder." The leading voice of American psychiatry was Dr. John P. Gray, superintendent from 1854 to 1886 of the Utica State Lunatic Asylum in upstate New York, the largest mental hospital in the country. Gray had been the first asylum superintendent to employ a pathologist to look for lesions in the brains of deceased patients. Like many psychiatrists and neurologists of his day, Gray was firmly convinced that mental illness was due to the biological events that produced these lesions. Known for his fine wine cellar as well as his absolute certainty that he was correct, Gray dominated American psychiatry through his position as editor of the *American Journal of Insanity* and also by his commanding 300-pound presence.

As psychiatrists and neurologists searched for means of controlling the alarming increase in insanity, other areas of medicine were making major advances in understanding the causes and prevention of disease. Bacteria had been discovered and were suspected of being responsible for many illnesses. In 1882 Robert Koch in Germany showed that the tubercle bacillus was the etiology of tuberculosis, which was the leading cause of

death in the United States. In 1883 the organisms causing chol-
era and diphtheria were found, and in 1885 the bacterium causing tetanus was isolated. That same year Louis Pasteur devised
a vaccine to treat rabies. By 1890 Koch had developed the tu-
berculin skin test for the diagnosis of tuberculosis, and public
health measures to prevent the spread of this disease were underway.

Logically and inevitably, the concept of preventing mental
diseases arose during this period. Its initial impetus began in 1880
with the foundation of the National Association for the Protection of the Insane and the Prevention of Insanity (NAPIPI).
Founded by reform-minded psychiatrists, neurologists, and laypersons, the organization's primary purpose was to improve conditions in mental hospitals, but it also hoped to prevent insanity.
The constitution of the organization stated explicitly that insanity
was rapidly increasing and that efforts were needed to reverse
that trend. NAPIPI disbanded after just four years because its
leaders could not get along. During its brief life, however, it
initiated a public inquiry into conditions in New York State asylums and introduced legislation into Congress to investigate the
causes and treatment of insanity. Its main legacy was the idea
that mental diseases could be prevented, and that idea continued
to grow in the minds of professionals and laypersons as they
watched with alarm the continuing rapid rise in numbers of the
hospitalized insane.

By the beginning of the twentieth century prevention had
become the dominant idea in American medicine. In 1904 W. C.
Gorgas eradicated yellow fever in the Panama Canal Zone,
demonstrating how effective prevention could be. The following
year Koch was awarded the Nobel Prize in Medicine for his work
on tuberculosis, and the cause of syphilis, a spirochete, was discovered. In 1906 August von Wassermann in Germany developed a blood test for the diagnosis of syphilis. Psychiatrists and
neurologists, aware that many patients in the asylums had syphilis of the brain, talked enthusiastically of possibilities for preventing not only brain syphilis but all mental diseases.

FREUD COMES TO AMERICA

It was at this time that the ideas of Sigmund Freud were introduced to the United States. Freud was an introspective, ambitious man who, during a period in which he used and advocated cocaine, turned away from his previous laboratory studies of neurology and became preoccupied with unconscious thought processes and subjective psychic phenomena. He was especially enthusiastic about a theory that early experiences in childhood are crucial to the causation of mental disorders that develop later in life. All children, said Freud, go through stages of development centering on important parts of their bodies, specifically the mouth, anus, and genital organs. If normal development through these stages is in any way arrested, then the child may develop symptoms of neuroses or psychoses (including schizophrenia) later in life. Especially important in Freud's theories was the Oedipal stage during which the young boy, in competition with his father, becomes attached to his mother and wishes to have sexual intercourse with her.

It should be pointed out that Freud offered no proof for his theories other than what he said his patients had told him. Many of his theories, furthermore, were not based on his own clinical experience but rather on what he was told the patient had told somebody else. For example, little Hans, whose analysis was crucial to Freud's ideas of the Oedipus complex, was seen by Freud only once; the rest of the information about him was relayed to Freud by little Hans's father. Daniel Paul Schreber, whose case Freud relied on to develop his ideas about paranoid schizophrenia and homosexuality, was never examined by Freud at all; Freud drew his conclusions solely from Schreber's published autobiography.

There was, then, no experimental or scientific evidence to support Freud's theories about the causes of mental illness at the time he published his ideas. And Freud himself pointed out one major problem—that "investigation into the mental life of normal persons . . . yielded the unexpected discovery that their infantile history in regard to sexual matters was not necessarily different in essentials from the neurotic." In other words, the problems in development reported by individuals with mental illnesses were no different than the problems reported by individuals without mental illnesses.

Almost one hundred years after Freud published his theories about the causes of mental illness, scientific evidence to support these theories is still nonexistent. There *is* evidence that some individuals have the constellations of personality traits that Freud called oral (e.g., dependent, passive) or anal (e.g., compulsive, acquisitive), but such constellations are much more likely to be genetic than developmental in origin, given the results of recent studies on identical twins and adoptees. Drs. Seymour Fisher and Roger P. Greenberg, in an exhaustive review of scientific evidence for Freud's theories, write that "the etiological aspect of the oral character theory is the vaguest and least verified" of Freud's theories. Similarly, regarding the anal stage, "The studies that have looked at extreme toilet training procedures . . . have largely failed to establish that they are correlated with the existence of anal character traits." And about the Oedipal stage, it has been verified that small children are more closely attached to their mothers than to their fathers, but that is hardly surprising in view of the mothers' greater caregiving role in most families.

On the other hand, within the last two decades scientific evidence has emerged to indicate strongly that major mental illnesses—especially schizophrenia and manic-depressive psychosis—are caused by biological factors and not by early childhood experiences. The evidence consists of studies of brain structure (e.g., CAT scan, neuropathology) and brain function (e.g., electroencephalograph, psychoneurological testing) and has demonstrated irrefutably that such mental diseases are truly brain diseases just like multiple sclerosis, Parkinson's disease, and Alzheimer's disease. After a long and circuitous detour through the Freudian hinterlands we have returned to the position of Dr. John Gray and his late-nineteenth-century colleagues, only now there is proof that they were correct.

How, then, should Freud's theories of mental diseases be regarded? Sir Peter Medawar, Nobel laureate in medicine, said that Freud's theories "will remain forever one of the saddest and strangest of all landmarks in the history of twentieth-century thought." And Dr. Hans Eysenck, a relentless critic of Freudian psychology, assesses the current status of these theories as follows:

> The Freudian unconscious, populated like a medieval morality play by such mythological figures as the ego, the id, and the super-ego, the censor, Eros, and Thanatos, and imbued by a variety of complexes, among them the Oedipus and Electra complexes, is too absurd to deserve scientific status . . . [Freud's] place is not, as he claimed, with Copernicus and Darwin, but with Hans Christian Anderson and the Brothers Grimm, tellers of fairy tales.

It is interesting to speculate about why Freud's theories were so warmly received in America compared to Europe where they were relatively ignored. One reason is that American psychiatrists were avidly looking for a means of stemming the increasing tide of the mentally ill; Freud's theories, by postulating remediable causes of mental illnesses, promised such means. Furthermore, American psychiatrists, held in low esteem by their medical colleagues whose specialties were advancing into the scientific era, were willing to accept any theory that promised scientific respectability. In 1894, for example, prominent neurologist S. Weir Mitchell had publicly excoriated American psychiatrists for their isolation and lack of scientific method in "one of the most blistering attacks" ever levied in American medicine. That the psychiatrists responded a few years later by embracing the totally unscientific theories of their colleague from Vienna is one of the great ironies of medical history.

Freud's theories became available in America soon after they were published in German. F. W. H. Myers gave an account of Freud's ideas in English as early as 1893. Five years later Havelock Ellis published a summary of Freud's theories about arrested sexual development as the cause of hysteria. By 1904 Dr. James J. Putnam, Professor of Neurology at Harvard, had become the first American to utilize psychoanalytic psychotherapy, and shortly thereafter he published a paper describing the technique. In 1905 Dr. Morton Prince, writing to Freud from Boston, called his ideas "well known." By 1907 Dr. Adolf Meyer, one of the most influential American psychiatrists, had "introduced psychoanalytic theory and techniques into the New York State Hospital system" (Manhattan State Hospital) and "insisted that his staff use psychoanalytic principles in diagnosis and treatment."

Meyer, like Ellis, Putnam, and other early followers of Freud in America, believed Freud's theories and thought they applied as much to the psychoses as to the neuroses. As one psychoanalyst summarized the view of his colleagues:

They all had in common the conviction that many psychoses represented forms of adaptation to intolerable stresses of the personality, that mental symptoms were intimately related to the prepsychotic personality of the individual, and that study of childhood development, especially family relationships, should be the basis for understanding the development of major personality problems.

It is clear, then, that even before Freud arrived in the United States in September 1909 to give a series of lectures at Clark University in Worcester, his theories about the causes of mental diseases had been widely disseminated. Freud was interviewed by reporters when his ship docked in New York, and his presence in America elicited great interest among psychiatrists and psychologists. One of those attending Freud's lectures in Worcester was the eminent psychologist William James who, after completion of the lectures, said to Freud's followers: "The future of psychology belongs to your work." Freud was pleased with his reception and later wrote: "In Europe I felt as though I were despised, but in America I found myself received by the foremost men as an equal."

THE NATIONAL COMMITTEE FOR MENTAL HYGIENE

As Freud's theories were being disseminated throughout American psychiatry and psychology, and interest in preventing diseases was coming to dominate American medicine generally, a third set of events was underway that would ultimately fuse the first two under the rubric of "mental health." Clifford W. Beers was a graduate of Yale University who had attempted suicide and been hospitalized for manic-depressive psychosis from 1900 to 1903. Deeply disturbed by the indignities and abuses he experienced and observed during his incarceration in several public and private mental hospitals, Beers vowed to expose hospital conditions and work for their reform once he was released. The result was a manuscript, *A Mind That Found Itself,* which Beers circulated to William James and Adolf Meyer for suggestions and which was eventually published in 1908.

Out of his discussions with James, Meyer, and others, Beers conceived of a national association of professionals and laypersons to help carry out his reform mission. It was a logical development; the Association for the Study and Prevention of Tuberculosis had been formed in 1904, and the American Association for the Study and Prevention of Infant Mortality was in process of formation. James, Meyer, and others agreed to help Beers, and the National Committee for Mental Hygiene was officially inaugurated on February 19, 1909. Its goals, as outlined in its first publication, were to serve as a "clearinghouse for the nation on the subject of mental health, the prevention of nervous and mental disorders, [and] the care and treatment of the insane."

Beers's primary interest in forming the National Committee was to promote the reform of mental hospitals. But as later described:

his doctor friends of those days were more interested in the possibilities of *preventing* mental illness, inspired by the examples set in the control of epidemic diseases through sanitation and immunization . . . Beers apparently was persuaded of the superiority of the preventive approach, particularly when psychiatrists told him that early treatment might have prevented his [own] major breakdown.

Dr. Meyer in particular was by then an enthusiastic promoter of Freud's theories; he suggested to Beers the term "mental hygiene" as the name for the national committee and urged Beers to develop a broader vision of what could be done in addition to reforming mental hospitals. At the same time that it was being launched, therefore, the National Committee for Mental Hygiene was shifting its focus from Beers's goal of reforming mental hospitals to the broader goal of "mental hygiene" as it was then called.

The future direction of the National Committee for Mental Hygiene became clearly established in 1912 when Dr. Thomas W. Salmon was hired as the director of special studies. Salmon was a bacteriologist with no special training in psychiatry. He had failed in private practice and had been suspended from duty by the United States Public Health Service because of his public criticism of open immigration policies, which he contended were contributing to the increasing number of mentally ill in America. As summarized by one historian, "Salmon was an individual whose reputation far exceeded his accomplishments." Salmon was also an enthusiastic and uncritical advocate of Sigmund Freud. Accepting Freud's theories as fact, Salmon argued that mental diseases are "dependent very largely upon errors of education, unsuitable environment, and the acquisition of injurious habits of thought and the suppression of painful experiences, usually in the sexual field, which later in life form the basis for psychoses." Prevention of psychoses could be accomplished, reasoned Salmon, by attention to early childhood experiences and family relationships, for it was these that led, in Salmon's words, to the "psychic infection." Salmon, as a bacteriologist, was well trained to recognize an infectious agent when he saw one, and there it was—the Oedipal bacillus—just as infectious and deadly as the tubercle bacillus or the spirochete.

By 1917 the National Committee for Mental Hygiene had completely disavowed Beers's original purpose of hospital reform. At its annual meeting, Salmon called the reform of the hospitals "a field of mental hygiene which all of us believe is less important perhaps than any other when the broader conception of mental hygiene is borne in mind." Instead, Salmon urged greater attention to "extending the frontiers of psychiatry" to prisons and especially to schools. For the prevention of mental diseases, he said, "practically all the hopeful points of attack . . . exist in early childhood, and if the psychiatrists are to take up such work they must be permitted to enter the schools." Salmon believed that psychiatrists should play an important role in social reform and urged that they be major players "in the great movements for social betterment." Salmon's was by this time one of the most influential voices in American psychiatry, and he would later become president of the American Psychiatric Association. When the United States entered World War I in 1917, he was appointed director of neuropsychiatric programs for the military. His complete acceptance of Freud's theories and willingness to work for "mental hygiene" based on those theories were not unique, and his beliefs were shared by many of his colleagues.

Dr. William A. White was one such colleague. As superintendent of St. Elizabeths Hospital in Washington, D.C., White had introduced psychoanalysis to the hospital's wards even before Freud came to America, and in 1913 he co-founded the first English-language psychoanalytic journal. White strongly supported the concept of mental hygiene and believed that the task of psychiatrists in preventing mental illnesses should include treatment of "all forms of social maladjustment and even of unhappiness."

Similar views were held by Dr. C. Macfie Campbell, who had visited Freud in Vienna in 1908, become a psychiatric colleague of Adolf Meyer at Johns Hopkins University, and was an active member of the National Committee for Mental Hygiene. "Mental hygiene," wrote Campbell in 1916, "aims to develop those qualities which give to human life its value and without which the preservation of the most superb physique loses all its meaning." Campbell was especially interested in insuring that psychoanalytic principles be incorporated into schools.

By 1917, then, "mental hygiene" had evolved beyond the prevention of mental diseases into a far loftier vision—that of promoting ideal human behavior. If, as psychiatric experts claimed, early childhood experiences were the cause of most undesirable behavior as well as most mental diseases, then the undesirable behavior could be changed. As described in the 1917 annual report of the National Committee for Mental Hygiene:

> May we by taking thought hasten the time when the minds of men will be capable of adjustment which will permit the spirit of humanity and charity to rule instead of envy and malice, vengeance to give way to justice, war to peace, despair to hope? It is to assist in the work of realizing these great objects by work in one important field that the National Committee for Mental Hygiene has been organized. The expectation of ultimately attaining these ideals is a reasonable one, but their final triumph depends upon the degree of intelligent interest and effort that we put forth in the attempt to know ourselves.

The one who would lead the world toward this vision was, of course, the psychiatrist, for only the psychiatrist understood the roots of undesirable behavior and mental illnesses. This may have seemed like a large responsibility, but some professionals were apparently prepared for the task. A remarkable paper, published in 1913 by Dr. Charles L. Dana, outlined the role envisioned for the new psychiatrist who, in addition to being a neurologist and psychiatrist, would also be "educator, preacher, sociologist":

> [The psychiatrist] has not only to be the diagnostician and the prescriber of drugs and diet, or surgery and mechanical therapeutics, but he has to be the educator and instructor of his patients . . . He must join with the teachers showing how children should be educated and taken care of while they study. He should follow them at the period of their youth

and maturity, correct mental faults, advise them as to marrying, even marry them at times and tell them about the management of the children. He must help and uplift the religion of those who have any and give a religion or high and positive ideals to those who have not. He must show them how to live happily and to use with scientific efficiency the forces which nature has given them; which two things are often the same . . . It is, in other words, necessary that we now proceed to develop a kind of social and economic neurologist as well as one of clinical and laboratory attainments . . . He must be a kind of superman, one with higher ideals, more potent inhibitions and wiser in life and wider in outlook than those whom he is trying to guide.

Although it had been barely ten years since the unproven theories of Freud were introduced to the United States, the Clark Kents of American psychiatry had donned their costumes and were ready for roles as supermen.

MENTAL HYGIENE AND THE PROTESTANT ETHIC

Following World War I, some of the ideas of the mental hygiene movement began to be implemented in the form of child guidance clinics. Although the origins of such clinics actually date to the Juvenile Psychopathic Institute begun in Chicago in 1909, the clinics only began to spread in 1922, when the National Committee for Mental Hygiene, with a grant from the Commonwealth Fund, began to finance demonstration projects. Juvenile delinquency, like all abnormal behaviors, was believed at the time to be the result of faulty emotional development, and it was hoped that through psychotherapy the child's life course toward crime could be reversed. As time went on, the professionals running these clinics became discouraged at their results in working with delinquents and shifted their energies increasingly to children with more minor problems, "children who are in distress because of unsatisfied inner needs or are seriously at outs with their environment—children whose development is thrown out

49

of balance by difficulties which reveal themselves in unhealthy traits, unacceptable behavior, or inability to cope with social and scholastic expectations."

Despite the proliferation of child guidance clinics and their popularity, no evidence was brought forth to suggest that the clinics prevented mental illness. The idea of preventing such illnesses, in fact, was largely ignored or forgotten during these years, and when it was raised at all it was done so with embarrassment. In 1932, for example, Frankwood E. Williams, who had succeeded Salmon as director of the National Committee for Mental Hygiene, published an article entitled "Is There a Mental Hygiene?" Williams noted:

> The basic question with which psychiatrists and particularly those interested in mental hygiene start is—What are the causes of mental and nervous disease? This question has been repeatedly raised during the twenty-two years of organized mental hygiene until it has almost become a ritual and like a ritual has led to nothing except repetition—not even a start.

This was the era of the Great Depression, which the National Committee for Mental Hygiene was attempting to counter by promoting "such trite and bromidic formulas as 'keep smiling,' 'A man may be down but he's never out,' 'Keep your chin up,' and 'Every cloud has a silver lining.' "

Probably the most devastating attack on mental hygiene in the years between the wars was a 1938 analysis by sociologist Kingsley Davis. Mental hygiene, Davis announced bluntly, had nothing whatsoever to do with mental illness. Rather it was a system of values, which, not coincidentally, was the same system of values espoused by the Protestant ethic. Davis argued that "mental hygiene hides its adherence behind a scientific facade . . . The mental hygienist is really enforcing in a secular way and under the guise of science the standards of the entire society . . . [Mental hygiene is a] social movement and a source of advice concerning personal conduct." In essence Davis was accusing the mental hygiene movement of being a secular religion and its leaders of being priests cloaked in the pseudoscientific garb of Freudian theories.

Meanwhile, despite the proliferation of child guidance clinics and the rhetoric of the National Committee for Mental Hygiene, the number of patients in the nation's mental hospitals continued to climb at an unprecedented rate. In 1909, when the National Committee for Mental Hygiene began its work, there were approximately 180,000. By 1923, there were 255,245 and in 1931, 318,821. In 1943, when Clifford Beers died in a mental hospital after having relapsed into manic-depressive psychosis four years previously, the number of patients had risen to over 450,000, an increase of 270,000 since the National Committee had been formed. The rate of increase of mental patients during those years was double the rate of increase for the population generally. One wonders what Beers thought; not only had mental illness not been prevented, but the hospitals he wanted so much to reform had not been reformed. The hospitals were, in fact, considerably worse than when Beers had first been a patient at the turn of the century because they had become much more overcrowded.

3

The "Conchies" and General Hershey Create NIMH

On September 18, 1945, the headlines of the *Washington Post* read: "MacArthur May Reduce Forces to 200,000." The bombs had dropped on Hiroshima and Nagasaki just six weeks earlier, and the formal surrender of the Japanese aboard the *USS Missouri* had occurred on September 2.

Newspaper headlines during the following week echoed the fact that the war was over: " 'Beast of Belsen' Will Be Tried by British Today," "25 of 39 Japs on Wanted List Arrested." It had been a war in which over 400,000 Americans were killed and another 671,000 wounded. The boys were coming home, and the nation was ready to get on with its business. Increasingly the attention of Americans was turning from the debris of the war to Phil Cavaretta's .358 batting average as he led the Cubs toward a pennant, or to *Anchors Aweigh* with Gene Kelly and Frank Sinatra playing at the Loew's Palace in downtown Washington.

On September 18, hearings opened before a subcommittee of the House of Representatives on the subject of H.R. 2550, the "National Neuropsychiatric Institute Act." According to the bill's synopsis, it was "a bill to provide for, foster, and aid in coordinating research relating to neuropsychiatric disorders; to provide for more effective methods of prevention, diagnosis, and treatment of such disorders; to establish the National Neuropsychiatric Institute; and for other purposes."

The proposed legislation was the product of an optimistic America, a nation that had prevailed over Hitler and the forces of evil in its most difficult challenge, a nation that believed itself strong enough to solve all the problems facing it, including the problem of mental illness. Dr. Thomas Parran, Surgeon General of the United States Public Health Service, reflected this sentiment in his opening statement in support of the bill:

I might say that every adult in the country has known intimately, in his family or among his friends, the tragedy of mental illness. Certainly no other type of illness is so disruptive to the family, to its economic security, or so prolonged and costly in its disabling effects. The achievements of our country during the war have demonstrated our ability to accomplish miracles. With such a heritage we can begin now, I am confident, to undertake an even greater task, the conquest of mental disease.

Throughout the House hearings, and during the Senate hearings that were to follow six months later, there were frequent allusions to the Manhattan Project, which had resulted in the successful creation of the atomic bomb. The problems of mental diseases, it was implied, would yield to a similar governmental research program. This "can do" attitude carried over to other social and medical problems as well, for ten days before the psychiatric hearings opened President Truman had proposed to Congress a massive employment and housing plan, and in November he would propose a compulsory national health insurance program. As the atom had yielded its secrets, so would mental illness and the other problems facing Americans at home.

Probably the most remarkable fact about the hearings was that they were being held at all. The care of the mentally ill in America had been a responsibility of the states since even before the Constitution had been written—since 1766, in fact, when Governor Francis Fauquier had gone before the Virginia House of Burgesses and asked funds to open a public psychiatric hospital because of the accumulating numbers of mentally ill individuals who could be seen on the streets of Williamsburg.

During the intervening 180 years there had been only one serious attempt to get the federal government involved in the care of the mentally ill. That occurred in the middle of the nineteenth century when Dorothea Dix advocated the use of funds derived from federal land sales to build better state mental hospitals. Dix claimed that mental patients, beset by "miseries and disqualifications brought upon them by the sorest afflictions with which humanity can be visited . . . are the wards of the nation." Through vigorous lobbying she persuaded Congress to pass legislation in 1854 that gave such federal aid to the states. President Franklin Pierce vetoed the bill, however. He believed the Constitution explicitly forbade the federal government from assuming such responsibilities and feared that if the precedent was established all the poor, sick, and indigent—"the whole field of public beneficence"—would become the responsibility of "the care and culture of the federal government."

At the time of the 1945 hearings, the federal government's involvement in the problems of mental illness was still very modest. Narcotics addiction and its relationship to crime had become a federal concern during the early years of the twentieth century. This had led to the investment of federal funds for research on addiction, the creation of a Narcotics Division in the United States Public Health Service, and ultimately to the building of two federal hospitals for the treatment of those addicted to drugs. In 1931, Congress enlarged the mandate of the Narcotics Division to include research on mental diseases and, with strong lobbying by the National Committee for Mental Hygiene, renamed it the Division of Mental Hygiene. Despite this fact, the federal government had virtually no involvement in problems of mental illness; those problems had been and still were the responsibility of the states.

THE "CONCHIES" GO PUBLIC

Federal responsibility for the mentally ill changed dramatically following the war because of both the "conchies" and the draft. "Conchies" was the name popularly given to the 3,000 conscientious objectors who, refusing to take up arms in the war, were assigned to alternate duty in state mental hospitals. These were Methodists, Quakers, and Mennonites, idealistic young men who had the courage of their convictions despite the popularity of the war and the taunts of their townspeople. They worked as aides and attendants in "nearly one-third of all state hospitals in twenty states from Washington to Virginia, from Maine to Utah."

But the conscientious objectors did more than work in the mental hospitals. They were appalled by the conditions they found there and started writing reports. They documented the beatings, degradation, and lack of medical care for patients, the long hours and low pay for attendants (the starting base pay in Pennsylvania was $900 a year plus maintenance), and the incompetence of many doctors employed in the hospitals ("alcoholics and psychotics who could hold no position in well-run institutions where cure is the objective"). At first the conchies just sent their reports to each other, but as their numbers and indignation grew, a few of them began to raise the issues publicly.

In 1943, for example, "a group of conscientious objectors stationed at Cleveland State Hospital interested two leading Cleveland citizens, the Rev. Dr. Dores R. Sharpe, executive secretary of the Cleveland Baptist Association, and Walter Lerch of the *Cleveland Press*. Before these men the conchies laid a stack of affidavits a foot high." Lerch confirmed the authenticity of the documents and reported the story on the front page of the *Press*. "Day after day he brought forth more evidence—proving the beating and shackling of patients, proving the inadequacy and revolting nature of the food, the overcrowding, the low salaries, the neglect of treatment."

The governor of Ohio ordered an investigation. Two attendants were arrested for beating patients. Then the superintendent of the hospital tried to fire the conscientious objectors, but newspapers and religious groups rallied behind them. Reporter Lerch, receiving daily reports from conchies working on the wards, publicized the plight of four women patients in a seclusion room who had died of pneumonia, thirteen patients with advanced tuberculosis who had not been seen by a physician for at least two weeks "except the superintendent on a routine tour," and conditions in the hospital's morgue where "rats ate away the face of an aged patient while his body awaited burial."

Charges and denials continued month after month, with public awareness slowly being raised despite the war going on. In mid-1944 the superintendent of Cleveland State Hospital was forced to resign. The governor's investigatory commission then issued a scathing report on conditions at the hospital, confirming the worst of the conscientious objectors' allegations. Finally, in January 1945, Dr. Dores R. Sharpe was serendipitously appointed foreman of a Cuyahoga County Grand Jury and a public investigation of the hospital was undertaken. In an unprecedented outcome the Grand Jury indicted the State of Ohio itself for "the uncivilized social system which enabled such an intolerable and barbaric practice to fasten itself upon the people."

By the end of the war the conscientious objectors were organized on a national level, with over 2,000 of their reports collected under the jurisdiction of the National Mental Health Foundation. Several prominent individuals lent public support, including Pearl Buck, Henry R. Luce, Reinhold Niehuhr, J. Robert Oppenheimer, Mrs. Franklin D. Roosevelt, and Mrs. Harry S. Truman. But it was the attention of Congress that the conscientious objectors were seeking:

A United States congressman from a midwestern state was presented with a few facts and pictures showing conditions in mental hospitals. After considering the materials for a moment he dropped them on his desk and said, "It isn't true. It just isn't true!" His informant replied, "It's true, all right, sir. For two years I have worked in these conditions, and I know whereof I speak." The congressman shook his head. "No," he said, "not in the United States. It just isn't true!"

Two members of Congress were enlisted as National Sponsors for the National Mental Health Foundation—Senator Claude Pepper from Florida and Rep. Percy Priest from Tennessee; both would become important advocates of federal legislation for the mentally ill.

The reports collected by the conscientious objectors might be denied but they could not be ignored. They described conditions that on the best of days were merely uncivilized but more usually were barbarous. The following is an example:

He opened the door to another room. I stood frozen at what I saw. Here were two hundred and fifty men—all of them completely naked—standing about the walls of the most dismal room I have ever seen. There was no furniture of any kind. Patients squatted on the damp floor or perched on the window seats. Some of them huddled together in corners like wild animals. Others wandered about the room picking up bits of filth and playing with it.

Near my feet was a little old man trying to shine my shoes. He had stepped in some of the human excrement and it was oozing out between his toes. A patient was eating some food from a tray which had been placed on the floor beside a urinal into which a patient had recently defecated.

With such documentation it was not difficult to persuade some members of Congress to respond, and it was in fact Percy Priest's Public Health Subcommittee of the Committee on Interstate and Foreign Commerce that held the initial hearings on the National Neuropsychiatric Institute Act. Conditions in state hospitals were referred to regularly during the hearings, including the fact that they were spending, on the average, only $306.62 per patient *per year*. (Kentucky spent the least, at $146.11 per patient per year.) Allegations submitted as testimony by the American Equity Association of Washington, D.C., claimed that "from July 1, 1916, to February 20, 1928, twenty patients in St. Elizabeths Hospital were killed by attendants and no convictions were had in respect of any such cases . . ."

Exposés of conditions in state mental hospitals became much more public in the months following the initial hearings while the legislation was still being considered by Congress. On May 6, 1946, the article by Albert Q. Maisel referred to in chapter 1 appeared in Henry R. Luce's *Life* magazine; Maisel gave full credit to conscientious objectors as the source of his information. The text and pictures etched the problem of the mentally ill into the consciousness and conscience of the nation as nothing had previously done. In *Reader's Digest,* also in May of 1946, there appeared the condensation of a new novel by Mary Jane Ward called *The Snake Pit.* The epigraph of the book read: "Long ago they lowered insane persons into snake pits; they thought that an experience that might drive a sane person out of his wits might send an insane person back into sanity." The horrifying experiences of fictional Virginia Stuart, confined to a mental hospital, had become a proper subject for America's readers. Finally, in July 1946, *Reader's Digest* carried a condensation of Maisel's *Life* magazine story. The work of the conchies in exposing conditions in state mental hospitals was being faithfully carried on by the media.

GENERAL LEWIS B. HERSHEY TESTIFIES

In addition to indirectly exposing conditions in state mental hospitals, World War II also had a direct effect on federal involvement in the problem of mental illness by exposing the magnitude of the problem. This came about through the draft. The majority of the testimony during the hearings on the proposed National Neuropsychiatric Institute concerned the number of men who had been rejected for military service because of psychiatric disorders as well as the number who, once in the uniformed services, had been discharged for the same reason. Major General Lewis B. Hershey, director of the Selective Service System, was a major witness at both the House and Senate hearings. Hershey gave detailed testimony showing that 18 percent of the men rejected for induction had been rejected because of "mental illness" (856,000 out of 4,800,000); another 14 percent (676,000) because of mental deficiency; and 5 percent (235,000) because of neurological diseases. In terms of disability discharges once in the service, Hershey and other military witnesses said that 38 percent of all such discharges "were due to mental disease." "Mental illness," it was said, "was the greatest cause of noneffectiveness or loss of manpower that we met." Another witness pointed out that "the war has not created, but it has revealed in a truly startling way, the need for the passage of this measure."

The creation of a National Neuropsychiatric Institute "where all phases of the problem can be investigated" was claimed to be the answer to the problem of mental illness. Dr. Thomas Parran, the Surgeon General, in his opening summary of the proposed legislation, pointed out that the Institute would have three functions: research on neuropsychiatric diseases, the training of personnel, and "aid to the States in developing mental health services." Several witnesses, including Dr. Parran, compared the proposed legislation with that which had set up the National Cancer Institute eight years previously: "This bill would do with the field of mental ill health what the Cancer Institute has been attempting to do and has been doing successfully in connection with that great problem."

Throughout the hearings it was made clear, both implicitly and explicitly, that the primary target group that would benefit from the proposed National Neuropsychiatric Institute was the seriously mentally ill, especially those confined to state mental hospitals. Dr. Parran emphasized this in his opening statement when he said:

An example of the seriousness of the mental-disease problem is the fact that half of all hospital beds in the country, some 600,000, are occupied by mental patients . . . Some 125,000 new cases of mental disease are admitted annually, and it has been estimated that 10,000,000 of the current population will require hospitalization for mental illness at some time in their lives.

59

The following day, on page one of the *Washington Post,* it was this aspect of the hearings that was singled out for headlines: "Half of All Hospital Patients Are Mental Cases, Parran Says." These same statistics were featured again in November 1945, when President Truman publicly addressed the problem of mental illness:

> Accurate statistics are lacking, but there is no doubt that there are at least two million persons in the United States who are mentally ill, and that as many as ten million will probably need hospitalization for mental illness for some period in the course of their lifetime.
>
> A great many of these persons would be helped by proper care. Mental cases occupy more than one-half of the hospital beds, at a cost of about $500 million a year—practically all of it coming out of taxpayers' money. Each year there are 125,000 new mental cases admitted to institutions.
>
> We need more mental hospitals, more outpatient clinics. We need more services for early diagnosis, and especially, we need much more research to learn how to prevent mental breakdown. Also, we must have many more trained and qualified doctors in this field.

Hospitals belonging to the Veterans Administration were also said to be overrun by psychiatric cases, with "60 percent of veterans' hospitalizations" being "due to psychiatric causes."

The largest group of the seriously mentally ill was those with schizophrenia, still frequently referred to as dementia praecox. It was claimed that this disease "occupies half the population of our mental hospitals" and thus one-quarter of all the hospital beds in the nation. Individuals with schizophrenia also accounted for 4 percent of disability discharges from the armed forces.

Finally, it was made clear that some individuals with serious mental illnesses such as schizophrenia could become dangerous if they were not treated; newspaper columnist Albert Deutsch, who published a series of articles in the New York newspaper *PM* in the spring of 1946, recited a litany of headlines to illustrate this point during his testimony; for example: "Deranged Mother Kills Son, 7, with Brother's Axe," "Girl, 16, Sent to Insane Asylum for Killing Tailor," "He Had a Queer Smile—Crazed Husband Kills Four."

THE "MENTAL HEALTH" LOBBY

Although it was clear that the major beneficiaries of the proposed National Neuropsychiatric Institute were intended to be the seriously mentally ill, it was also clear from the beginning that some witnesses who testified in support of the legislation saw it as the start of much grander things. Improving the treatment of the mentally ill in state hospitals was indeed a laudable goal, but much more important was the prevention of mental diseases. In some cases, it was noted, prevention could be accomplished by physical means such as an adequate diet to prevent pellagra or interrupting the transmission of the spirochete to prevent syphilis of the brain. But in most cases, in the words of Surgeon General Parran, "the mental illness or mental maladjustment seems to be purely psychic."

The theories of Sigmund Freud about the causes of mental diseases had continued to dominate thinking in American psychiatry despite the fact that no evidence had appeared to support them. At the time of the 1945 hearings, for example, a standard textbook of psychiatry described the cause of schizophrenia as "a maladapted way of life manifested by one grappling unsuccessfully with environmental stresses and internal difficulties" whose specific causes included "early conditioning experiences, intrapsychic conflicts, insistent but consciously rejected demands of various instinctive drives and urges, feelings of guilt or of insecurity, as well as various other long-standing, troublesome problems and frustrated purposes."

Because of their belief that "intrapsychic conflicts" were the root cause of mental diseases, some of America's most influential psychiatrists testified at the hearings and urged Congress to broaden the mandate of the proposed National Neuropsychiatric Institute to include "mental health" as well as mental illness.

Foremost among these psychiatrists were the trio of Francis J. Braceland, William Menninger, and Robert H. Felix. Although it was not widely known at the time, these three men had, at the request of Surgeon General Parran, designed the legislation being considered by Congress. All three were devoted to the psychoanalytic theories of Freud and favored extending those theories to schools, courts of law, and the community generally. Each of the men would eventually serve a term as president of the American Psychiatric Association.

Braceland was at the time chief of the Neuropsychiatry Division of the United States Navy. He was a versatile and literary man who had grown up in Philadelphia, been a semiprofessional baseball player, and come to medicine comparatively late in his career. His psychiatric training had included a year of study under Carl Jung at the Burgholzli Institute in Zurich, and he was devoutly committed to the canons of psychoanalysis. The role he envisioned for psychiatry was not a modest one, and in later years he described it as follows: "Modern psychiatry . . . no longer focuses entirely upon mental disease, nor the individual as a 'mental patient,' but rather it envisages man in the totality of his being and in the totality of his relationships." Psychiatry, said Braceland, had "become a *humanistic* discipline" and "an essential part of an overall science of man . . . One might even say the ideal goal of the psychiatrist is to achieve wisdom."

In his testimony in support of a National Neuropsychiatric Institute, Dr. Braceland quoted a report of the Rockefeller Foundation, which said: "It is not too much to assert that in its actual and potential contribution to general medicine, to education, to sociology, indeed to the general business of living, psychiatry, without claiming omniscience in itself, is cast for a role of fundamental importance in helping to shape any world which may come out of the present one." Dr. Braceland had earlier called for "an all-out attack on the problem of mental illness and human behavior," which he described as follows:

Up to now the job of psychiatry has been to apply scientific techniques and methods to the problems of mental illness and human behavior. Its task has been not only the recognition and treatment of the mentally sick but also the discovery of better ways and means to prevent these illnesses. Again and again the war has demonstrated that in order to understand mental illness, what is first required is an understanding of men; how they live, what they want from life, where they have come from, and what their backgrounds have been. Men do not get mentally sick "out of the blue," so to speak; ... their illness or well-being depends upon their relations with other men.

The war's smashing climax at Hiroshima and Nagasaki hammered into the consciousness of all men one irrefutable fact: More than ever before, man's very existence is dependent upon his fellow men. This realization, great though it is, is not enough. Ways and means have to be created for better understanding human behavior and doing something about its training. It is tragically significant that our civilization found it easier to split an atom than it has to join man with man.

The National Neuropsychiatric Institute, in short, was being assigned by Dr. Braceland the task of educating human beings to live with each other and bringing about world peace.

Dr. William Menninger, a year older than Braceland, was a fully trained psychoanalyst who would be president of the American Psychoanalytic Association from 1947 to 1949. He had grown up in Kansas and, with his father and older brother Karl, had founded the private Menninger Clinic in the 1920s. At the time of his testimony in support of the National Neuropsychiatric Institute he was chief of the Neuropsychiatric Division of the United States Army and thus Dr. Braceland's counterpart. His belief that psychiatrists "have some knowledge of the unconscious dynamics [of human behavior] which appear so mysterious to the layman" led him to urge his colleagues "to participate in community affairs in order to apply our psychiatric knowledge to civic problems" and to:

assume citizenship responsibilities for policy forming at whatever level we can—in the Board of Education, City Council, civic clubs, welfare groups, legislative committees, Congressional hearings . . . As psychiatrists, we are expected to provide leadership and counsel to the family, the community, the state, welfare workers, educators, industrialists, religious leaders, and others.

The third member of the mental health trio, Dr. Robert H. Felix, would turn out to be the most influential, for he would become the first director of the Institute that had been proposed to Congress. Like Menninger, Dr. Felix had grown up in Kansas, but following psychiatric training he had chosen a career in public health rather than private psychiatry. At the time of the 1945 congressional hearings, Felix, age 41, had completed assignments at the Hospital for Federal Prisoners, the USPHS Lexington Hospital for narcotics addicts, and the Coast Guard Academy, and he was chief of the Division of Mental Hygiene, United States Public Health Service. Felix, Braceland, and Menninger were the highest ranking psychiatrists in the United States government.

Dr. Felix blended a deep interest in the principles of public health (he had obtained a masters degree in public health from Johns Hopkins University) with an interest in the principles of Freud and psychoanalysis (he would complete his formal psychoanalytic training at the Washington-Baltimore Psychoanalytic Institute). "Mental hygiene," he argued, with echoes of the 1880s, "bears a relationship to clinical psychiatry similar to that which tuberculosis control, for example, bears to the treatment of clinical tuberculosis." He also wrote, "Prevention of mental illness implies not only the reduction of those factors which tend to produce mental and emotional disturbances, but also the provision of a climate in which each citizen has optimum opportunities for sustained creative and responsible participation in the life of the community and for the development of his own particular potentialities."

Dr. Felix urged his colleagues to become involved with "education, social work, industry, the churches, recreation, the courts," so that "mental health services" would be "fully integrated into, and a regular and continuing part of, the total social environment." He compared the role of the psychiatrist in the community to that of an insurance agent or clergyman; just as people "consult their clergyman before getting married" and "consult their insurance agents before embarking upon a new insurance program," so they should also consult their psychiatric professional "when they plan for retirement, when they consider having a relative live with them, or when they prepare a child for hospitalization. All these situations can lead to emotional problems if people are not prepared to cope with them adequately."

The end result, in Dr. Felix's thinking, was a vision of a brave new psychiatric world. As individuals increasingly came to know themselves better and achieved mental health, the world would improve, since the world was merely a collection of individuals. Dr. Felix conveyed this vision graphically in a story he told to illustrate a 1948 lecture on "mental hygiene and public health":

> One evening, a man was trying to read the newspaper. His little boy was making so much noise that he could not concentrate. Finally, in desperation, the father took a page of the newspaper showing a big map of the world and cut it into small pieces. "This is a puzzle," he said to his son. "Put the world together right." The little boy worked quietly in the next room, and in only a few minutes he returned with the map of the world put together exactly right. "How did you do it so quickly?" asked the father, in great surprise. "Oh," said the little boy, "there was a picture of a man on the other side of the page. I found that when I put the man together right, the world was just right, too."

"MENTAL HEALTH" BECOMES INSTITUTIONALIZED

The 1945 and 1946 congressional hearings on the proposed National Neuropsychiatric Institute set a pattern that would be repeated many times during the next thirty years. Psychiatrists and other interested parties first got the attention of lawmakers by focusing on state hospitals and the plight of the seriously mentally ill. Once this had been accomplished, testimony shifted to preventing mental diseases and eventually to promoting "mental health." It was a seductive vision that was not easily resisted; the nation's foremost psychiatrists were claiming that they had the knowledge to make a better world by eliminating the organism responsible not only for mental diseases but for delinquency and unhappiness as well. The infectious disease model still appealed to the public in 1945 as it had earlier in the century, and witnesses like Dr. Braceland did not hesitate to utilize it:

> The entire matter of the prophylactic measures which can be used to prevent mental illness brings to the fore a most important phase. Psychiatry in the future will not content itself with the belief that it is doing a full job when it merely provides care for disease. The job of tomorrow's psychiatry is, as Dr. Parran said, large-scale prevention. The conquest of the infectious diseases—and certainly our war statistics testify to this—did not come about until there were such measures as vaccination and immunization. In the same manner in which medicine has overcome such diseases as lockjaw and smallpox by prophylaxis, psychiatry can do like-wise by providing information and a public understanding which will prevent much unnecessary unhappiness. We believe that the technique of more successful living can be taught.

Such a vision was of course also compatible with the rhetoric of the National Committee for Mental Hygiene, which had champ-pioned its cause since 1909. At the time of the 1945 hearings, the National Committee was launching public education campaigns with slogans such as "Mental Health Is Everybody's Business" and "Build Mental Health—Our Children's Birthright, The Nation's Strength." Dr. George S. Stevenson, medical director of the National Committee, testified at the hearings that one "problem in need of solution," which the Institute might help solve, was the problem of "retirement and stagnation [for individuals] in the middle and late 60s." Similarly, Dr. Edward A. Strecker, testifying for the American Psychiatric Association, foresaw the Institute as a place where a progressive judge might come to learn "about juvenile delinquency and its management."

Also testifying in support of the bill was a representative of the National Congress of Parents and Teachers who said that organization "would like to see mental health services organized on the basis of a preventive health program that starts with the pre-school child and is carried through the entire school period." Child development specialist Dr. Arnold Gesell sent a letter in support of the bill also urging "more stress on prevention and on anticipatory forms of management. Adequate diagnostic and supervisory measures should be extended downward into the years of infancy and childhood."

After much discussion during the hearings, it was agreed that the name of the proposed Institute, the National Neuropsychiatric Institute, was too narrow, too medical, for the tasks it would be asked to do. Proposed alternatives included the National Psychiatric Institute, the National Mental Hygiene Institute, and the National Institute of Mental Health. The last eventually won out and "mental health" achieved official status in the United States government.

The act creating the Institute, which was signed into law by President Truman on July 3, 1946, authorized three kinds of activities to accomplish "the improvement of the mental health of the people of the United States." First was "the conducting of researches, investigations, experiments, and demonstrations relating to the cause, diagnosis, and treatment of psychiatric disorders"; second was "training personnel in matters relating to mental health"; and finally was "developing and assisting states in the use of the most effective methods of prevention, diagnosis, and treatment of psychiatric disorders." This tripartite division of the National Institute of Mental Health (NIMH) into research, training, and service assistance to the states would become a hallmark of the Institute.

THE ORIGINS OF COMMUNITY MENTAL HEALTH CENTERS

Although little noticed at the time, the hearings that led to the creation of the National Institute of Mental Health in 1945 and 1946 contained within them the seeds of the community mental health centers that would blossom forth twenty years later. Surgeon General Parran, in his opening statement, advised Congress:

I wouldn't want to see the major program under this act bogged down merely in the care of patients in state mental institutions. I would hope you would have a public health approach to the problem, particularly in regard to mental health clinics. Child-guidance clinics and services for veterans are tremendously important. Such clinics, I am sure, should be operated under public health auspices.

Later the same day, Dr. Stevenson of the National Committee for Mental Hygiene noted:

Under the provisions of this bill it will be possible for the federal government to assist in the development of preventive services. In the field of psychiatry this, in essence, means outpatient clinics . . . The outpatient clinic may be an all-purpose clinic or it may be specialized to serve children, or schools, or courts, or college student bodies, or other groups of the population at large . . . Empirically on the basis of experience already obtained we should have one clinic of the size referred to previously for approximately every 100,000 of our population . . .

When Dr. Felix testified, he reiterated this idea:

As I shall indicate later on in my testimony, there is a need for outpatient clinics in order to treat individuals before they reach the point where they must avail themselves of such asylum as is provided. If it would assist to stimulate the states to provide those outpatient facilities, I think it is proper for the federal government to contribute a certain amount of money . . . One of the first objectives [of the proposed Institute] would be to assist, through grants, the organizing and operation of treatment facilities of this nature in communities not already served by such a center . . . It is possible that sufficient trained personnel will be available to assist the states, through grants-in-aid, in establishing one hundred additional clinics.

In an article published in 1947 Dr. Felix again echoed Dr. Stevenson's call for "one outpatient mental health clinic for each 100,000 of the population." Such clinics, said Felix, would care for the seriously mentally ill by "providing supervision and follow-up treatment of provisional-discharge or convalescent posthospitalization cases," but the clinics would also "serve the community by providing outpatient psychiatric treatment or psychological counseling for patients not in need of hospitalization."

The ultimate purpose of the proposed outpatient clinics, all witnesses agreed, was to prevent mental illness. Dr. Braceland phrased this hope eloquently in response to a question from a Senator:

I feel sure, sir, there are thousands of brilliant young minds lost every year because of the fact that we have been unable to get to those people before the mental illness has proceeded so far that they had to be incarcerated in mental hospitals.

According to Dr. Felix, the proposed psychiatric outpatient clinics would be cost-effective by eliminating some of the need for costly hospitalization:

We have roughly calculated, however, that if 10 percent of the cases now going to mental hospitals could be prevented from going, considerably more money would be saved than would be expended in this program.

This was an argument that would be heard many times in future years as the mental health lobby tried to persuade Congress to spend ever-increasing sums of money on community mental health centers. And it was an argument that had appeal to members of Congress, since public psychiatric services were said to comprise a large percentage of state budgets in 1945: for example, 28 percent of the cost of state government in New York State.

QUESTIONS AND DOUBTS

To the members of Congress who listened to the testimony in support of the Institute that would become the National Institute of Mental Health, the proposal must have seemed reasonable enough. There was abundant evidence that the number of seriously mentally ill persons in the nation was alarmingly high, and equally convincing evidence that conditions in most state mental hospitals were abysmal. America was in an optimistic mood; it had helped defeat the Germans and Japanese, and surely mental diseases could not be more difficult to overcome than such enemies. Some of the most eminent psychiatrists in the nation had agreed that the proposed Institute was a good idea, and nobody had proposed any alternatives. How could a member of Congress vote against such a proposal? And yet questions arose and doubts were expressed in the course of the hearings, questions and doubts that would prove to be prophetic.

The first question that came up was the time-honored constitutional question about federal versus state responsibilities. Services for the mentally ill had been vested in states for almost two hundred years, and although they were admittedly doing a poor job of delivering those services, that did not automatically mean that the federal government would do any better. Representative Clarence J. Brown, a newspaper publisher and four-term congressman from Ohio, raised the question most forcefully:

I agree with everything that has been said as to the necessity for research and study of this problem, but it seems to me that we must always draw the line somewhere, or build a fence to define the field of activity in which the federal government can participate and the field in which the responsibility rests with the local and state governments and with the individual citizens themselves. I believe the federal government should lead the way in research, in furnishing information and advice to the people of the states and their local subdivisions, but I don't think the federal government should take the responsibility of administering aid to the individual all the way through.

Representative Brown observed that local and state governments would be quick to seize upon federal funds as a means of saving their own funds:

That is . . . because a lot of our citizens are very short-sighted and don't seem to realize that when the federal government spends the money it costs them just as much, if not a little more, as when the local government spends the money, and they have to pay for it in the end anyhow.

A second question that arose during the hearings concerned the federal role in training psychiatric professionals. Everyone agreed that there was an insufficient number of such professionals; indeed testimony was introduced that "entire states, including Idaho, Montana, Wyoming, and Utah are without the services of a single qualified specialist practicing psychiatry." There were clearly differences of opinion, however, about whether federal funds should be used to support such training or whether such responsibility should reside at the state and local (e.g., university or medical school) level.

One aspect of this that was also brought out by Representative Brown of Ohio was whether physicians, once trained in psychiatry using federal funds, might not simply go into private practice instead of working in state mental hospitals and public psychiatric clinics. He posed this hypothetical possibility to Dr. Robert Felix:

> REP. BROWN: Let me ask you another question, doctor. I am a graduate medical student. This law is in operation. I decide I want to specialize in psychiatry. I apply for a fellowship. If I get that fellowship the government will spend $15,000 educating me. Then, as soon as I get it, I go into private practice.
>
> DR. FELIX: No.
>
> REP. BROWN: Can't I do that? If so, is there any arrangement made, whereby a man who gets a subsidy from the federal government must pay back or in some way compensate the government or is it your idea that this training will be only for men who will go into public service?
>
> DR. FELIX: That is exactly what my thought is, and the selection of the men would be by the states. I would think that a reasonable requirement of these men would be that they would spend at least one year in public service for every year they spent in training at public or State expense.
>
> REP. BROWN: I think that would be very reasonable, if you spend $7,000 a year on them. Offhand, I would suggest perhaps that they should be required to spend a little more time in the public service.
>
> DR. FELIX: I think that would be reasonable. I was trying not to be fantastic in specifying a larger number of years, but I would certainly say one year.

A third question that arose during the hearings on the proposed Institute was that of its proper province. Was it to be an institute for the study of the causes, treatment, and prevention of mental diseases or for the study of all human behavior? Ms. Lee Steiner, speaking for the American Association of Psychiatric Social Workers, strongly urged that "emotional distress" be differentiated from "psychiatric disorders." Under the former category Mrs. Steiner said:

I refer to the personal problems involved in domestic dishar-
mony—quarrels between parents, between children, between in-laws, relatives. They are the unhappiness over
maladjustments in work, the problems of love and courtship,
the conflict over relationship to one's religion—and one
could go on and on and on. If we include these problems as
"preventive psychiatry," then all problems of life and living
fall into the province of the practice of medicine.

Such problems, said Ms. Steiner, were not the same as mental
illness:

The two should be differentiated. They are not synonymous.
They call for different treatment. The psychiatrist is not the
specialist here. Even the best trained psychiatrists do not
necessarily have an internship in the problems of normal
living. They are primarily physicians, trained to treat illness
and to prevent illness. There are other members of the
clinical team better qualified than the psychiatrist to handle
the usual problems of daily living.

In fact no satisfactory answers to any of the three questions
were presented at the hearings, and the lack of their resolution
contributed greatly to the eventual failure of the National Institute of Mental Health and community mental health centers.
Federal and state authorities never coordinated their activities or
plans: no payback obligation was ever attached to federal training subsidies, following which most psychiatrists did go directly
into private practice; and to this day the National Institute of
Mental Health is a jungle of programs spanning every conceivable aspect of human behavior and mental illness.

It would have been nice, if unrealistic, if one of the members
of Congress listening to the testimony of the psychiatrists had
asked in 1945 and 1946 the harder questions that seem so obvious
in retrospect: What do you mean by "mental health," doctor?
What kind of training do you have that allows you to tell other
people how to achieve happiness? What kind of evidence do you

have that you can in fact prevent mental diseases and hospitalizations? And what about those theories about arrested childhood development and the Oedipus complex—may I please see the data that support such theories? Nobody, of course, asked these questions, although Representative Brown of Ohio, one of the more astute members of Congress, appears to have had a suspicion that what was being proposed by the psychiatrists rested more on hopes than on facts. Brown at one point observed: "Men get strange ideas; they get hobbies and they decide the only way in the world they are going to solve all the problems of mankind is to do a certain thing and that their field is the most important." "Mental health" was both a hope and a hobby, nothing more.

In summary, then, the National Institute of Mental Health was a product of World War II, both indirectly, because conscientious objectors exposed conditions in state mental hospitals, and directly, because the draft revealed how many men had serious psychiatric disorders. The Institute was set up to do research, train more professionals, and assist the states in improving services. Those tasks might have improved conditions for the mentally ill in the United States if they had been carried out with mental illness in mind. Instead, the Institute adopted Mental Health as its last name and rode off madly in all directions.

4

Freud and Buddha Join the
Joint Commission

"Mental health" had acquired a home in 1946, but one that existed on paper only. The lack of enthusiasm that many members of Congress felt toward their new creation was reflected by the fact that, following passage of the legislation, Congress adjourned without allocating any funds for NIMH's operation. Not until 1948, in fact, was $6.2 million finally made available so that NIMH could begin its official existence.

As in the past, it was exposés about appalling conditions in state mental hospitals that finally mobilized Congress to fiscal action. In 1948 the exposés came from the pens of two reporters from New York, Mike Gorman and Albert Deutsch. Gorman, a graduate of New York University who had served in the army in Oklahoma, stayed on after the war and joined the staff of *The Daily Oklahoman*. In July 1946, the same month in which *Reader's Digest* reprinted Maisel's *Life* magazine article about mental hospitals, Gorman's editor assigned him the task of investigating Oklahoma's state hospitals.

Gorman did so with a vengeance, producing a series headlined "Misery Rules in State Shadowland," which opened with the following: "In many ways the treatment of our mentally ill in Oklahoma today is little better than in the times when they were chained in cages and kennels, whipped regularly at the full of the moon, and hanged as witches." Gorman's stories mixed hyperbole and invective in a way that could hardly be ignored ("That dining room made Dante's *Inferno* seem like a country club . . . [the kitchen] was more gruesome than the Black Hole of Calcutta"). It was a good story and mobilized Oklahoma's citizens to action. But it remained a local story until 1948 when Gorman's book, *Oklahoma Attacks Its Snake Pits,* was condensed in *Reader's Digest.*

At the same time that Mike Gorman's writings were coming to national attention, Albert Deutsch published an equally shocking account of the nation's state mental hospitals. Deutsch, the son of poor Latvian emigrants, had grown up in New York City tenements and later wandered the country working as a longshoreman and farmhand. Returning to New York during the Depression, he obtained a job researching historical documents for the New York Department of Welfare and became interested in the problems of the mentally ill. In 1937 he published a history of the subject, *The Mentally Ill in America,* which established him as a leading writer on mental illness.

In 1948 Deutsch's exposé of mental hospitals, *The Shame of the States,* was published and caused a sensation. He had visited hospitals in twelve states and, more importantly, had taken a cameraman along. The book was illustrated with photographs of naked men and women confined like cattle in overcrowded hospital wards, and Deutsch left little to his readers' imagination:

In some of the wards there were scenes that rivaled the horrors of the Nazi concentration camps—hundreds of naked mental patients herded into huge, barnlike, filth-infested wards, in all degrees of deterioration, untended and untreated, stripped of every vestige of human decency, many in stages of semi-starvation. The writer heard state hospital doctors frankly admit that the animals of nearby

piggeries were better fed, housed, and treated than many of
the patients in their wards . . .

Actual physical brutality toward patients is not the rule
and plays a small part in the real complaint against our state
hospital system. The most serious defects arise from the
deadly monotony of asylum life, the regimentation, the de-
personalization and dehumanization of the patient, the
herding of people with all kinds and degrees of mental sick-
ness on the same wards, the lack of simple decencies, the
complete lack of privacy in overcrowded institutions, the
contempt for human dignity.

Deutsch concluded rhetorically: "Could a truly civilized community permit humans to be reduced to such an animal-like level?"

The publications of Gorman and Deutsch assured the National
Institute of Mental Health funds to begin operations. It began
modestly and quietly, for those were years in which wise advocates of mental health were both modest and quiet. Not only had
the Korean War gotten underway in June 1950, but Senator
Joseph McCarthy and the House Un-American Activities Committee were looking assiduously for Americans who might be
sympathetic to Communist causes. Jews were especially suspect,
especially after Julius and Ethel Rosenberg were convicted of
giving top-secret information on nuclear weapons to Russia, and
it was not an auspicious time to be publicly advocating the theories of a Jewish psychiatrist from Vienna. Furthermore, some of
the more prominent members of the mental health lobby were
in fact sympathetic to socialist causes, and one of the best known
had been a card-carrying Trotskyite in his university years.

It was not until late 1953, in fact, that the mental health forces
again began lobbying for their idea. By then the Rosenbergs had
been executed, an armistice had been signed halting the Korean
conflict, and the nation was wearying of Joseph McCarthy. In
October 1953, hearings were held before the House Committee
on Interstate and Foreign Commerce on "The Causes, Control,
and Remedies of the Principal Diseases of Mankind." Mental

illness (not mental health) was of the principal topics for discussion.

Compared to later congressional hearings, the 1953 hearings on mental illness were restricted to narrow scientific and economic considerations. Mental illness was being grossly unresearched, witnesses attested, getting "less than 2 cents of every dollar spent for medical research." Research funds per patient under treatment in 1951 were said to be as follows:

Polio	$44.90
Cancer	26.60
Tuberculosis	15.13
Mental illness	4.75

Furthermore, mental diseases were exceedingly expensive diseases to treat, costing the states more than a billion dollars a year in treatment costs alone. Dr. S. Bernard Wortis, professor of psychiatry at New York University College of Medicine, testified that "approximately from one-sixth to one-third of state budgets in our larger states is for the care of the mentally ill,"; the true figure was less than one-tenth, but the exaggeration got the point across.

Although mental illness was the focus of the 1953 hearings, Dr. Robert Felix and other advocates of mental health continued to work behind the scenes to bring about the day when their cause would be properly recognized. In a progress report by the staff of the NIMH in 1949, its first year of operation, goals virtually identical to mental hygiene movement principles of thirty years earlier were given great prominence. They included the following:

1. *Strengthening public health aspects of professional training,* by schooling psychiatrists, psychologists, social workers, and nurses who intend to enter the public mental health field in community organization, community relationships, public education, and other techniques for mobil-

izing the community in support of measures that will promote positive mental health.

2. *Strengthening mental health aspects of public health training,* by grounding health educators in mental hygiene principles.

3. *Expanding programs of public education,* through constructive use of films, radio, press, and other mass media resources.

4. *Developing more research,* for the purpose of evaluating and improving mass preventive techniques.

During the 1953 hearings, Felix urged, as he had earlier, that government funds be used to establish mental health clinics throughout the United States, at least one clinic for each 100,000 in population. He also scrambled the issues of mental illness and mental health into an all-purpose omelet, which he promised would solve most of the problems of mankind: "If the whole nation would begin to understand; if people would work for their state hospitals and mental health clinics in their communities and assist their schools to develop better guidance programs for the students who are having problems; if we could do something in the field of marriage counseling to save homes that are breaking apart because of psychological reasons; much could be done."

MENTAL HEALTH STUDY ACT

As the pious comminations of Joseph McCarthy receded further into the background in 1954, the mental health lobby decided that a national commission would be a useful means of furthering their cause. A harbinger of this development had appeared in 1953 when Dr. Kenneth Appel, president of the American Psychiatric Association, publicly called for the appointment of a national commission which would "study current conditions and develop a national mental health program. Patchwork stopgap programs are keeping us on a treadmill and actually doing little or nothing to reduce and prevent mental illness." The following year, the Council of State Governments held a national governors' conference on the problems of mental illness. In the keynote speech Governor G. Mennen Williams of Michigan observed: "I have never been able to understand why we spend only 5 percent of our medical-research investment on mental illness, a disease which fills more than 50 percent of our hospital beds, and costs us more in taxes than all other afflictions combined." The governors urged more research on how services for the mentally ill might be improved.

By early 1955 the stage was set for a new federal initiative. In February, Representative Percy Priest of Tennessee and Senator Lister Hill of Alabama introduced legislation entitled "The Mental Health Study Act of 1955." Priest, a former schoolteacher and newspaperman, had continued to be a strong supporter of the National Institute of Mental Health ever since his subcommittee hearings helped to create the Institute ten years earlier. Hill, named Joseph Lister Hill after the famous surgeon, was a lawyer who was emerging as a staunch congressional ally of all health programs. The proposed Study Act called for "an objective, thorough, and nationwide analysis and reevaluation of the human and economic problems of mental illness." Other legislation was also introduced to increase training funds for professionals working with the mentally ill, to provide construction funds for psychiatric research laboratories, and to increase federal funds for improvement of state mental hospitals.

Hearings on the legislation were held before Priest's House Subcommittee on Health and Science (Committee on Interstate and Foreign Commerce) on March 8 to 11, 1955, and before Senator Hill's Subcommittee on Health (Committee on Labor and Public Welfare) on March 30 and April 13. The timing was fortuitous. On March 6 the Hoover Commission issued a report written by Dr. Braceland claiming that mental illness was the "single greatest problem in the nation's health picture." The following day, on March 7, *Time* magazine reported on two new drugs, reserpine and chlorpromazine, which were said to be effective in treating some mental illnesses. The new drugs, it was said, may "(1) nip in the bud some burgeoning outbreaks of emotional illness; (2) treat many current cases far more effectively, and (3) in some instances reverse long-standing disease so that patients can be freed from the hopeless back wards of mental hospitals where they have been 'put away' for years."

It was a period of optimism in medicine generally. On April 12, the day prior to the final day of hearings in the Senate, a report was made public by the University of Michigan on the effectiveness of the Salk polio vaccine. The milieu of the hearings, then, was one of hope that the problem of mental illness was a solvable one. As expressed by Mike Gorman, who had moved from Oklahoma to Washington to become a lobbyist: "There is a feeling we can lick it. It is a medical problem, it requires research, but it is no longer something to be stigmatized and something that we treat as a superstition. It is something that must enlist the full support of government."

The congressional hearings on the proposed Mental Health Study Act were basically a rerun of the hearings that had led to the creation of NIMH ten years earlier. Both Drs. Braceland and Felix testified prominently. The third member of the trio, Dr. Menninger, was said to be unable to testify because he was in Phoenix, Arizona, "trying to get money" for his research facility, which was housed in "a converted tombstone facility and two barns." The message was clear—research funds for studying mental illness were grossly inadequate.

Dr. Braceland characterized the proposed Mental Health Study Act as "phase two" of the fight against mental illness. Alluding to statistics showing the extent of mental illness in the United States, he said the figures were so alarming that if they were "for any other condition it would be regarded as a national emergency immediately, but with mental disease peculiarly in many cases we meet with only a sympathetic and respectful apathy."

The statistics referred to were detailed by many of the witnesses at the hearings, including Representative Priest in his opening statement:

Approximately 750,000 mentally ill persons are now hospitalized in the United States on any given day, according to the figures I have; 47 percent of the hospital beds of the nation are occupied by mental patients. The direct economic cost of mental illness to the taxpayers of the nation is over $1 billion a year and has been increasing at the rate of $100 million a year.

In view of the tremendous scope of the problem facing us, the federal government must be prepared to cooperate wholeheartedly and effectively with state governments and voluntary agencies in making a positive approach by dealing not only with the mentally ill but by emphasizing its concern for the maintenance and improvement of the mental health of the American people.

Oveta Culp Hobby, Secretary of the Department of Health, Education and Welfare, noted that "unless something more is done to prevent and control mental illness one out of every twelve children born today will spend part of his life in a mental hospital." Mental illness was used during the hearings virtually synonymously with serious mental illness, especially schizophrenia, which was noted by several witnesses to be the diagnosis of "approximately one-half of the patients in our mental hospitals."

Dr. Robert Felix, director of the National Institute of Mental Health, introduced dismaying statistics on the fate of patients in state mental hospitals. He asserted that of all such patients 75 percent "have been in the hospital for two years or more; 50 percent of them have been in for over eight years; and a quarter of them have been in for more than fifteen years." Furthermore, "by the time the patient has been in the hospital for two years his chances of getting out alive . . . are about 16 to 1. By the time the patient has been in the hospital for eight years his chances against getting out alive are poorer than 99 to 1."

Both the human costs and the economic costs of the mentally ill in state hospitals were stressed by many witnesses. Mike Gorman recalled:

I remember, Mr. Priest, a terrible shock going to a hospital in Oklahoma one day to see a man who I knew was the finest newspaperman in Oklahoma. I had never heard about him for seven years. They said he was 'away somewhere.'

In seven years this man had lost 40 pounds. He was a shell of himself. He still carried the *New York Times* with him. He read vastly. He had a brilliant mind. He was in a pigsty.

This was the man I sat next to at the copydesk. This was my conscience. This just makes me a little angry.

In this hospital, said Gorman, the patients "were fed out of tin buckets and the food was dispensed out of a big iron bucket . . . They went around and kind of slopped it in the [patient's] bucket. If it managed to stay in the bucket that was all right. If it hit the floor, that was too bad." The economic costs of this kind of treatment came up for discussion repeatedly; in New York State it was said that the budget for state mental hospitals comprised 35 percent of the entire state budget.

Many solutions to the problem of mental illness were proposed by those testifying before the House and Senate subcommittees in 1955. They all had in common the need for an increased expenditure of federal funds for research, training, and services. Mike Gorman described "research being carried out in basements, in closets, in converted tombstone factories," referring to the facility being used by Dr. Menninger. Furthermore, argued Gorman, potential researchers were going to work in private industry because of the paucity of funds for research into mental illness: "They can go to work for DuPont and make nylon stockings and this is more productive economically for themselves and maybe more esteemed by society."

Possibilities for more effective treatment and even prevention of mental diseases were put forth by some witnesses. As they had done in the past and would do in the future, they drew parallels between mental diseases and infectious diseases:

It is just like the conquest of the infectious diseases which at one time were hopeless. Pneumonia and influenza killed thousands of Americans and today have been conquered by research dollars. Tuberculosis is another story of how new

83

drugs have conquered disease . . . The New York State budget saved $2.5 million last year through the closing of three
TB hospitals. I don't see why the same thing cannot be done
in this area if we apply the same money.

The lack of trained psychiatric manpower, especially psychiatrists, was discussed by many witnesses. It was noted that the
American Psychiatric Association had set a minimum standard of
"1 psychiatrist for 150 chronically ill persons and 1 for each 30
acutely ill persons," yet state hospitals were described, such as
Rusk State Hospital in Texas, which had only "2 psychiatrists for
approximately 3,000 patients." Representative Martin Dies of
Texas noted that in such circumstances the psychiatrists "mainly
perform functions of counting people in the hospital."

Dr. Felix described the NIMH training grant program, then at
a level of $4.5 million a year, and said that "more than 3,000
trainees have received individual support since the program
started." He also described how NIMH had spent an average of
$4.2 million a year for the first eight years of the program provid-
ing "technical assistance and consultation" to the states as well
as grants-in-aid to assist the states "in the development of community mental health services." Reintroducing the idea of outpatient community mental health centers, Dr. Felix described
them as alternate facilities to state hospitals and said that "it
would, in my opinion, be fruitful and useful for the federal government to encourage further experimentation along these
lines." Dr. Felix also asked for federal funds to support "pilot
studies and demonstrations" for the improvement of care in the
state hospitals, but it was clear that Congress was wary, as it had
been previously, of the federal government becoming directly
responsible for patients who had traditionally been taken care of
by the states.

Although most of the testimony and discussions during the
1955 hearings focused on the treatment of patients with serious
mental illnesses, especially those confined to state hospitals, there
were allusions to prevention as well and further foreshadowings
of the directions NIMH wished to take. Dr. Braceland, for exam-

ple, spoke enthusiastically about the possibility of preventing mental illness:

> We need men with ideas to visualize what the future will be so that we may treat people before this happens, and I think in this phase two, which I spoke about earlier, prevention is the watchword, because otherwise we simply expand hospitals and put more and more people in and that is not the answer to this problem . . . But I do think that by means of prevention and starting early with mental hygiene, perhaps in the schools, we can cut down the load and then with the help you gentlemen will give eventually train enough physicians and nurses to take care of the patients.

Similarly, Dr. Felix extolled efforts "to detect mental illness in youth . . . working through the schools, and working in the health departments, through the maternal and child-health program . . . After all, as a tree is bent so it grows. And we like to do what we can while the youth is, figuratively speaking, a sapling."

The outcome of the proposed Mental Health Study Act was never in doubt, as it was clear that Congress and the public both viewed the problem of mental illness as serious and neglected. By unanimous vote the act was passed and then signed into law by President Dwight D. Eisenhower on July 28, 1955. NIMH was authorized to appoint a joint commission to evaluate the needs of the mentally ill and to make recommendations to Congress for future programs.

THE JOINT COMMISSION

If there has ever been a more hydra-headed national commission than the Joint Commission on Mental Illness and Health, it has not come to light. The Commission not only had forty-five individual members representing every conceivable constituency in the mental illness–mental health community, but it also had thirty-six "participating agencies," including the American College of Chest Physicians, American Personnel and Guidance

Association, American Psychoanalytic Association, Catholic Hospital Association, National Education Association, Department of Defense, and Department of Justice. As a final touch of ecumenicism, the American Legion was persuaded to contribute $10,000 to the Commission to cover publication costs of the report, thereby blunting potential criticism from conservative groups that the Commission was a creation of the liberals.

Dr. Robert Felix, as director of NIMH, had responsibility for selecting the Commission's director, and after consulting with his colleagues, he chose Dr. Jack R. Ewalt. Ewalt, like Felix, had come from a small town in rural Kansas and had also gone to the University of Colorado for his medical training. He was well known to Bill Menninger, also from Kansas, who had used Ewalt as an assistant on the Hoover Commission. Ewalt was a fully certified psychoanalyst and at the time of his appointment was the commissioner of mental health in Massachusetts. He was thought to have excellent organizational skills, which balanced personal traits characterized by his close friends as "brusqueness." Francis Braceland was appointed a member of the Commission, and Dr. Felix and his staff at NIMH had continuing input to the Commission's deliberations.

Another member of the Commission, and one who was becoming increasingly powerful in shaping national policies on psychiatric matters, was Mike Gorman. Gorman had gone to work full time as a mental health lobbyist for Mrs. Mary Lasker, a wealthy philanthropist who had graduated cum laude from Radcliffe and done graduate work at Oxford University. Lasker's husband had amassed a fortune as a businessman, and Mary Lasker was developing a career as a contributor of her husband's money to senators and representatives who supported her interests in mental health, birth control, and, later, cancer and hypertension. Mary Lasker was "known to be one of the nation's more generous campaign contributors" and worked in tandem with another wealthy philanthropist, Florence Mahoney, who regularly entertained Washington's political elite in her Georgetown home. Both Mary Lasker and Florence Mahoney were friends of the

Trumans and had ready access to the White House when it was occupied by the Kennedys and the Johnsons.

Gorman's position as point man for Mary Lasker made him extremely powerful. He boasted of having "a warm relationship" and being "on a first-name basis with 150, 175 members of the House." Gorman was especially close to Senator Lister Hill of Alabama, chairman of the Committee on Labor and Public Welfare and one of the most powerful men in the Senate. During the 1955 hearings on the Mental Health Study Act, Senator Hill extolled his friend Mike; Gorman in turn dedicated his 1956 book, *Every Other Bed*, to "Senator Lister Hill, valiant legislator for, and compassionate friend of, the mentally ill of this nation." The citizens' lobby of Gorman, Lasker, and Mahoney worked in concert with Senator Hill and also with the NIMH–American Psychiatric Association professional axis to shape the recommendations of the Joint Commission. Gorman in later years implied that the recommendations of the Commission had been predetermined from the very beginning: "I was very happy to be a member of that [Commission] and really made only one contribution although it was a five-year study; I had the good fortune to write my suggested recommendations for Senator Hill in 1956. Old Chinese proverb—'If you appoint Commission, have all the recommendations finished before you appoint it.' "

During the years when the Joint Commission was preparing its report, the mental health lobby demonstrated its effectiveness in obtaining greater federal spending for its projects. Between 1955 and 1961 the NIMH budget for research increased over sixfold (from $6.5 to $41 million) and the budget for training increased over ninefold (from $4.5 to $42.5 million). Only in the services area was NIMH not growing as rapidly; prior to 1955 federal expenditures on psychiatric services had averaged $4.2 million a year, and by 1961 this had only increased to $7.7 million.

Simultaneously with the deliberations of the Joint Commission and the increasing budget of NIMH, a miracle was taking place in state mental hospitals. The miracle had nothing to do with either the Joint Commission or NIMH but would profoundly influence both of them. The new antipsychotic drugs were proving to be extremely effective in controlling some symptoms of psychosis, especially for individuals with schizophrenia, and for the first time in almost two hundred years the patient population of the mental hospitals was decreasing. The first decrease had been noted between 1955 and 1956 (from 558,922 to 551,390 patients), the same year the drugs had been introduced, and this had continued each year until by 1961 the number of patients had decreased to 527,456. It was clear that psychiatrists had, for the first time, effective medication for treating some cases of serious mental illness.

THE RIGHT-WING ANTI–MENTAL HEALTH LOBBY

Despite the official successes of the mental health lobby in Washington, there continued to be a deep distrust of psychiatry elsewhere in the nation in the late 1950s. The strength of this distrust became clear in 1956 when forces emerged to oppose an apparently innocuous bill introduced in Congress to allow Alaska, which had not yet achieved statehood, to build a public psychiatric hospital. Because Alaska had no hospital of its own, Alaskan residents who needed psychiatric hospitalization had to be sent to Portland, Oregon, an obviously confusing experience for a psychiatrically impaired Alaskan native from a rural village.

Right-wing groups across the United States organized a campaign to oppose the hospital legislation, claiming that the proposed psychiatric hospital would really be "a concentration camp for political prisoners under the guise of care and treatment of mental cases." A housewife in California labeled the proposed hospital "Siberia, U.S.A." and the name became a battle-cry. Mental health advocates were said to be part of a broad Communist conspiracy to subvert American liberties and seize political power. Racists tied the alleged Communist plot to a broader Communist-Jewish conspiracy. For example, John Kaspar, a racist agitator, segregationist, and protege of Ezra Pound (who corresponded with Kaspar regularly from his room at St. Elizabeths Hospital in Washington, D.C.), argued that the proposed Alaskan psychiatric hospital was another attempt by Jews to brainwash

Americans: "Psychiatry is a foreign ideology; it is alien to any kind of American thinking . . . its history began with Sigmund Freud who is a Jew . . . almost 100 percent of all psychiatric therapy and 80 percent of the psychiatrists are Jewish . . . one particular race is administering this particular thing."

The bill to build a psychiatric hospital in Alaska ultimately passed Congress, but an anti–mental health lobby had been established. Across the country, local initiatives to open mental health clinics ran the risk of encountering fierce opposition. In Delaware, thirty-five young men in black leather jackets disrupted an organizing meeting of a local mental health organization shouting that mental health was a Communist plot. In Utah, anti–mental health lobbyists packed a meeting of the state legislature that was considering setting up mental health services. In Wisconsin, opponents "caused the defeat of some twenty mental health measures that seemed certain of passage." The magazine of the Daughters of the American Revolution published a two-part series on mental health describing it as "a Marxist weapon" and alleging not only that 80 percent of American psychiatrists were foreigners but that "most of them [were] educated in Russia." The executive director of the Dallas Association of Mental Health received threatening telephone calls, and an academic symposium on mental health in Lubbock was picketed.

The heartland of the anti–mental health movement, however, was Southern California. There the movement was adopted by some members of the John Birch Society and was well financed. Literature was widely distributed with allegations such as: "Mental health programs are part of a Communist plot to control the people's minds." "Mental hygiene is a subtle and diabolical plan of the enemy to transform a free and intelligent people into a cringing horde of zombies." "Do we want to be become a regimented nation, brain-washed and brain-fed through a powerful army of psychiatrists?" In the suburbs of Los Angeles a large billboard was erected in July 1958 with the following message: "It is amazing and appalling how many supposedly intelligent people have been duped by such COMMUNIST SCHEMES as FLUORIDATION and 'Mental Health' especially since both the AMERI-

CAN LEGION and the D.A.R. have publicly branded 'Mental Health' as a COMMUNIST PLOT to take over our country." And when the Los Angeles City Council was asked to vote on a proposal to allow an unoccupied health center to be used as a mental health clinic, the measure was defeated by 11 to 0. One of the senators from California at the time was Richard M. Nixon, who had been elected in 1950 and would play an important role in opposing the mental health movement when he became president. It would become clear in later years that both Nixon and members of his staff (many of whom came from Southern California) were overtly antagonistic to psychiatry as well as to the concept of mental health.

Although the right-wing lobby was ridiculed as a lunatic fringe by the mental health establishment, some of its members were asking such cogent questions as "What is mental health?" and "By whose standards can we deduce that one person is normal and another is not?" They sensed intuitively what sociologist Kingsley Davis had described twenty years earlier, that "the mental hygienist is really enforcing in a secular way and under the guise of science the standards of the entire society." Mental health professionals claimed that they had revealed truth regarding such things as child-rearing practices and interpersonal relations, and the anti–mental health forces were asking where the revealed truth had come from. Unfortunately, these questions were usually so mixed in with anti-Communist and anti-Semitic slogans as well as with other issues such as the fluoridation of water and theories of a grand conspiracy, that the legitimate questions about the nature of mental health were never heard.

ACTION FOR MENTAL HEALTH

Throughout the late 1950s the work of the Joint Commission on Mental Illness and Health went forward. By getting the American Legion to agree to help sponsor the Commission, the mental health leaders had cleverly blunted much right-wing opposition to their deliberations. The report was complete by early 1960, but Dwight Eisenhower was still in the White House and it was thought that the recommendations being made by the Commission—recommendations for much greater federal investment in psychiatric services—would not be sympathetically received by a Republican administration. A decision was made to delay release of the report in hopes that a Democratic administration would be elected in November and would provide more fertile ground. The report of the Joint Commission, then, was finally issued two months after the election of John F. Kennedy.

The title of the report, *Action for Mental Health,* was significant in that the Commission responsible had been the Joint Commission on Mental Illness *and* Mental Health. The report itself was as strange and confused an entity as its motley array of authors. It contained sections of insightful analysis regarding problems of mental illness in the United States, yet its recommendations were often logically inconsistent with this analysis. There was something in the report for everyone, as if each of the forty-five individual members and thirty-six participating agencies had taken turns writing paragraphs. In future years, advocates for the mentally ill as well as those for mental health programs would both quote the report as favoring their position; both would be correct.

Mental illness, said the report, is characterized by its "staggering size" and "peculiar nature . . . that differentiates its victims from those with other diseases or disabilities." The report continued:

A national mental health program should recognize that major mental illness is the core problem and unfinished business of the mental health movement, and that the intensive treatment of patients with critical and prolonged mental breakdowns should have first call on fully trained members of the mental health professions. There is a need for expanding treatment of the acutely ill mental patient in all directions, via community mental health clinics, general hospitals, and mental hospitals, as rapidly as psychiatrists, clinical psychologists, psychiatric nurses, psychiatric social workers, and occupational, physical, and other nonmedical therapists become available in the community. There is a related need for revision of commitment laws to ease the movement of patients through the various treatment facilities.

The major institutions for treating mental diseases for almost two hundred years—the state hospitals—were relegated to a secondary role in the treatment system recommended by the Joint Commission. "No further state hospitals of more than 1,000 beds should be built, and not one patient should be added to any existing mental hospital already housing 1,000 or more patients." Furthermore, the existing large state hospitals should be "converted into centers for the long-term and combined care of chronic diseases, including mental illness." Mike Gorman, who played a prominent role in formulating the Joint Commission's recommendations, confirmed in later years that his "hidden agenda was to break the back of the state mental hospital."

In place of state mental hospitals, the proposed cornerstone for treatment of the mentally ill would be community mental health clinics "operated as outpatient departments of general or mental hospitals, as part of state or regional systems for mental patient care, or as independent agencies." There would be one such clinic for each 50,000 in population, and they would be "a main line of defense in reducing the need of many persons with major mental illness for prolonged or repeated hospitalization." Elsewhere in the report it was clearly stated that the community mental health clinics "must concentrate on providing psychiatric treatment for acute mental illness cases and for patients who can be helped either short of admission to a mental hospital or following discharge. The job of community education and mental health promotion should be left to the health departments and mental health associations."

In addition to community mental health clinics for the mentally ill, the Joint Commission report proposed a greater utilization of psychiatric beds in general hospitals and intensive inpatient psychiatric treatment centers. Emphasis was also placed on aftercare and rehabilitation for mentally ill persons once they had left the hospital: "Aftercare and rehabilitation are essential parts of all service to mental patients, and the various methods of achieving rehabilitation should be integrated in all forms of services, among them day hospitals, night hospitals, aftercare clinics, public health nursing services, foster family care, convalescent nursing homes, rehabilitation centers, work services, and ex-patient groups."

Perhaps the most controversial aspect of the report was its recommendation for financing public psychiatric services: "It is self-evident," said the report, "that the states, for the most part, have defaulted on adequate care for the mentally ill, and have consistently done so for a century." Since the states did not have the necessary fiscal resources to provide adequate services, "the federal government should be prepared to assume a major part of the responsibility for the mentally ill insofar as the states are agreeable to surrendering it."

At the same time that the proposed community mental health clinics were supposed to "concentrate on providing psychiatric treatment for acute mental illness cases," other portions of the Joint Commission report suggested that the function of these centers would be much broader. The centers, it said, should also serve "people who are emotionally disturbed—that is to say, under psychological stress that they cannot tolerate" and who need "skilled attention and helpful counseling . . . if the development of more serious mental breakdown is to be prevented." Furthermore:

Nonmedical mental health workers with aptitude, sound training, practical experience, and demonstrable competence should be permitted to do general, short-term psychotherapy . . . Such therapy, combining some elements of psychiatric treatment, client counseling, "someone to tell one's troubles to," and love for one's fellow man, obviously can be carried out in a variety of settings by institutions, groups, and individuals, but in all cases should be undertaken under the auspices of recognized mental health agencies.

How activities utilizing techniques such as "love for one's fellow man" were supposed to relate to the recommended concentration on "psychiatric treatment for acute mental illness cases" was not addressed by the Joint Commission.

MENTAL HEALTH IS OFFICIALLY DEFINED

In addition to making recommendations regarding treatment programs for acute mental illness cases and for the emotionally disturbed, the Joint Commission on Mental Illness and Health tried to do what nobody had yet done—define mental health. The task was certainly overdue since "mental health" had already acquired its own National Institute with an annual budget of over $91 million.

The definition was published by the Joint Commission as a report entitled *Current Concepts of Positive Mental Health*. (The implication that there was a negative mental health as well was never explored.) The first thing the Joint Commission did in its attempt at definition was to state categorically that mental health was *not* merely the absence of mental disease. This statement was not satisfying to all consultants on the project, however, and Dr. Walter Barton, superintendent of Boston State Hospital, wrote a dissenting opinion. He stated that the absence of disease was the criterion for health in medicine generally. Furthermore, said Barton, "I believe most patients would settle for the absence of illness. If they are not sick, they are well."

The logic of Dr. Barton's position escaped the Joint Commission, however, and it summarized positive mental health as consisting in:

1. the attitudes of the individual toward himself
2. the degree to which the individual realizes his potentialities through action
3. unification of function in the individual's personality
4. the individual's degree of independence of social influences
5. how the individual sees the surrounding world

6. the individual's ability to take life as it comes and master it

There was a strong psychoanalytic tone to the group's deliberations, as if Freud had been a Commission member in absentia. An underlying assumption was made that knowledge of oneself (including one's unconscious motivations) and honest assessment of oneself are valuable and desirable ends in themselves, although recent research in psychology has shown that this is not always so. Combined with this assumption were overtones of various philosophical and religious belief systems, especially a Buddhist calm acceptance of life. Some parts of the report encouraged striving to better oneself and the power of positive thinking as preached by Norman Vincent Peale, while other parts urged flowing with the tide of life in the what-me-worry posture of Alfred E. Newman.

Most aspects of positive mental health could be summarized quite satisfactorily by two homilies that had been around for a few hundred years before the Joint Commission undertook their task: "Know thyself" and "To thine own self be true." The definition of mental health arrived at by the Joint Commission was also consonant with the definition advocated by the National Committee for Mental Hygiene, which had modernized its name in 1950 to become the National Association for Mental Health. In 1951 it had described people with mental health as follows: "They feel comfortable about themselves; they feel right about other people; they are able to meet the demands of life."

Also of interest in the Commission report was the definition proposed by Dr. Jack R. Ewalt, the director of the Joint Commission. Dr. Ewalt said that mental health was:

. . . a kind of resilience of character or ego strength permitting an individual, as nearly as possible, to find in his world those elements he needs to satisfy his basic impulses in a way that is acceptable to his fellows or, failing this, to find a suitable sublimation for them . . .

This resilience of character should be such that he can

adapt himself to the vicissitudes of fortune, bouncing back to find new ways of satisfaction or sublimation after defeat . . .

Another definition was proposed by Dr. William Menninger, one of the most influential advocates of the mental health concept. He borrowed his definition from his brother, Karl Menninger:

> Mental health is the adjustment of human beings to the world and to each other with a maximum of effectiveness and happiness. Not just efficiency, or just contentment—or the grace of obeying the rules of the game cheerfully. It is all of these together. It is the ability to maintain an even temper, an alert intelligence, socially considered behavior, and a happy disposition. This, I think, is a healthy mind.

The only thing missing from the National Institute of Mental Health, it appeared, was a smiling face for its logo.

The 1961 report of the Joint Commission on Mental Illness and Health pointed the way for future psychiatric services in the United States. State mental hospitals would no longer be the main treatment centers; this responsibility would be shifted to community mental health clinics. And the proper purview of psychiatry was not merely to treat disease. Mental health was more than that—much more.

5

From the Suffering Sick to the
Worried Well

The year 1961 was a watershed year for psychiatric services in the United States. It was not only the year that the Joint Commission on Mental Illness and Health issued its report but also the year in which Erving Goffman published *Asylums,* Thomas Szasz published *The Myth of Mental Illness,* and Gerald Caplan published *An Approach to Community Mental Health.* By the end of 1961 three axioms had been established that would profoundly influence services for the mentally ill: (1) psychiatric hospitals are bad and should be closed; (2) psychiatric treatment in the community is better because cases can be detected earlier and hospitalization thereby avoided; and (3) the prevention of mental diseases is the most important activity to which psychiatric professionals can aspire. From that point onward it was all downhill for the mentally ill; the debacle of deinstitutionalization and the tragedies that accompanied it became virtually inevitable.

Goffman, a sociologist funded by the National Institute of Mental Health, formulated his theories about mental hospitals during a year spent at St. Elizabeths Hospital in Washington, D.C., as "an assistant to the athletic director." Goffman observed that mental hospitals were "total institutions" in which patients learned certain behaviors that helped them to live better and get along within that setting. But Goffman went further and reasoned that *most* of the behavior of the patients was a reaction to the institutional setting, implying that if somebody would just open the gates and let these people out (there were over 7,000 patients in St. Elizabeths at the time Goffman did his study), the patients would not have to behave strangely anymore.

This "King of Hearts" approach to the problems of the mentally ill had a romantic appeal to individuals who knew nothing about the problem. One such individual was Ken Kesey, a writer in California who was a rising guru of psychedelic drugs and who had worked as a psychiatric aide in the Menlo Park Veterans Administration Hospital. Out of his experiences came *One Flew Over the Cuckoo's Nest* in 1962. It became an instant underground best-seller, idealizing the heroics of Randle McMurphy as he challenged Nurse Ratched. In the end McMurphy lies dead, but his death has stimulated Chief Broom to escape from the hospital and, implicitly, live happily ever after.

Equally important in determining the future direction of deinstitutionalization and psychiatric services were the writings of Dr. Thomas Szasz. A psychoanalyst by training and a historian by inclination, Szasz postulated that mental diseases do not actually exist but are merely labels assigned by society to condemn behavior the society does not like. *The Myth of Mental Illness,* published in 1961, was widely quoted by many of the same people who were reading Goffman and Kesey. Two years later Szasz published *Law, Liberty and Psychiatry,* which carried his argument further, advocated the abolition of all involuntary psychiatric hospitalization, and urged mental patients to take "legal action against their oppressors," the hospital psychiatrists.

The attacks on mental hospitals, appearing concurrently with the report of the Joint Commission recommending a phasing down of these hospitals, were reinforced by psychiatrists representing the American Psychiatric Association. In 1958 Dr. Harry C. Solomon, as president of that organization, had publicly called for the abolition of state mental hospitals: "I do not see how any reasonably objective view of our mental hospitals today can fail to conclude that they are bankrupt beyond remedy. I believe, therefore, that our large mental hospitals should be liquidated as rapidly as can be done in an orderly and progressive fashion."

In the minds of the American public, the first axiom of modern psychiatric care was becoming clear: "Psychiatric hospitals are bad." Fifteen years earlier, when *Life* magazine, Mike Gorman, and Albert Deutsch had exposed the abysmal conditions in these hospitals, the corollary of "psychiatric hospitals are bad" had been "and should be improved." With the ideas of Goffman, Kesey, and Szasz stirring in the minds of the public, however, an alternate corollary emerged: "and should be closed down."

TREATMENT IN THE COMMUNITY

The second axiom of the emerging psychiatric ethos was formulated by Dr. Gerald Caplan, who in 1961 published *An Approach to Community Mental Health.* Caplan, a psychoanalyst from England, held the title Associate Professor of Mental Health and Head of the Community Mental Health Program at Harvard University School of Public Health. This was indeed academic sanction for mental health; despite the fact that most professionals appeared to be uncertain what mental health was, Harvard University had an associate professorship and program in it.

Caplan's thesis was that psychiatric treatment in the community permits cases to be detected earlier and hospitalization thereby avoided. He accepted the premise that hospitalization was bad—"hospitalization as such is an important cause of disability"—and, like other psychoanalysts, focused on the mother-child relationship as crucial to the development of mental diseases. Since mental illness arose out of the mother-infant relationship, the prevention of mental illness therefore consisted of educating mothers and treating the child's neurosis before it grew into a full-blown psychosis. Both neuroses and psychoses were caused, Caplan believed, by a failure of the individual to resolve early developmental problems, so that, when confronted with stress, the individual regressed. Mild regression led to neurosis, but severe regression led to psychosis:

> In other words, in order to avoid facing the tensions that his unified, integrated personality would face if dealing with this unsolved problem, he [the patient] just smashes up his personality, as it were. This gives him a psychosis. One of the most typical of these is schizophrenia ... If your personality is fragmented you cease to exist from a certain point of view, and cease to feel then the tensions of the unsolved problem. This is a way to escape, and is a quite primitive way. Sometimes there is a complete and absolute disorganization of the personality.

Elsewhere Caplan made it clear that he accepted the belief that schizophrenogenic mothers caused their children to develop schizophrenia.

Caplan's writings became widely accepted as the theoretical basis for the community mental health movement. Dr. Robert Felix called Caplan's second book, *Principles of Preventive Psychiatry,* which was published in 1964, "not only a primer for the community mental health worker—it is a Bible." The theories espoused by Caplan were in reality little different from those advocated by Freud fifty years earlier. For mental health professionals in the 1960s, however, it seemed more modern to quote an associate professor at Harvard University than a deceased Viennese psychoanalyst.

Caplan's advocacy of treating mental illnesses in the community was directly contradictory to his (and other psychoanalysts') belief that experiences in the home *caused* most mental illnesses, however. Dr. Lawrence Kubie, a prominent psychoanalyst, pointed out this contradiction in a paper published in 1968:

> This assumption [treating mental illness closer to home] ignores elementary common sense and familiar clinical experience. The very words "normal contacts" are surprising. The patient became ill in the midst of these normal contacts

with home, job, and community, among family and friends, among work and school associates. Why assume that this is where to help him find the road back to health? Would it be wise to launch the treatment of a malarial patient in the very malarial swamp in which he had contracted his illness?

Caplan, however, should not be blamed any more than Freud for the uncritical use of his theories to formulate public policies for the mentally ill. Caplan readily acknowledged that "mental health as a concept is a very fuzzy one and it is really not a useful scientific concept at all." In the introduction to *An Approach to Community Mental Health,* he defined mental health simply as "the potential of a person to solve his problems in a reality-based way within the framework of his traditions and culture." Despite Caplan's reservations about the scientific basis of mental health, however, his writings produced a union of "community" with "mental health." The myth now had an official place to live.

PRIMARY PREVENTION

The third axiom of modern psychiatric treatment that acquired the status of accepted fact in the early 1960s was that prevention of mental diseases is the most important activity to which psychiatric professionals can aspire. In Caplan's terminology this was called "primary prevention," which he defined as "the processes involved in reducing the risk that people in the community will fall ill with mental disorders."

Caplan used the model of infectious diseases, as had many mental health advocates before him, to illustrate primary prevention. In a low-income housing project near his office, for example, healthy families moving into the housing units were exposed to unhealthy families already living there. "A healthy family comes in and gets infected, as it were, like putting a new apple in a barrel where there are a lot of rotten ones." Caplan urged psychiatrists to become involved in social issues, which he believed had a direct causative effect on mental illness (e.g., housing, mandatory retirement laws, unemployment among high school graduates) and "to join pressure groups for their elimination . . . as a citizen leader." He was *not*, Caplan added, "advocating government by psychiatrists."

Another model of primary prevention was put forth by psychologists Nicholas Hobbs and M. Brewster Smith, both of whom had been members of the Joint Commission of Mental Illness and Health. Community psychiatrists, said Hobbs and Smith, were like police officers and firefighters: "Just as a modern police or fire department tries to prevent the problems it must cure, so a good mental health center would look for ways of reducing the strains and troubles out of which much disorder arises." The difference, of course, was that police and fire departments had a scientific basis for some of their preventive activities (e.g., narcotics addiction increases theft, faulty wiring increases the chances of fires). Psychiatrists, by contrast, had only theories derived from Freud regarding early childhood experiences and mental diseases. Police officers and firefighters also had specific training for their preventive activities, whereas the training of psychiatrists (medical school and residency) taught them nothing about housing, retirement laws, or unemployment. Their knowledge in the areas where they were claiming special expertise was no more and no less than that of any other informed citizen.

The emphasis on primary prevention in the emerging treatment ethos of the 1960s had two important consequences. By defining prevention as the sine qua non for being a good psychiatrist, it further reduced the already low status of psychiatric professionals who were actually working with the mentally ill. State hospital psychiatrists especially were relegated to the bottom of the status hierarchy, a development which would have tragic results (see chapter 8). The other consequence of the emphasis on primary prevention was the emergence of psychiatrists who aspired to be kings, as will be discussed in the next chapter.

MENTAL ILLNESS IN THE KENNEDY FAMILY

The election of John F. Kennedy in November 1960 appeared auspicious to the mental health lobby. The Democrats had included concerns about the mentally ill in their party platform, and Kennedy was thought to be sympathetic to social causes generally. The report of the Joint Commission on Mental Illness and Health, which had lain dormant for months awaiting the hoped-for election of a Democratic administration, was immediately dusted off and laid on the new president's desk.

What was not known to most of the psychiatric professionals seeking federal support for community mental health clinics was that mental illness had profoundly affected the Kennedy family, through Rosemary Kennedy, the third Kennedy child, born after Joseph Jr. and John. She had been born at the height of the 1918 influenza epidemic, which, given present knowledge, might have been consequential for her later problems.

According to biographers of the Kennedy family, it was suspected from her earliest years that Rosemary was neither as bright nor as coordinated as her brothers and sisters. Her intellectual deficits were confirmed in kindergarten when her teacher would not recommend her for advancement to first grade, and thereafter she attended private schools.

Rosemary's mental retardation would today be classified as mild. She reached a fifth-grade level of achievement in English and a fourth-grade level in math. She was included in the family's social occasions and, watched over by her older brothers, attended tea dances and other activities with her younger sisters. At age 19 she traveled in Europe accompanied only by her 16-year-old sister, Eunice. One year later, living in England where her father was the United States Ambassador, Rosemary accompanied her mother to Paris to buy a gown, was presented to the Queen at Buckingham Palace, and was presented at a coming-out party in London for three hundred guests. According to one biographer, through all of this "Rosemary's retardation" went "unnoticed" by the press.

Between the ages of 21 and 23 Rosemary's behavior appears to have changed dramatically. While she was still at the convent school in Hertfordshire in late 1939, where she remained after all the other Kennedys except her father had returned to the United States following the outbreak of World War II, her letters were noted to be "filled with eerie ellipses," probably indicating the onset of a thought disorder. Her intellectual abilities deteriorated: "The basic skills she had labored so hard to master in her special schools were deteriorating." "In the eighteen months following Rosemary's return from England, there had been a marked deterioration in her mental skills." More ominously, she began to have "wild moods" and "tantrums, then rages which developed into near clonic states during which she smashed objects and struck out at people around her." "Pacing up and down the halls of her house, she was like a wild animal, given to screaming, cursing and thrashing out at anyone who tried to thwart her will . . . Every day there would be one terrifying incident after another: physical fights where Rosemary would use her fists to hit and bruise people, long absences at night when she'd be out wandering the streets and violent verbal exchanges." There are also suggestions of psychotic, probably delusional, behavior: "In one traumatic incident during the summer of 1941, Rosemary, who was sitting on the porch at Hyannis, suddenly attacked Honey Fitz, hitting and kicking her tiny white-haired grandfather until she was pulled away." Rosemary Kennedy apparently had developed a psychosis, either schizophrenia or manic-depression psychosis, in addition to her mild mental retardation.

In 1941, thinking about the causes of schizophrenia and manic-depressive psychosis was undergoing a change. Biological and genetic theories had predominated in the earlier years of the twentieth century, especially a suspicion that the endocrine system of the body was involved, and such theories were still prevalent in Europe. In the United States, however, psychoanalytic concepts were taking over thinking about the psychoses as they had taken over thinking about normal human behavior during the preceding three decades. When the Kennedy family queried experts about what was causing Rosemary's bizarre behavior, therefore, the answers they received would have been deeply disturbing.

John White, a journalist researching a series about mental illness and a friend of Kathleen Kennedy, recalled being "quizzed rigorously" on the subject; Kathleen acknowledged to him that "it was because of Rosemary." What White found in the leading American textbooks of psychiatry at the time would not have pleased the Kennedys. Noyes's 1939 edition of *Modern Clinical Psychiatry,* for example, claimed that "schizophrenia represents a special type of personality disorganization, a maladapted way of life manifested by one's grappling unsuccessfully with environmental stresses and internal difficulties." Among the causative factors, said Noyes, were "early conditioning experiences, intrapsychic conflicts, insistent but consciously rejected demands of various instinctive drives and urges, feelings of guilt or of insecurity, as well as various other longstanding troublesome problems and frustrated purposes."

Rosanoff's *Manual of Psychiatry and Mental Hygiene,* published in 1938, was more directly to the point. Conditions like schizophrenia and manic-depressive psychosis were no longer categorized as diseases, according to Rosanoff, but were instead manifestations of "chaotic sexuality." The causes of these conditions included an "inborn psychosexual ill-balance . . . mainly between the factors within the individual which make for maleness and those which make for femaleness." Rosanoff cited Freud's "contribution of fundamental importance" to thinking about the causes of psychoses, specifically "that the principal actuating factor in the mechanism was *repressed and unconscious homosexuality.*"

One can imagine the distress that such theories would have caused for the Kennedys or any other family. The shame and stigma associated with such diagnoses even today are significant, but in 1941 for a socially prominent family like the Kennedys they would have been devastating.

It is hardly surprising that Joseph Kennedy Sr. would have tried anything that promised to improve his daughter's condition. Prefrontal lobotomy was one possibility, having first been used by Dr. Egas Moniz in Europe in 1936 and being promoted in the United States by Dr. Walter Freeman, professor of neurology at George Washington University in Washington, D.C. Freeman advocated lobotomy for the psychoses and claimed excellent results: "Disturbed patients often become friendly, quiet, and cooperative. They retain their basic psychotic dissociation and often their delusional ideas, but they no longer react to them so vigorously. Hallucinations are reduced or suppressed in about half the cases . . . the results are usually quite good, especially from an administrative point of view." Even before leaving England Joseph Kennedy Sr. had discussed the advisability of this new procedure with physicians there.

In the fall of 1941 Rosemary Kennedy underwent a lobotomy, probably by Dr. Freeman himself. The results were a disaster: "She no longer realized who she was" and "her capacity to speak was almost entirely gone." One member of the family claimed that the operation "made her go from being mildly retarded to very retarded." Since 1941 she has been confined to a nursing convent in Wisconsin except for brief visits outside.

The issues of mental illness and mental retardation, then, were exceedingly sensitive ones for the Kennedy family. President John F. Kennedy's decision to become an advocate for the mentally ill must have been a very complicated one both for him and for his family. Intimately involved in that decision was Eunice Kennedy Shriver, Rosemary's younger sister, with whom she had traveled in Europe. All accounts of the shaping of the community mental health center legislation which followed President Kennedy's election make it clear that Eunice was an active participant in the decision-making. She specified that there would be no presidential support for the mentally ill without equal support for the mentally retarded but that the two programs must be entirely separate. In the intervening years Eunice Shriver has become the nation's leading public advocate for the mentally retarded.

THE CELEBREZZE COMMITTEE

One strategy every president of the United States learns early is, when in doubt about an issue, appoint a committee to study it. Kennedy, faced with an extremely sensitive subject for his family, did exactly that with the report of the Joint Commission on Mental Illness and Health. He asked Anthony Celebrezze, the

Secretary of Health, Education and Welfare, to chair an inter-agency committee to study the report and make specific recommendations regarding possible legislation. The working members of the committee were Boisfeuillet Jones, a medical administrator representing Celebrezze; Daniel P. Moynihan, representing the Secretary of Labor; Robert Manley of the Veterans Administration; Robert Atwell of the Bureau of the Budget; and Rashi Fein of the Council of Economic Advisors. Dr. Robert Felix and the staff of NIMH were invited to participate as well and played major roles in formulating the committee's recommendations.

The major issue faced by the Celebrezze committee was, not surprisingly, the same one that had preoccupied the Joint Commission—the future of state mental hospitals. They had been the center for treatment of the mentally ill for almost two hundred years. If they were to be phased out, what would do their job? Could the proposed community mental health centers do it? Would they do it? Where would the professionals come from to staff the proposed centers? How would the centers be financed?

The outcome of the Celebrezze committee's deliberations was a foregone conclusion, since there were no members to represent the states' point of view. Atwell and Moynihan both believed that state hospitals were too discredited to survive; in addition, Moynihan's deep interest in preserving the integrity of families must have been aroused by NIMH staff descriptions of what the proposed new centers would do to provide unified psychiatric and social services close to home. Fein was on record as favoring federal investment in psychiatric services. The fear of some committee members that support of the centers might turn into a permanent federal subsidy was assuaged by proposals to use federal funds only for start-up costs and to phase out the funds over three to five years. Dr. Felix and his staff from NIMH were enthusiastic about the proposed centers. Behind the scenes Mike Gorman and Mary Lasker generated political pressure in favor of the NIMH position.

Meanwhile at the White House, Eunice Kennedy Shriver negotiated the position of the Kennedy family vis-à-vis mental

107

retardation and mental illness. There would also be legislation for the mentally retarded, it was decreed, and that legislation would be separate and distinct from the legislation being proposed for the mentally ill. Furthermore, NIMH would not administer the programs for the mentally retarded; instead a new institute, the National Institute of Child Health and Human Development, would be created as part of the National Institutes of Health (of which NIMH was also a part at that time). There would be no confusion about the mentally retarded and the mentally ill. Word circulated quietly that President Kennedy was interested in the problems of the mentally impaired because his sister, Rosemary, was mentally retarded; there was no mention of mental illness among the Kennedys.

By the end of 1962, the necessary compromises had been forged and the Kennedy initiative was ready to go forward. In January 1963, in his State of the Union message, President Kennedy spoke of "the abandonment of the mentally ill and the mentally retarded to the grim mercies of custodial institutions" and the following month delivered his historic special message to Congress entitled "Mental Illness and Mental Retardation." Kennedy proposed community mental health centers (CMHCs) as "a bold new approach" and promised that "when carried out, reliance on the cold mercy of custodial isolation will be supplanted by the open warmth of community concern and capability . . . It has been demonstrated that two out of three schizophrenics—our largest category of mentally ill—can be treated and released within six months." No longer would it be necessary for the mentally ill to undergo "a prolonged or permanent confinement in huge, unhappy mental hospitals . . . If we launch a broad new mental health program now, it will be possible within a decade or two to reduce the number of patients now under custodial care by 50 percent or more." CMHCs, then, were set up for the seriously mentally ill as alternatives to the state hospitals. Kennedy made no mention of services for married couples having difficulty communicating, young adults concerned about their relations with the opposite sex, or

108

middle-aged individuals undergoing existential crises. This was a program for the suffering sick, not for the worried well.

CONGRESSIONAL HEARINGS ON CMHC'S

On March 5, 1963, one month after President Kennedy's special message to Congress, hearings began on the proposed community mental health centers (CMHCs) before the Senate Subcommittee on Health of the Committee on Labor and Public Welfare. The mood of the nation was buoyant; the previous year John Glenn had become the first American to orbit the earth, and President Kennedy had won a tense showdown with Soviet Premier Kruschev over missiles being placed in Cuba. The Democrats had retained control of the House and Senate in the November elections, and one of the newly elected senators was the president's brother Edward, now a member of the committee before which the CMHC hearings were being held. Two weeks prior to the opening of the CMHC hearings President Kennedy had proposed a domestic Peace Corps (to become VISTA) and a Youth Conservation Corps. There was a sense in America that everything was possible in terms of improving life for disadvantaged citizens.

The Senate hearings lasted three days and were followed on March 26 to 28 by hearings on the House side before the Subcommittee on Public Health and Welfare of the Committee on Interstate and Foreign Commerce. In July, two more days of hearings were held before the House subcommittee to discuss a compromise bill and to resolve some of the questions that had arisen, especially those concerning funds for staffing the centers. Finally, on March 2 to 5, 1965, additional hearings were held before the House subcommittee specifically on the proposed staffing funds. Altogether, the testimony of those four hearings filled 1,330 pages, with the vast majority of it devoted to discussions of mental illness and the proposed CMHCs.

At the outset of the hearings, Anthony J. Celebrezze, Secretary of Health, Education and Welfare, made it clear that the CMHC "proposals are the outgrowth of an exceptionally thorough and competent study of our national mental health needs . . . the work of the Joint Commission on Mental Illness and Health." As explained to the Senate subcommittee at the initial hearing by Dr. Jack R. Ewalt, who had been the director of the Joint Commission, the Commission's "report recommends planning at the local level the erection of general purpose mental health centers, and the gradual abandonment of the large isolated mental hospitals."

The conditions in state mental hospitals came in for severe criticism during the hearings as they had in the Joint Commission's report. Secretary Celebrezze noted that "three-fourths of the state mental institutions were opened prior to World War I. Many are fire and health hazards. Almost all are understaffed. The average expenditure per patient in state institutions is only $4 a day, and in some states the average is less than $2 a day." In Missouri it was said that the average stay in the state mental hospitals was thirteen years and "our study shows us if you spend four years in one of Missouri's hospitals you have only 1 chance in 20 of ever leaving that hospital." Senator Lister Hill of Alabama, chairman of the Subcommittee on Health, introduced an article about one hospital at which "41 percent of the patients had not had a visitor within the last year and 16 percent had not had a visit since hospitalization. Several had no visit for twenty-five years."

It was precisely because the state mental hospitals had failed that the new CMHCs were needed. Dr. Luther Terry, Surgeon General of the Public Health Service, testified that the CMHC legislation was an opportunity "for making one of our greatest health advances," while Senator Hill added that "at long last after all these years we are really going to move in now and try and wage a battle for the care of the mentally ill."

THE TARGET POPULATION

Throughout the hearings, both implicitly and explicitly, it was emphasized that the target population of the proposed CMHCs

110

was to be the seriously mentally ill. Secretary Celebrezze, in his initial statement, characterized the state hospitals as "primarily institutions for quarantining the mentally ill, not for treating them." He continued:

> While new therapies have considerably improved the prospects for cure and rehabilitation for many patients, and further improvements can be expected, it is clear that huge custodial mental hospitals are not suitable for the treatment of mental illness.
>
> Given what is now known about the treatment of mental illness, the magnitude of the problem, the human, economic, and social loss to the nation resulting from millions of mentally disabled persons, we cannot afford to continue to support mental health activities in the traditional manner. Rather, if we are to plan for the mental health needs of the nation, we must embark upon a bold and imaginative new program.
>
> Therefore, the national program for mental health is centered on a wholly new emphasis and approach—care and treatment of most mentally ill persons in their own home communities. Recognizing, of course, that our state hospitals will still have a major role to play during a period of transition, however, the program also makes provision—under existing authority—for limited project grants to develop and establish improved programs in existing state institutions.

Other spokesmen for the Kennedy administration were just as unambiguous. Mr. Boisfeuillet Jones, the special assistant to Secretary Celebrezze who had headed the interagency committee, stated that "the basic purpose of the president's program is to redirect the focus of treatment of the mentally ill from state mental hospitals into community mental health centers" with "the objective stated in the president's message of reducing the population of state mental hospitals by 50 percent within a decade or two."

Dr. Robert Felix, the director of NIMH who had worked so

hard to bring the CMHC program into existence, was also convinced that the state hospital population could be cut in half if
the CMHC legislation was passed:

> If you will do this, sir, I am as certain as I am that I am sitting
> here that within a decade or two we will see the size of these
> mental hospitals, the population of these mental hospitals,
> cut in half. I wish to God I could live and be active for
> twenty-five more years, because I believe if I could, I would
> see the day when the state mental hospitals as we know
> them today would no longer exist, but would be a different
> kind of institution for a selected few patients who needed
> specialized types of care and treatment.

The chairmen of the Senate and House Subcommittees hold-
ing the hearings indicated that they understood the purpose of
the proposed CMHCs. Senator Hill said:

> Thirty years ago in our economic distress period during the
> Depression, we spoke much of our forgotten men. I have
> long felt that our mentally ill were the forgotten people. We
> put them in state institutions, we closed the doors, and they
> were forgotten. That was the end.
> Now you come to us today with a program resolved to put
> an end to this forgetfulness; to do something about these
> people; to do our best where possible to cure them, care for
> them, rehabilitate them, and restore them to society; and
> better still, try to prevent mental illness and mental retarda-
> tion.

Similarly, Rep. Kenneth A. Roberts of Alabama clarified his understanding of the program:

> I take it that you envision replacement of the present state
> services which are in your opinion primarily custodial . . .
> We will bring these services back to the grassroots, so to
> speak, or back to the hometown of the patient who is af-

112

fected, and gradually large institutions that are concentrated maybe in one or two or more places in each state will be out of the picture, so to speak, as far as the overall treatment of this problem is concerned.

Others, such as Representative Oren Harris of Arkansas, chairman of the Committee on Interstate and Foreign Commerce, offered similar justification for supporting the CMHC legislation:

> What you ultimately hope to accomplish by this program is to reduce the number of patients in the big state hospitals to a minimum, and ultimately down the line to more adequately take care of the patients in the local center, and thereby increase the opportunities or possibility of that patient then getting back into society instead of being sent to the state hospital where he becomes a life patient?

Finally, Philip S. Hughes, from the Bureau of the Budget, testified about the intent of the legislation from the point of view of President Kennedy:

> As the president indicated in his message, if a broad new mental health program such as he has suggested is enacted, it will be possible within a decade or two to reduce the number of patients now under custodial care in state mental institutions by 50 percent or more. Accordingly, the major purpose of the president's proposals is to encourage the development of comprehensive community mental health centers "which will return mental health to the mainstream of American medicine."

DOUBTS AND QUESTIONS

Despite strong endorsement of the proposed CMHC legislation by witnesses from virtually every segment of the mental health community, and unanimous agreement regarding the target population and intent of the CMHCs, several doubts and questions were raised during the course of the hearings. These included:

· *Staffing:* Questions about using federal funds to pay CMHC staff salaries were a source of contention and disagreement from the outset. The original legislation included funds for both construction and staffing, but only the former funds were appropriated in 1963; funds for staffing had to wait until 1965. The question of whether psychiatrists would be attracted to work in the CMHCs was raised repeatedly. Mr. Boisfeuillet Jones, speaking for the Department of Health, Education and Welfare, assured Congress that "some of the psychiatrists who are now working in clinics and in private practice will undoubtedly move to staff, full time and part time, the new comprehensive community mental health centers as they become the locus of care of the mentally ill in the community." Dr. Jack Ewalt of the joint commission was even more reassuring: "I have no worry at all about our ability to staff these mental health centers." It was projected that by 1970, when 290 CMHCs would be operational, some 2,900 psychiatrists would be needed.

· *Costs:* Several witnesses who testified at the hearings asserted that CMHCs would save the states large amounts of money by reducing the number of patients in costly state hospitals. In his initial testimony, for example, Secretary Celebrezze said that "since the development of effective community-based programs will predictably reduce the utilization, and hence the costs, of state-operated mental hospitals, it is reasonable to expect the states to share in some manner in the costs of providing community service programs."

Later, Representative Kenneth A. Roberts and Mr. Boisfeuillet Jones agreed that the savings would be significant:

> MR. ROBERTS: So any way you look at it states are going to be relieved of a considerable amount of financial burden that they have been under for the last several years. Is that not correct?

114

MR. JONES: That is the full and reasonable expectation demonstrated already in a few communities.

In another exchange, Representative Leo W. O'Brien from New York asked Dr. Harold Visotsky, director of the Illinois Department of Mental Health, whether "every state in the union" might not save "billions of dollars" by "avoiding [the] wasteful expenditure [of] throwing it down a rattrap concept of the madhouse." Dr. Visotsky said he "could not agree more strongly."

MR. O'BRIEN: If by some miracle overnight the money that is now being spent on an archaic system could be brought to a local level and properly spent curing people, you would not need a nickel of federal money, would you?
DR. VISOTSKY: No, I might even say "Amen."

Other questions were raised regarding whether the federal dollars proposed for CMHCs would merely replace dollars currently being spent by states and thus amount to a federal subsidy, and whether it was appropriate to use federal dollars at all, which would have to be borrowed, when many states were at that time reporting budget surpluses.

• *Phase-out:* Several members of the Senate and House subcommittees expressed skepticism that the federal funds for CMHCs could really be phased out over three to five years as the legislation proposed. Dr. Felix testified that the proposed CMHC funds were "grubstake money," which "gets you on the road and from there on you take it on your own." Representative Ancher Nelson of Minnesota observed, however:

I have never seen a temporary government program that didn't become permanent, and I see no way that you can terminate this financing of staffing in the future. It seems to me the very reason that you propose it be terminated at a future date is an admission of the fact that it shouldn't continue, and if it shouldn't continue, why start?

In fact, many of the NIMH staff involved in the CMHC planning effort privately advocated and foresaw continuing federal fiscal support. Similarly it was the conscious strategy of Secretary Celebrezze to project the total number of CMHCs as 400 to 500 by 1970 and not to mention the projection of 2,000 centers by 1980 that had been emphasized by his interagency committee.

Representative William Springer of Illinois attempted to extract a promise from Secretary Celebrezze that he would not return asking for more money:

> MR. SPRINGER: Mr. Secretary, you are probably going to be here for at least four more years. Will you guarantee me you won't come back in here, if I support this bill, four years from now asking for another extension of this?
>
> SECRETARY CELEBREZZE: I am sure this Congress—and, after all, we can only suggest and Congress passes the law. What the circumstances will be at that time, I don't know. I wouldn't try to guess on conditions four years from now. I am hopeful, based on past experiences, that it will phase out. On the other hand, we have had some experience where things haven't phased out, so I wouldn't try to guarantee you about anything that would happen four years from now . . .

• *Dropping state hospital population:* The reduction of the population of state mental hospitals was unanimously agreed to be the principal objective of the proposed CMHC legislation. Yet at several points during the testimony it was noted that the state hospital population was already dropping and had been doing so consistently since 1956. Dr. Stanley Yolles, director of NIMH, asserted that "the number of resident patients in state mental hospitals . . . [has] been coming down for the last nine years in a very startling fashion." Former NIMH Director Felix, in the same hearings, testified "that the public mental hospital population in this country has dropped over 12 percent in the last ten or twelve years . . . this last year was the largest single drop, about 2 percent."

• *Other doubts and questions:* Since it was alleged that the CMHCs would save so much money for the states, one congressman asked why the states did not implement the program on their own. Questions also arose about why Hill-Burton Act hospital construction funds could not be used to construct the CMHCs rather than having to implement a new program. Another congressman was skeptical that the CMHCs would treat the indigent. Finally, Representative John B. Bennett of Michigan expressed serious doubt that the Department of Health, Education and Welfare needed any more money and accused it of wasting funds it already had on "projects which I won't characterize as ridiculous because maybe that is only my opinion." He specifically cited research "on why a monkey loves its mother, and other similar things, which have no tangible benefits as far as I can see." Dr. Yolles of NIMH retorted quickly in defense of the research, which was in fact Dr. Harry Harlow's research on maternal deprivation among monkeys: "I will stand on both my feet on top of the Empire State Building and shout with pride that we put the money into that one. You picked the wrong one, Mr. Bennett."

Ultimately, however, the most important question never got asked—"What evidence do you have, sir, that your program will work?" And the answer would have been startling: "None." There was almost no evidence that the care of mentally ill persons could be shifted en masse from state hospitals to the community, no evidence that the projected CMHCs either could or would provide care for the patients already being discharged from state hospitals, no evidence that the CMHCs could reduce admissions to the hospitals, and no evidence that the CMHCs could prevent mental illnesses. Furthermore, no pilot projects to test the feasibility of CMHCs were proposed.

The closest anyone who testified at the CMHC hearings came to citing evidence for the effectiveness of CMHCs was to make vague allusions to programs in Europe. In fact, there had been at that time only one reported study of discharged psychiatric patients, and that had been carried out in England by Dr. John K. Wing. It had involved a total of twenty patients with schizophrenia who had been *selected as high-functioning* and capable of working; the study had shown that with job training many such patients could live in the community and be self-supporting. In addition, Mike Gorman recalled during the hearings that "when I was in Amsterdam in 1957 I saw there a very remarkable community mental health center." The reference was to a program developed by Dr. Arie Querido in which 24-hour emergency psychiatric services were available to make home visits and prevent some psychiatric hospitalizations. The program was an integral part of the Dutch national health insurance plan and thus not comparable to administrative or funding mechanisms available in the United States.

In the end, however, it was not evidence of the efficacy of community mental health centers that carried the day but blind hope. Dr. Felix said he could "see a new day dawning." Despite opposition from the American Medical Association, which saw CMHCs as another example of socialism creeping into American medicine, the CMHC legislation passed Congress easily and was signed into law by President Kennedy. The date of the signing was October 31, 1963; the legislation would bring much "trick" but little "treat" for the nation's seriously mentally ill.

6

Psychiatrists Who Would Be Kings

The assassination of President John F. Kennedy on the streets of Dallas just twenty-two days after he had signed legislation creating community mental health centers deeply affected the psychiatric professionals and mental health advocates who had fought so hard for the program. Kennedy had been their leader, the first president to publicly proclaim support for their principles, their hope for the future. Suddenly he was gone. The community mental health centers became, in the minds of many, a Kennedy legacy to them, and to honor their fallen president they vowed to carry on his program.

Carrying on initially was easy, for it was the era of President Lyndon B. Johnson's Great Society. Legislation declaring a war on poverty was passed in July of 1964, quickly followed by legislation creating Medicare, low-income housing, job training, loans for education, and the protection of civil rights and voting rights of Blacks. Johnson was given a further mandate when he demolished Barry Goldwater in the November presidential election. It was the Age of Aquarius in which everything worthwhile would be legislated and the federal government would fly in by sleigh from the North Pole bringing gifts for all.

In this atmosphere the CMHC legislation was translated into operational reality. The National Institute of Mental Health was charged with the task of writing regulations to determine what services a CMHC would provide and which programs would receive federal money. By May 1964, initial regulations had been agreed upon by NIMH staff, and five essential services were prescribed in order to qualify for funds as a community mental health center:

1. inpatient services
2. partial hospitalization (e.g., hospitalization during days only)
3. outpatient services
4. emergency services available 24 hours a day
5. consultation and education services

The services were to be delivered to a catchment area of between 75,000 and 200,000 people.

In what would turn out to be an egregious error, the regulations failed to include any provision for a mandatory working relationship between CMHCs and state mental hospitals despite the fact that CMHCs were supposed to assume responsibility for patients from the hospitals. As noted by a 1974 study of CMHCs done by the Health Research Group:

Perhaps the most striking aspect of the regulations is what they omit. They describe no plans, mechanisms, nor procedures to guide centers in determining their relationship to state hospitals; no methods to divert potential state hospital admissions to community mental health centers; and no procedures whereby patients released from state hospitals could be rehabilitated and assisted back into the community. Indeed, the regulations contain not a single reference to the goal of supplanting state hospitals!

120

PUBLIC HEALTH PSYCHIATRISTS

Instrumental in NIMH decision-making in 1964 were two young psychiatrists who, between them, would provide leadership for NIMH over the next fourteen years. They were Dr. Stanley F. Yolles, who was director from 1964 to 1970, and Dr. Bertram S. Brown, who followed him from 1970 to 1978. Like Dr. Felix, both men had masters degrees in public health, and they were hand-picked by the retiring NIMH director to insure that the prevention of mental illness and promotion of mental health would continue to be the number-one priorities of the Institute.

Although Yolles and Brown would be criticized in later years for their programs, it should be kept in mind that they were carrying on the dreams and hopes of a half century of their predecessors beginning with the leaders of the mental hygiene movement. The mandate of Yolles and Brown had been implicitly given to them by the leaders of American psychiatry—Braceland, Menninger, Ewalt, Felix, *et al.* Felix himself had clearly indicated the future direction of NIMH as early as 1947 when he said that, in order to prevent mental disorders, community mental health programs "would require the active cooperation of other community agencies in carrying out, where indicated, plans for modification of the patient's environment." The fact that nobody knew how to prevent mental diseases (except for a few rare conditions such as pellagra psychosis) or how to promote mental health (because nobody knew what it meant) was ignored not only by Yolles and Brown but by an entire generation of American psychiatric leaders.

For Dr. Yolles, 45 years old when he became NIMH director, "the next frontier for mental health is the prevention of illness." To this concept he attributed the rapid acceptance of the CMHC program: "As the months of community mental health planning went by," recalled Yolles, "it became increasingly apparent that no mental health program could meet the needs of the population unless it began to work to prevent mental illness and improve the mental health of populations as well as of individual persons." The responsibility of mental health professionals, claimed Yolles, is:

> to improve the lives of the people by bettering their physical environment, their educational and cultural opportunities, and other social and environmental conditions. In accepting such a responsibility, mental health professionals do not claim omnipotence. They are trying to act as community catalysts, helping to bring the best thinking available in all relevant fields to bear on common needs and objectives.

Dr. Yolles pointed with pride to activities of CMHC staff members who "in addition to treating the classic range of mental illness, are helping clients with problems about housing, bill collection, reading difficulties . . ."

It was not merely prevention of mental illness that interested Yolles, however, but *primary* prevention, which had been defined by Gerald Caplan as reducing "the incidence of mental disorder." In order to accomplish this goal, psychiatrists would have to become involved in improving the social conditions that, according to Yolles, were known to cause mental disorders. Foremost among these conditions was poverty:

> The psychiatrist is aware that a man's mind, assaulted by poverty in either its acute or chronic form, is susceptible to mental disturbance, disorder or disease . . . The conditions of poverty, since they constitute a breeding ground for mental disease, require the professional involvement of the modern psychiatrist. Working with community leaders and specialists in other professions, we, as specialists in the art of psychiatry, have skills and knowledge which can help the statesman, the politician, and the poor man himself to intervene in this condition of poverty before it creeps into the fiber and style of a man's thoughts and behavior.

In fact there was no evidence that poverty *per se* caused mental disorders; a review of the literature in 1972 concluded that such studies "have not clearly supported an etiological link between poverty and mental disorder."

Dr. Bertram S. Brown was only 33 years old in 1964 when he helped write the CMHC regulations. Three years earlier he had strongly argued the merits of primary psychiatric prevention using "mental health education and mental health consultation." The latter could be done with the community's "caretakers," both unofficial, such as bartenders, and official, such as clergymen, physicians, and nurses. Brown asked at the time:

> Shall we extend this concept to include the true caretakers—the political forces? Here we get into such areas as the role of mental health personnel in such things as city planning. Such psychiatrists as Dr. Leonard Duhl are actively involved in this field. It is more than fantasy to conceive that one form of assistance to a mayor may be a psychiatrist, since this has already happened in New Orleans.

Both Yolles and Brown believed firmly that state mental hospitals had failed and should be replaced by the new CMHC delivery system for psychiatric services.

The new breed of public health psychiatrists that took command at NIMH in the mid-1960s was also typified by Dr. Leonard Duhl, cited by Dr. Brown for his work in city planning. Duhl was chief of planning for NIMH. In 1968, he represented the position that mental disease was "a socially defined condition and mental health must be conceived of as a social problem." The role of a mental health professional, argued Duhl, should be as "change agent in society" with the goal of helping "construct a social system that produces mentally healthy individuals."

Duhl recognized that the role of psychiatrist as change agent meant that he would become involved in community politics:

> Such a role requires that he undertake action to persuade a majority to support his decision, and to involve people in implementing his ideas. This, by any definition, is political action . . . It requires those involved in the mental health

program on whatever level—federal, state, or local—to understand the breadth of the problem and to become deeply involved in its total policies. It means making alliances within the social structure so that one can influence political decisions.

Such a strategy also requires that the mental health professional stretch his imagination to embrace the concept of a national mental health effort through an evolution of programs all the way across the board in every government agency.

Duhl's special interest in urban conditions as mental health problems found expression in statements like the following:

The city . . . is in pain. It has symptoms that cry out for relief. They are the symptoms of anger, violence, poverty, and hopelessness. If the city were a patient, it would seek help . . . The totality of urban life is the only rational focus for concern with mental illness . . . our problem now embraces all of society and we must examine every aspect of it to determine what is conducive to mental health.

Another young NIMH psychiatrist of that era was Dr. Matthew Dumont, who became assistant chief of the NIMH Center for Studies of Metropolitan Mental Health Problems. Dr. Dumont shared Dr. Duhl's interest in the problems of cities, an interest that sharpened as Watts, then Newark, Detroit, and other inner cities burst into racial conflagrations in the mid-1960s. Dumont viewed a city "as an organism capable of health or suffering":

It isn't too difficult to view the city in this way. Like any organism it has a circulatory system in its streets, railroads, and rivers; a brain in its universities, and planning offices; a digestive system in its food distribution and sewerage lines; muscles in its industrial centers; and any city worthy of the name has an erogenous zone . . .

The first question a physician must ask himself about an

organism is whether it is suffering or not. There would seem little doubt that the urban organism is indeed distressed; it is feeling symptoms. There have been choking sensations, blackout spells, uncontrolled and uncoordinated growth patterns, and painful tissue destruction. By the last, of course, I mean the riots that have become the most conspicuous part of summertime in the city.

Poverty was another concern of Dumont, and he maintained that "study after study has demonstrated the relationship between poverty and mental illness." If, argued Dumont, social factors like poverty, unemployment, and social discrimination cause mental illness, "then it will be the responsibility of mental health professions to devote at least some of their attention to these issues, or the battle against mental illness will be lost." Duhl reasoned that, in terms of achieving mental health, "a dollar's worth of effort in low-income housing may pay off more than a dollar invested in psychiatric treatment."

It is not surprising that both Duhl and Dumont had been trained as psychoanalysts. Mental diseases, they believed, were caused by the environment around them. Duhl and Dumont focused not only on the mother and family as crucial environmental variables, but on the broader societal environment in which they lived. Duhl illustrated this line of reasoning when he argued:

To operate in the larger system of mental health concerns one must deal with the total society rather than with the individual's emotional problem as the key to restoring mental health. For the individual's mental health is formed by the total society in which he exists. If you cure a mentally ill patient from a low-income background in a hospital, you must then return him to the poverty community. If he goes back to the poverty community, conditions in the community can undo everything that you have done. It is therefore the total society that needs a mental health treatment program and, almost more important than what you do in the individual psychiatric treatment is how you treat the total environment.

Given the staff and milieu at NIMH when regulations were being written for community mental health centers, it was inevitable that prevention of mental disorders and promotion of mental health would be of greatest interest. The vision of "mental hygiene" had finally become a reality.

Dissenting voices were present within NIMH, arguing that the primary focus of the CMHC program should be the seriously mentally ill, but such voices were in a minority. Two small federal grant programs aimed at state mental hospitals (the Hospital Staff Development and Hospital Improvement Programs) had been enacted at the same time as the CMHC program, and it was hoped that such programs would improve the hospitals sufficiently that the seriously mentally ill would no longer be a problem. Community mental health centers could therefore get on with the real business of mental health.

The message conveyed by NIMH to potential applicants for community mental health centers was clear—prevention, not treatment, was what was valued. This message was conveyed by the director, Dr. Yolles, when in 1966 he wrote:

The community mental health center has been designed as a public health facility, which means that it is basically concerned with disease as it affects groups of people in a community and with prevention of such disease . . . Through community planning on a comprehensive basis, through crisis intervention and other methods, mental health professionals can share with other community leaders in environmental manipulation to eliminate known producers of stress as well as loci of stress such as urban slums and rural depressed areas—potential breeding grounds of mental disease.

All of these are perfectly legitimate methods of treatment and no longer have the overtones of quackery which have in the past been attributed to them.

The message from NIMH was also conveyed by staff members in charge of the CMHC program, such as Dr. Saul Feldman, who urged his colleagues to extend their psychiatric activities ever further afield: "For some mental health professionals, environmental concerns are viewed as 'not mental health,' as if mental health had somehow been immutably defined. It is worth noting that in many areas of contemporary science, the boundaries of traditional disciplines are rapidly disappearing."

Finally, the message from NIMH was conveyed by the activities of the Institute itself, which every month appeared to espouse yet another social cause—urban studies, poverty, crime and delinquency, racism, sexism, unemployment, divorce, school dropouts, terrorism—there seemed no limit to what could be pursued in the name of mental health. In a typical conference, such as one sponsored by NIMH in May 1966, to which seventy-five "leading people in community mental health" were invited, three days of papers and discussions produced virtually no mention of the seriously mentally ill except in passing. Rather, a consensus developed that "primary social systems" must be "treated . . . and sometimes altered functionally or structurally." Professionals would need to:

> intervene in those aspects of community life which have a demonstrable effect on mental disorders and mental health . . . It means assisting all members of the community to function optimally in terms of their values. It means reducing social breakdown to a minimum . . . Thus, community mental health programs must be broad in scope, yet they need not be fuzzy, and their boundaries may be established.

Probably at no time in American history, however, has a federal program been conceived that more deserved the adjective "fuzzy."

It should be added that the social causes that NIMH urged psychiatrists to take up were all worthy causes. Indeed, it was difficult to oppose NIMH, for, as sociologist Morton Wagenfeld pithily observed in writing about the period, "who wants to be labeled as a conscientious objector or a draft evader in the war on poverty, racism, and human suffering?" But despite the good intentions of NIMH, there was no more scientific basis for psychiatrists to assume a leadership position on social problems than for anyone else to do so. Psychiatrists had no special knowledge, no special training, and no special competence in social problems. And, tragically, the one area in which psychiatrists *did* have special knowledge, training, and competence—the treatment of the mentally ill—was implicitly held by NIMH to be relatively unimportant.

THE PROMOTION OF MENTAL HEALTH BEGINS

The community mental health center movement of the 1960s was not the first time in this century that psychiatrists had laid claim to the special knowledge needed to prescribe social and political change. In 1941 Dr. George S. Stevenson, president of the American Psychiatric Association and medical director of the National Committee for Mental Hygiene, had asserted that wars were "mental health problems" because they had their roots in "psychological and psychopathological factors." Similarly, in 1946 Dr. G. Brock Chisholm, president of the World Federation for Mental Health, outlined a less than modest role for his colleagues: "If the race is to be freed from its crippling burden of good and evil, it must be psychiatrists who take the original responsibility . . . With the other human sciences, psychiatry must now decide what is to be the immediate future of the human race. No one else can. And this is the prime responsibility of psychiatry."

Although there had been such claims by psychiatrists before, there was now one important difference. Past reformers had to carry out their mission on their own time and money, which tended to act as a natural brake on their activities. With the federal funding of CMHCs and official interest in preventing mental illness and promoting mental health, the betterment of society could be carried out by psychiatrists in government-funded offices on government-funded salaries. Psychiatrists were being, in a sense, deputized by the United States government to enforce the laws of mental health.

In retrospect it is remarkable how few voices of dissent were raised as psychiatry embarked on its journey down the yellow brick road toward prevention. The lobbyists who had fought so hard to get the CMHC program through Congress thought the idea of prevention was wonderful. Mike Gorman, for example, commended CMHCs for becoming:

> involved in housing committees and tenant councils, which force slumlords to improve living conditions . . . in establishing remedial educational courses . . . and, yes, even encouraging the previously alienated people to register and to vote so that they can truly participate in electing officials pledged to improve conditions which presently generate so much mental illness and mental disturbance.

Similarly, the National Association of Mental Health was so enchanted by the official pursuit of mental health that "in many mental health association programs the mentally ill were all but forgotten."

The first federally funded mental health centers opened in 1967. The centers were said by one pair of observers even at the time to be "a victim of the Babel syndrome . . . [community mental health] conveys many different things to different people." In Chicago, the organizers of the Woodlawn Community Mental Health Center called on community activist Saul Alinsky to help plan their approach to mental health. In Philadelphia, a CMHC community board proposed as its mission "to resolve the underlying causes of mental health problems such as unequal distribution of opportunity, income, and benefits of technical progress." In Los Angeles, a CMHC was described as follows by its psychiatric director:

> In planning services for the inner city, I use the broadest definition of the function of a community mental health center. The function of a community mental health center

is to serve the needs, mental health or otherwise, of the community while carrying out the mandate of their staffing and construction grants. If the community is in need of some type of organization to bring a basic service into the area, then the community mental health center should serve that function. It should find out if there are such organizations in the community to do the job or, if not, help the community to organize to bring this about themselves. An example in our area was the need for a red light on a busy street near a school. For a long time citizens were unable to get the Division of Traffic to put a light on the corner. Collectively, the center brought parents together and drew up a petition and circulated the petition to most of the parents of the neighborhood, and then a group led by the community service director of the center went down to the city councilman's office and from there to the Division of Traffic. Within a few days the traffic light was placed on the corner.

In pursuing such activities, CMHC directors were encouraged by NIMH. The prevention of mental disease and promotion of mental health covered all contingencies, and the initial direction of CMHCs was perfectly compatible with the definition of them given at the time by Dr. Jack Ewalt, who could lay claim to having fathered CMHCs in his capacity of director of the Joint Commission on Mental Illness and Health. Dr. Ewalt wrote:

A community mental health center is a concept or program of action, not a single organization or facility. Its purpose is to coordinate efforts to improve the community in ways that will enhance mental well-being, decrease to bearable limits the occurrence of personal and social stress, relieve troubled persons, prevent mental illness when possible, and treat and rehabilitate those who become ill or disturbed. The program should serve the troubled, the disturbed, the slow, the ill, and the healthy of all age groups, irrespective of race, religion, socioeconomic or educational status, or political affiliation.

THE PROMOTION OF MENTAL HEALTH ENDS

The noble ideal of preventing mental illness and promoting mental health lived a relatively short official life. Born in 1963 with President Kennedy's signing of the legislation that created community mental health centers, prevention was effectively dead by 1971 when Dr. Anthony Panzetta, one of the earliest enthusiasts of CMHCs, wrote:

> The preventive psychiatrist is a bits and pieces practitioner with built-in chutzpah. He takes this piece and that, fills the gap with maybe, packages his war on evil so that it will be funded, and sets out . . . When we in psychiatry wave our preventive banners, we must look ridiculous to even the gods on Mount Olympus who once held the key to the causal mysteries of human events.

The prevention of mental illness and promotion of mental health had become irreversibly entangled in their own conceptual flaws and had strangled to death.

Richard M. Nixon was the first to make community mental health advocates aware of the defects in their model. Elected on November 6, 1968, Nixon brought into power a Republican coterie of government officials with assumptions about human behavior that were sharply at variance with those held in the Kennedy and Johnson years. This became clear in 1970 when Dr. Leopold Bellak, a leading exponent of the principles of preventive mental health, proposed a national psychiatric register to detect cases of mental illness early in order to insure treatment. Dr. Bellak described his proposal as follows:

> One way this approach could be introduced on a large enough scale would be to set up a network of metropolis-wide or country-wide central registries. There, the social, emotional, and medical histories of every citizen who had come to attention in any way because of emotional difficulties would be tabulated by computer. When these persons

were divorced or widowed or encountered other difficulties, they could be offered guidance and treatment. These centers could also insure quick referral to an appropriate therapist and a follow-up on the success of treatment.

Bellak had been active in the community mental health movement and was author of a book entitled *Community Psychiatry and Community Mental Health* in which he claimed that "community psychiatry is designed to guarantee and safeguard, to a degree previously undreamed of, a basic human right—the privilege of mental health." Yet his proposal was met by his colleagues with resounding public silence and private expressions of alarm.

Logically Bellak was correct; what he was proposing was completely compatible with the principles espoused by Gerald Caplan and the other architects of community mental health. The problems were: who would decide what mental illness was, who would be in charge of the computer, and who would have access to the information? When John Kennedy was in the White House a national psychiatric case register had seemed like a good idea to many psychiatrists committed to the principles of preventive mental health. With Richard Nixon in the White House it seemed like a distinctly dangerous idea.

The possibilities for political misuse of preventive mental health became abundantly clear to psychiatrists a few months after Bellak made his proposal. President Nixon's former personal physician suggested that all 6-year-olds in the United States should be psychiatrically tested to determine their potential for future criminal behavior. Those found to be deviant would be sent to "camps" so they could receive intensive "treatment" of their problems. Previously this physician had proposed that all high school and college students be tested to detect mental illness, and that a "mental health certificate" be required for adults as a prerequisite for jobs of political responsibility.

The truly alarming thing about such ideas from the point of view of community psychiatrists was that the proposals were logical once the principles of preventive mental health had been accepted. As Bellak himself wrote in defending his psychiatric case register proposal:

> Some of my proposals may arouse violent reactions. For many, the suggestions of mental health legislation to control our lives in the areas we cherish most—freedom of thought and action—may invoke the image of Big Brother. And enforced treatment for emotional ills may cause the powers that be to fear brainwashing. But I am reminded that income taxes were once considered basic violations of personal freedom and fluoridation of water was held to be a subversive plot. If a Clean Meat Bill and a Truth in Lending Act were finally enacted, why should a "Sound Mind Bill" be far behind?

Another problem that rapidly became apparent as the prevention of mental illness and the promotion of mental health got underway was that these activities were very time-consuming. Getting one traffic light installed on a busy street near a school was feasible, but then action was needed on 10 more lights, and on 100 rundown buildings, and on 1,000 social injustices, and on 10,000 inequities, and on 100,000 personal missed opportunities, all in the same CMHC catchment area. Each social case that was undertaken took staff time, leaving that much less time for seeing patients with schizophrenia, depression, or other mental illnesses. In many community mental health centers the staff became divided on the question of how they should spend their time—preventing (at least in theory) mental illness or treating mental illness. Panzetta noted this dilemma in 1971 when he wrote of the "enormous consequence that has not yet dawned on many newer community mental health programs," which he said was the following: "Doing a good job of comprehensive and continuous care of the psychotics and mental retardates of a base population group of from 75,000 to 200,000 may very likely absorb every available manhour of resource . . . and then some."

As these conceptual flaws were becoming increasingly apparent, political events in several operating community mental health centers cast further doubt on the viability of community mental health. The most publicized of these events took place at Lincoln Hospital in the South Bronx. The setting was one of the worst slums in America, block after block of urban blight and burned out tenements that resembled, as it still does today, Dresden following the bombing in 1945. It is a ghetto of broken dreams, and the dream of promoting mental health shattered there as well.

Lincoln Hospital Mental Health Services had begun in 1964 with funds from the Office of Economic Opportunity (OEO), one of the programs in President Johnson's war on poverty. A series of storefronts, called Neighborhood Service Centers, were opened in the community and staffed with nonprofessional aides under the supervision of professional mental health workers. Their mandate was "to provide direct and accessible services to those individuals and families under psychological and social stress," a job description sufficiently broad to justify virtually any activity. The staff became involved in such problems as garbage collection services, rat control, housing code enforcement, and organizing tenant councils to force absentee landlords to make improvements in their buildings.

The Lincoln Hospital Mental Health Service program was directed by Drs. Harris Peck, Seymour R. Kaplan, and Melvin Roman, two psychiatrists and a psychologist, who planned the program on the principles of prevention being espoused by the National Institute of Mental Health. As Kaplan and Roman made clear in a later publication, the Lincoln program was a logical outgrowth of existing theory:

> The conceptual models for the Lincoln program were based upon extensions of these existing theories and practices in the fields of psychodynamic psychiatry, public health, and social work. The Lincoln program was not conceived as a program that was to attempt to establish new methods of treatment. Rather, it was directed toward the modification of established treatment methods to the needs of the patients in settings that heretofore had been relatively ne-

134

glected—the disadvantaged urban community with predominantly minority ethnic populations . . .

The theories and practices related to small group and family process concepts played a large part in the programs developed at Lincoln. The dynamic interrelationship of the individual and his significant social groups has been particularly stressed in the past twenty years. The studies that have evolved from this point of view have led to clinical treatment with the patient in conjunction with his family, in small group therapy, and in therapeutic communities; they have also led to the application of small group process concepts to social and work rehabilitation programs.

Dr. Peck and his colleagues proudly advertised the fact that they expected:

our centers and the aides to play a vital role in finding and developing indigenous leadership and involving those residents in the community who are usually not reached by other social action groups . . . We expect the Neighborhood Service Centers to contribute to the kind of fundamental changes envisioned by those community mental health and social action programs which hope to influence both institutions and their clients.

The program was considered to be a great success and was widely praised by supporters of community mental health centers in the late 1960s. In 1968 it was given a prestigious award by the American Psychiatric Association. By recruiting leaders of the surrounding Black and Puerto Rican communities for its staff and governing board, the program put into action the dictum of "maximum feasible participation," a concept that was strongly encouraged in Great Society programs for the poor. The Lincoln program was also promoting mental health by teaching "the dispossessed how to use the political process to ameliorate their own conditions." By 1968 the original OEO grant was scheduled to terminate, and NIMH agreed to continue funding the program. In addition, NIMH designated Lincoln as one of eight model community mental health centers in the nation and extolled its activities in promoting mental health.

On March 4, 1969, Lincoln Hospital Mental Health Services came to an abrupt end. Almost two hundred strikers, including 70 percent of the Lincoln staff, took over the offices of directors Peck, Kaplan, and Roman, locked them out, and declared a nonprofessional mental health worker the new director of the program. Many news services, including the *New York Times,* carried the story: "Community Takes Over Control of Bronx Mental Health Services."

There had been two immediate precipitating incidents. In one, the mental health workers in a Neighborhood Service Center had organized tenant councils in buildings owned by a man who was a major financial supporter of Yeshiva University, the parent academic institution for Lincoln Hospital; word circulated from the university administration that the workers' efforts had not been appreciated. The other incident had been the firing by Drs. Peck *et al.* of four mental health workers, who the strikers demanded be reinstated. Beyond these two precipitating factors there were additional allegations of racism, dead-end jobs, lack of job security, and fiscal mismanagement by the directors, but it was clear to everyone that the underlying issue was community control of the program.

The logic of the strikers was inescapable. Drs. Peck, Kaplan, and Roman had preached community control, so the community was taking control. The *New York Times* emphasized this aspect of the takeover prominently:

Dr. Harris B. Peck, director of the Lincoln Hospital Mental Health Service, used to pound the table at staff meetings and call for a "revolution." He urged community workers, one of them recalled, to wrest control of their South Bronx mental health project from him and other professional administrators and put him out of a job.

Yesterday, they did.

136

The newspaper also quoted Dr. Peck's previously published statements about the Lincoln program and the importance of community control: "Over a period of years the program is designed to move members of the community into positions within such agencies where they may appropriately and competently engage in decisions and policy-making roles in matters of vital concern to their own community's health and well being."

The strike dragged on for three weeks during which time negotiations took place with New York City and Yeshiva University as well as with Puerto Rican and Black leadership groups in the community. The strikers refused to yield control of the building or to negotiate on the leadership issue, and rhetoric on both sides became increasingly acrimonious as the Black Panthers and the Students for a Democratic Society lent support to the strikers. Finally, on March 20, police were sent in and arrested twenty-three strikers.

The strike was, for all intents and purposes, the end of Lincoln Hospital Mental Health Services. Drs. Peck, Kaplan, and Roman and much of the Lincoln leadership resigned. The National Institute of Mental Health, which had watched the events at its model CMHC with growing horror, issued a report critical of the program and tried to disassociate itself from Lincoln as quickly as possible.

Word of the Lincoln fiasco spread rapidly throughout the mental health community. CMHC directors previously committed to "maximum feasible participation" of community leaders suddenly reconsidered their position. Directors who had spoken out strongly in favor of maximizing the mental health of the community now muted their advocacy. Mental health was a fine ideal for other people as long as its achievement was not at the expense of the professionals' own mental health. To be publicly locked out of your office by your own mental health workers was humiliating, but to be hoisted on the petard of your own rhetoric and ridiculed in the *New York Times* went beyond the bounds of decency.

7

Signposts to a Grate Society

B y the early 1970s the ideas of preventing mental illness and promoting mental health had fallen into disfavor among mental health professionals. Richard M. Nixon was in the White House and was attempting to reverse the Kennedy-Johnson thrust toward a Great Society in which the federal government had taken increased responsibility for health and social programs. In such a milieu it might have been expected that community mental health centers would wither and die.

Instead, they flowered, watered by a strong coalition of Democratic Party leaders in Congress, psychiatric professionals, and laypersons in the mental health lobby that had successfully gotten CMHC legislation through Congress ten years previously. During the Nixon years and subsequent Ford administration the number of CMHCs increased each year, from 165 when Nixon took office in 1969 to 434 when he resigned in 1974 to 548 by the end of Ford's term in the White House. The increase in CMHCs during the eight years the Republicans controlled the White House, averaging 48 new CMHCs each year, was in fact greater than the increase during the four years of the Carter presidency, in which an average of 36 new CMHCs were opened each year (see the chart below).

At the same time community mental health centers were increasing in number, the exodus of patients from state mental hospitals, which had begun slowly in 1955, accelerated to a stampede. The census of state mental hospitals was reduced by 197,921 individuals during the 1960s, and this reduction continued during the 1970s by another 205,455 persons (see the chart on the next page). Altogether between 1955 and 1984 a total of 433,407 beds in state mental hospitals were taken out of use, or 80 percent of the 552,150 beds occupied in 1955. Some states were more aggressive in their policy of deinstitutionalization; as shown in Appendix A, Arkansas, Wisconsin, and Kentucky reduced the number of patients in public mental hospitals by 90 percent or more, while Rhode Island, Illinois, Vermont, Massachusetts,

Number of Operational Community Mental Health Centers
1965–1981

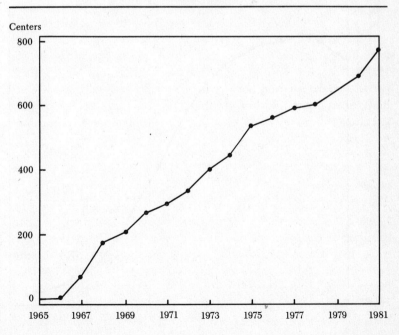

139

Nebraska, California, and Idaho reduced the number between 85 and 89 percent. New York State alone closed down 71,066 beds, a sufficient number of patients to make up a small city.

First one or two wards were closed in a building, then whole buildings closed, and in a few states entire hospitals closed. Hospitals that had been small cities unto themselves—Rockland State Hospital and Pilgrim State Hospital in New York, which had over 9,000 and 14,000 patients respectively in 1955—shrank each year until there were only a few thousand patients, and abandoned buildings far outnumbered occupied buildings on their sprawling grounds. It was a massive shift of patients from public hospitals to the community, a shift unprecedented in medical history.

Number of Inpatients in Public Mental Hospitals
1950–1984

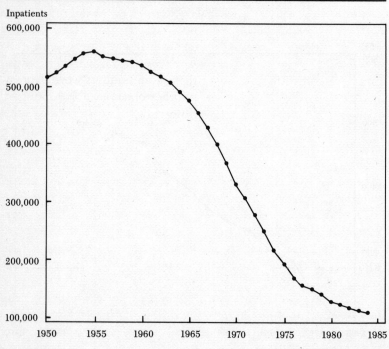

WHERE WERE THEY GOING TO LIVE?

The fact that 433,407 individuals who had been living in state mental hospitals were being moved out of the hospitals meant that 433,407 places for them to live must be found in the community. During the earliest years of deinstitutionalization, the finding of housing was not a major problem; the patients who were released first were those who were the best candidates for community living and those who had the closest ties to their families and relatives; in fact, about two-thirds of the released patients in the early years of deinstitutionalization went to live with their families or in their own apartments.

The problems began in the late 1960s when patients without close family ties began to be released. The number of halfway houses available for discharged patients was minimal; a 1971 NIMH survey identified only 196 such houses in the entire United States, with a total capacity of 6,170 persons. Therefore, some of the patients were placed in nursing homes and others went to boarding houses, single-room-occupancy hotels (SROs), and similar low-income housing. Such housing was often clustered in towns near the state hospital or in poorer areas of cities, and by the mid-1970s many of these communities were expressing concern about the increasing ghettoization of the mentally ill. Long Beach, New York, whose rundown boardwalk hotels were filling up with patients released from nearby Creedmore and Pilgrim State hospitals, attempted to pass an ordinance restricting their number. In New York City, one-quarter of the estimated 100,000 residents of single-room-occupancy hotels were said to be "severely mentally dysfunctional." In San Jose, California, the area around San Jose State College became overrun with patients released from nearby Agnews State Hospital, which was being closed. Some of the low-income housing for the mentally ill was decent and well maintained, but most of it was not.

As the mass movement of patients from state hospitals into low-income housing continued during the 1970s, important changes were taking place in the housing market. Redevelop-

141

ment and gentrification of inner cities accelerated sharply, with consequent demolition of low-income housing for highways, office buildings, and convention centers, as well as expensive condominiums and rental units. Changes in federal and state housing policies made it unprofitable to build or maintain low-income units, and in many cities landlords simply abandoned apartment buildings or had them "torched" to collect the insurance. At the same time, inflation led to rising rents and eroded the ability of individuals with fixed low incomes to compete for the increasingly limited number of low-income units.

The consequence of these changes was that "nationwide in the period 1970–82, 1,116,000 single-room units disappeared, nearly half of the total stock. During the same period New York City lost 110,000 units of low-rent SRO housing—representing 87 percent of the total low-rent SRO stock—because of rent inflation, conversion, or demolition." One study of homeless women in New York reported that half of them had been living in SROs immediately prior to becoming homeless.

Redevelopment and gentrification of the inner cities, then, was a major contributor to homelessness both among mentally ill individuals as they left state hospitals and among other low-income individuals who were not mentally ill. In retrospect one wonders where public officials, builders, and psychiatric professionals thought the individuals who had been living in the housing units being demolished were going to go.

WHERE WOULD THEY GET AFTERCARE?

In addition to adequate and decent housing, most individuals released from state mental hospitals need continuing psychiatric aftercare. This includes such activities as insuring that the person receives proper medication, encouraging participation in social activities, providing vocational counseling, pointing out community resources, and generally helping individuals live as normally as possible despite their illnesses. Community mental health centers had been specifically created to assume the responsibilities of state mental hospitals; aftercare of released patients was theoretically one of their most important functions.

From the earliest days of CMHCs, however, it was apparent that the centers were not providing aftercare for most patients being released from state mental hospitals. Data available from the NIMH from 1968 to 1978, the last year in which such data were collected, showed that only 3.6 to 6.5 percent of admissions to CMHCs were patients referred by state mental hospitals. Of even greater concern was the fact that the trend was downward and that the longer a CMHC was in operation, the smaller the percentage of its referrals from public mental hospitals. In 1976, for example, CMHCs that had been operational for one to two years had 5.5 percent of their admissions referred from public mental hospitals, whereas CMHCs that had been operational for six to seven years had only 2.6 percent of their admissions referred from public mental hospitals.

The fact that patients being released from state mental hospitals were not receiving aftercare at CMHCs was well known to the officials at the National Institute of Mental Health who had authority over the CMHCs. It recurs like a theme on a broken record on virtually every assessment of the CMHC program from its earliest years:

1972: A basic finding that emerges from the questionnaire survey is that relationships between community mental health centers and public mental hospitals serving the same catchment area exist only at a relatively minimal level between the majority of the two types of organizations.

1977: A coordinated system of care for the mentally ill through the centers program remains a goal rather than a reality. The centers program has developed separately from the public mental hospital system, making integration of the two care systems difficult. Funding for community-based mental health services has not grown in proportion to the number of patients in or transferred to communities.

1979: The relationships between the CMHCs and public

143

psychiatric hospitals are difficult at best, adversarial at worst . . . [emphasis in original] The centrality of this issue is compelling. As long as there are two such mental health systems operating by and large independently, the fundamental cost problems alluded to throughout our assessment have little chance of improvement, and the individuals caught up in the two systems are likely to remain poorly served.

That CMHCs and state mental hospitals were not working together was hardly surprising. NIMH had, after all, failed to mandate any relationship between the two in its original CMHC guidelines. Furthermore, the state hospitals had in essence been told they were to be abolished and their functions assumed by the newly created CMHCs. Funding for the CMHCs flowed directly from NIMH, bypassing state mental health officials. These officials were completely left out of the planning process and, quite understandably, often less than enthusiastic about cooperating with CMHCs. For a federal agency that claimed expertise in the behavioral sciences, NIMH showed shockingly poor judgment in the way the CMHC program was administered and funded. It would not have taken an advanced degree in psychology to predict that such an arrangement would fail.

Most patients, then, were moved out of state mental hospitals into the community without being referred to CMHCs for aftercare. The state hospitals ignored CMHCs, and the CMHCs were happy to reciprocate. One absurd example of this lack of relationship: A state hospital in Kansas refused to provide the CMHC theoretically responsible for its discharged patients with the name or any identifying information about the patients. The hospital dutifully sent the CMHC a notice of a patient's release but "all identifiable characteristics, including the patient's name, are blacked out." The CMHC was left to play a guessing game about who might have been discharged and returned to its catchment area.

There were, of course, exceptional CMHCs that accepted responsibility for seriously mentally ill patients being discharged from state mental hospitals. Such CMHCs were few in number but well known to psychiatric professionals for their excellence—Prairie View in Kansas, Weber County in Utah, Range in Minnesota, and Sacramento in California were examples. Prairie View CMHC, in fact, had originally been started as an outpatient clinic by some of the conscientious objectors who served in state hospitals during World War II and were appalled by their conditions. The vast majority of CMHCs, however, were not interested in seriously mentally ill patients but rather selectively accepted as patients those individuals who had interpersonal and intrapersonal problems. These were the patients amenable to counseling and psychotherapy, the treatment modalities that were valued at community mental health centers just as they were valued in the professional world of private practice.

A breakdown of patients seen at CMHCs in 1975 illustrates this focus:

Primary Diagnosis of Patients	Percent of Total
Schizophrenia	10
Alcoholism	10
Depressive disorders (includes broad range from manic-depressive psychosis to mild depressive neurosis)	13
Childhood disorders (not including mental retardation; vast majority were behavioral problems referred by schools)	13
Neuroses and personality disorders	21
Social maladjustment	7
No mental disorder	15
All others	11

Probably no more than 20 percent of the individuals seen in the CMHCs would ever have been treated in a state mental hospital; for many CMHCs the percentage was considerably lower. The CMHC system, set up to take over the function of state mental hospitals and treat the seriously mentally ill, had instead found a whole new group of patients, whom we might call the worried well. In fact, the patients were so unsick that most CMHCs stopped calling them patients at all and instead adopted the nonmedical term "clients." The implication was that community mental health centers were more like legal firms than they were like state mental hospitals.

By the mid-1970s it had become clear that the trend was away from CMHCs treating the seriously mentally ill. As seen in the accompanying chart, individuals who showed social maladjustment and no mental disorder progressively increased among CMHC admissions, while those diagnosed with schizophrenia decreased. So embarrassed was the National Institute of Mental Health by this trend that officials in charge of the CMHC program published a report arguing that:

the apparent decline in the proportion of CMHC admissions of patients with the diagnosis of schizophrenia does not itself reflect a "neglect" of patients with serious mental disorder. Rather, as has been shown, the substantial increase in admis-

Percent of Admissions to Community Mental Health Centers with Diagnosis of Social Maladjustment and No Mental Disorder vs. Schizophrenia, 1970–1978

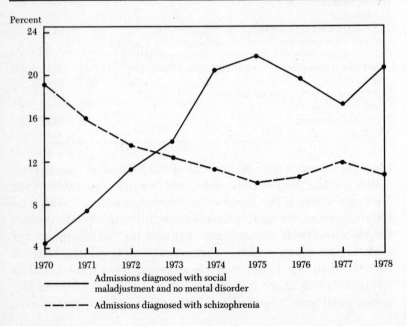

sion of patients with other diagnoses has diluted the proportion of admissions of patients with schizophrenia, and the rapid expansion of the number of CMHCs has diluted the average number of admissions of patients with schizophrenia per CMHC.

Translated, this says that there are proportionately fewer apples in the barrel because so many peaches and pears have been added, and besides there are more barrels.

Such verbal legerdemain could not conceal the fact that the CMHC program was failing in its primary mission—to take over the functions of state mental hospitals. This failing became even more dramatic when community mental health centers were compared with psychiatric outpatient clinics in operation before the CMHC program began. In 1961 the Report of the Joint Commission on Mental Illness and Health had indicated that 19.5 percent of patients being seen in the psychiatric outpatient clinics in existence at that time had diagnoses of "psychotic disorders." By 1975 a comparable figure for the CMHCs would have been no more than 15 percent. The CMHCs, then, had not even achieved the modest standard of 1961 in providing services to the seriously mentally ill. The strong implication of NIMH data collected during the 1970s was that patients with serious mental illnesses had gained virtually nothing from the CMHC program; they would, in fact, have been better off had CMHC funds simply been divided up and allocated to existing psychiatric outpatient facilities rather than being given to CMHCs.

During the 1970s there were several other indications that community mental health centers were not providing care for patients being discharged from state mental hospitals. One of the five essential services that CMHCs had agreed to provide as a condition of receiving federal funds was inpatient beds to be used by patients needing hospitalization. Approximately half of all CMHCs did not have such beds, and some centers simply referred patients needing hospitalization to the state hospitals. Partial hospitalization, such as day hospitals, was another mandated essential service, yet on the average only 6 percent of CMHC treatment fell into this category; one observer described the "poorly staffed day programs" as "thinly disguised day camps . . . where the primary therapeutic goal seems to be securing per diem reimbursement from the county or state." Another essential element, emergency services, was shown to be grossly deficient in a 1977 survey, which showed that 32 percent of CMHCs had no emergency services at all and another 39 percent handled emergency calls by using a telephone answering service, which referred the caller on, sometimes to a professional and sometimes not. As described in this report: "At one center the caller was referred to another number, which turned out to be a methadone clinic where he found himself talking to the security guard, who hung up on him."

The one essential service that CMHCs *were* providing in the 1970s was outpatient counseling and psychotherapy, which comprised 80 percent or more of all treatment activities in the centers. In 1978, the last year for which such figures are available, the six hundred operating CMHCs had almost 10 *million* counseling and psychotherapy sessions divided as follows:

Individual counseling and psychotherapy	8,120,344
Group counseling and psychotherapy	876,441
Family counseling and psychotherapy	727,520
	9,724,305

These sessions, according to NIMH data, did not include "medication or drug maintenance," and only a small proportion of them were for individuals with serious mental illnesses. Instead, most such sessions were for individuals with problems of living— the teenage son who refused to do what his parents told him, the wife whose husband was hinting at divorce, the man whose midlife crisis had made him depressed. These are certainly problems, and individuals with such problems have the right to seek counseling for them, but the resources that were being used to help them had been created primarily to provide care for individuals with serious mental illnesses. And since most of the resources of

CMHCs went to helping people with problems of living, few resources were left over to help the seriously mentally ill.

Since few resources of community mental health centers were going to patients with serious mental illnesses, and since most CMHCs had no working relationship with state mental hospitals, it was hardly surprising to find that CMHCs as a group had little effect on state mental hospital utilization. Politically this was very sensitive, however, because the original justification of federal funding for community mental health centers had been that they should replace state hospitals. With the population of state hospitals declining precipitously, NIMH was anxious to show that the decline was due to the CMHCs. But attempts to make this connection were futile. When 175 CMHC directors in one survey were asked to rank in order ten potential CMHC goals and objectives, the goal of reducing the utilization of state mental hospitals was ranked ninth. In another survey of CMHCs in sixteen states it was found that "there is no consistent relationship between the opening of centers and changes in state hospital resident rates." Admission rates to state hospitals, in contrast to the resident rate, or census, were also examined. In one study of five CMHCs in Texas "the centers investigated appear to have had a negligible impact on state hospital admissions." In the sixteen-state survey the "statistics showed slightly less increase in admission rates for areas with centers than for areas without, but the differences were not reliable statistically."

To be certain, a few CMHCs were having an effect on the admission rate and resident population in state mental hospitals, but such centers were the exceptions. One of the most successful, in Sacramento, California, reduced admissions from its catchment area to state mental hospitals from 1,100 per year to only 4 per year. Not uncoincidentally, the leadership in such CMHCs had a special interest in the seriously mentally ill and gave those patients priority for services. Two other successful CMHCs in Wyoming reduced admissions to the state hospital 400 miles away by admitting seriously mentally ill patients to the CMHCs instead. An indication of how anxious NIMH was for such data in 1976 is suggested by the title of the journal article describing the

Wyoming program: "Is NIMH's Dream Coming True? Wyoming Centers Reduce State Hospital Admissions." These exceptional CMHCs were very useful at appropriations time to convince Congress to continue expanding the CMHC program, but officials knew they were aberrations. Most community mental health centers had no more interest in state mental hospitals than they had in teahouses in China.

THE FISCAL SHELL GAME

If CMHCs as a group had virtually no relationship to the continuing exodus of patients from state mental hospitals, then what was the driving force behind this exodus? Why did the census of state hospitals decrease by another 205,455 patients during the 1970s despite increasing evidence that housing was insufficient and aftercare minimal. One would think that state officials and psychiatric professionals might have reversed the course of deinstitutionalization given the accumulating evidence that it was not working as planned. Such might have been the case except for the power of federal money, which was the real driving force behind deinstitutionalization.

In 1963, when CMHCs were first funded and deinstitutionalization had just begun, the total amount of public funds spent on the mentally ill was approximately $1 billion per year (see Appendix B). The vast majority of these funds—an estimated 96 percent—came from the states, which supported state mental hospitals and outpatient clinics whose patients were virtually all seriously mentally ill. The federal government through the Social Security Administration paid living expenses for a small number of "permanently and totally disabled" individuals with severe mental illnesses, while local counties and cities assumed the costs for some released patients through welfare, social services, subsidized housing, police, jail, and court costs. Both federal and local costs were limited, however; for all intents and purposes, fiscal responsibility for the mentally ill was a state responsibility.

Following passage of the Community Mental Health Centers Act, the configuration of fiscal responsibility for the seriously mentally ill changed dramatically. The first change was a liberalization of rules, which made mentally ill individuals living in the community eligible for federal benefits under the Aid to the Disabled program. These benefits consisted of monthly payments intended for rent, food, and other living costs. The Aid to the Disabled program was subsequently incorporated into the federal Supplemental Security Income (SSI) program for individuals who did not qualify for Social Security benefits, and into the Social Security Disability Insurance (SSDI) program for those who did qualify. In addition, a federal Food Stamps program was enacted in 1966, which could also be used by mentally ill individuals living in the community.

At the same time, other federal programs were begun that paid part of the costs for mentally ill patients in nursing homes and in the psychiatric units of general hospitals—but relatively little for such patients in state mental hospitals. These were Medicaid, enacted in 1965, and Medicare, enacted the following year. Medicaid and SSI require states to provide some funds to match the federal subsidy, whereas Medicare and SSDI do not have this requirement; even with the matching funds, however, states can save at least 50 percent of the costs of inpatient and outpatient psychiatric care by the use of such federal programs.

The consequence of these federal programs was to create an overwhelming incentive for states to empty state mental hospitals, where costs were borne almost exclusively by the states, and transfer patients to the psychiatric units of general hospitals, nursing homes, and community living facilities, where costs were borne predominantly by the federal government. As this took place, total expenditures by federal, state, and local governments on programs for the seriously mentally ill escalated sharply, from $1 billion in 1963 to $17.1 billion in 1985, *a fourfold increase even after inflation and increased population are taken into consideration* (Appendix B). For example, total expenditures for the Aid to the Disabled program in 1963 were only $3.8 million for patients with all diagnoses; in 1985, SSI and SSDI expenditures for the mentally disabled alone were estimated to be $2.4 *billion.*

151

Medicaid and Medicare costs for the seriously mentally ill, which were zero in 1965, were estimated to be approximately $3.6 *billion* in 1985. Accompanying the sharp increase in total expenditures was a shift of fiscal responsibility from state governments to federal, and to a lesser extent, local governments. This shift was approximately as follows:

FISCAL RESPONSIBILITY FOR THE SERIOUSLY MENTALLY ILL

	Federal	State	Local
1963	2%	96%	2%
1985	38%	53%	9%

At first glance, this shift appears reasonable enough. Why shouldn't the federal government share the cost of the seriously mentally ill, as Dorothea Dix had eloquently argued over one hundred years earlier? The major problem with this arrangement was that mentally ill individuals became pawns in a huge fiscal shell game.

State hospital administrators were urged to discharge ever more patients and to make it increasingly difficult for them to get readmitted. The hospital administrators were told that their job performance would be assessed based on how many patients they discharged and how many beds they closed down. Administrators in state capitals were not especially interested in where the discharged patients were going to live; the important thing was to get the patients out of the hospitals.

For patients who might need rehospitalization following discharge, officials in many states decreed that they must first go to psychiatric units of general hospitals (where Medicaid and Medicare would cover most of the costs) rather than return directly to state hospitals. Unfortunately, however, many general hospitals did not want the seriously mentally ill as patients. Patients needing rehospitalization were thus caught in a "Catch-22" situation in which they could not be readmitted to a state hospital without first going to the psychiatric unit of a general hospital that refused to accept them. The tragic consequences of such policies were, and continue to be, evident everywhere:

William M., age 47, had spent 19 years in Fairview
State Hospital in Pennsylvania. He was discharged
from the hospital to live in a boarding house in
Philadelphia. For the first month he did well, but then
stopped taking the antipsychotic medication that
controlled the symptoms of his illness. "He became
floridly psychotic, unkempt, malodorous, out of touch
with reality, and extremely paranoid about being
poisoned. His resulting physical problems included
infestations of lice and maggots." He moved from his
boarding house to live on the streets. Attempts to get
him rehospitalized at Fairview were unsuccessful,
because Pennsylvania had a rule that if the patient had
been out of the hospital for more than thirty days he
could not be readmitted without first being
hospitalized in the psychiatric unit of a local hospital.
But no local hospital would take him because he had
no fixed address and no money. Several weeks later
"William M. was found dead behind a Philadelphia
crisis center, his feet bitten by rats."

Little attention has been given to the importance of federal
funds as the driving force behind deinstitutionalization. As seriously mentally ill individuals who had been living on back wards
of mental hospitals for twenty, thirty, or even forty years were
hastily marched off to nursing homes or boarding houses, state
officials and psychiatric professionals piously extolled the virtues
of community living and the advantages of the "least restrictive
environment." The fact that most nursing homes offered no psychiatric care and less freedom than state hospitals, and the fact
that most boarding houses offered only a television set and a
neighborhood inhabited by human piranhas, were discreetly ignored. When state officials were asked who was going to provide
aftercare for the discharged patients, they replied, "Why community mental health centers, of course." This was to be the
ultimate revenge for state administrators. They had been told by
federal officials that because they had done such a poor job, state

hospitals were to be closed and new CMHCs would take care of the mentally ill. They had been completely bypassed in the funding of CMHCs. Now they would hand the problem over to the CMHCs. Unfortunately the mentally ill paid a tragically high price for this revenge.

Knowledgeable officials at both the federal and state level have known for many years that the availability of federal money, not the availability of CMHCs, was the motivation for deinstitutionalization. There was no definite proof of it, however, until 1985 when economist William Gronfein at Rutgers University published an analysis of data on deinstitutionalization from 1973 to 1975. Comparing the development of CMHCs with the availability of Medicaid funds (which he used as representative of federal funds), he concluded:

> These results do not support the hypothesis that CMHC size, utilization, or coverage are positively associated with state hospital inpatient decline net of population. The number of CMHC inpatient beds is not significantly associated with inpatient decline between 1973 and 1974 or 1973 and 1975, and the percentage of catchment areas served by CMHCs is not statistically significantly correlated with inpatient decline in any of the three intervals.

On the other hand, the availability of federal Medicaid funds was strongly correlated with the rate of deinstitutionalization state by state:

> Clearly, then, Medicaid payments are very strongly associated with the amount of deinstitutionalization experienced by a state in the early 1970s. A correlational analysis of this type does not, of course, permit us to draw causal conclusions. Nonetheless, the data are consistent with a model in which Medicaid funds are used as a way of transferring costs from the states to the federal government, and in which one of the influences on the degree to which state

hospital systems declined in the early 1970s was a state's involvement in the Medicaid program.

What had become clear was that if federal money was provided as an incentive to empty state mental hospitals, then the hospitals would get emptied. What federal and state officials thought was going to happen to the hordes of discharged patients is one of the abiding mysteries of our time.

In addition to the shift in fiscal responsibility from state governments to the federal government, the allocation of fiscal resources within state governments has also been detrimental to the interests of the seriously mentally ill. In New York State, for example, between 1955 and 1981 the number of patients in state mental hospitals decreased from over 94,000 to under 24,000, yet during those same years the number of state hospital staff members *increased* from 24,000 to almost 37,000. Since salaries comprise approximately three-quarters of state hospital budgets, the failure to move hospital staff to positions in community psychiatric facilities meant that most of the money remained in the hospitals as well. This can be seen in the total expenditures for public mental hospitals in the United States in 1969 and 1981: despite a reduction of patient population by 66 percent during those years (from 369,969 to 125,246) the total hospital expenditures in constant dollars decreased only 3 percent (from $1.81 to $1.76 billion).

Improvement in the hospital staff-patient ratio was one reason for leaving most staff in the hospitals as patients were moved out, but politics and unions also played prominent roles. In rural communities, state mental hospitals are often major employers, and in states such as New Mexico, state hospital jobs have been used as patronage by county political leaders. State politicians have therefore strongly resisted moving staff out of the hospitals. This is sometimes referred to as the "Rusk syndrome" after Rusk State Hospital in Texas, where efforts to decrease staff or close part of the hospital have been fiercely opposed by powerful state politicians. As recently as 1985, State Senator Roy Blake announced publicly, "They won't close Rusk State Hospital as long as I am in the Senate," while an official of the State Department of Mental Health and Mental Retardation at the same meeting assured listeners that "we will reduce the number of patients [in Rusk State Hospital] but there have been no staff cuts. We expect a continuation of what we have been experiencing the past few months."

Even in states that were successful in closing down some of the mental hospitals as patients were moved to the community, the money that was saved was not necessarily reinvested in community programs for mental patients. California, for example, transferred some of these savings into state general revenues, where they were used to build roads. Although counties were given full responsibility for the care of seriously mentally ill individuals living in the community, they were given only partial fiscal support to do the job. To compound the confusion, in many states the hospitalized mentally ill remained the responsibility of the department of mental health, while those living in the community became the responsibility of other state departments such as social services, vocational education, or corrections.

In short, the introduction of federal funds to support the care of the seriously mentally ill has produced fiscal and administrative chaos. In 1963 it was clear that state departments of mental health were both administratively and fiscally responsible for such patients. By 1985 fiscal responsibility for the seriously mentally ill was spread among a convoluted array of federal, state, and local government programs that would make Rube Goldberg proud. Administrative responsibility was difficult to ascertain at any level, with each government program pointing fingers at the next program. Care for the seriously mentally ill continued to deteriorate.

LEGAL IMPEDIMENTS TO CARE

Given the scarcity of housing and lack of psychiatric aftercare for discharged patients, and given federal fiscal incentives to encourage indiscriminate emptying of state mental hospitals, deinstitutionalization was a predictable disaster. The disaster was further compounded, however, by civil liberties lawyers who filed suits against states, forcing the release of still more patients. Once the patients had been released, the lawyers filed additional suits making it difficult to rehospitalize them involuntarily when they became sick again or to treat them against their will. The net effect of these legal actions can be likened to prohibiting the use of life support systems for a man who has been shot three times and is lying critically wounded; the man will probably die anyway, but the lack of life support systems makes it certain.

The first important court case to accelerate the pace of deinstitutionalization was the 1971 *Wyatt v. Stickney* decision in Alabama. In that case the court ruled that involuntarily hospitalized mental patients had a legal right to adequate treatment. The court also established minimum standards for such treatment, including a minimum staff-to-patient ratio, and the decision was hailed by many as an important step toward better care for the seriously mentally ill. In some states, including Alabama, the effect of *Wyatt v. Stickney* was clearly positive and did indeed lead to better care. Other states, however, faced with a court mandate to improve the staff-to-patient ratio, achieved the target not by hiring more staff but simply by discharging more patients. What had begun as a positive reform evolved in some states into another excuse to empty the hospitals.

A further impetus to deinstitutionalization came from the 1975 *O'Connor v. Donaldson* case in Florida in which a court awarded $20,000 in compensatory damages to a patient who had been kept in a hospital for nearly fifteen years without proper treatment. Making a state monetarily liable for lack of hospital care was a strong incentive for discharging more patients. Also in 1975 a judge in the District of Columbia ruled in the case of *Dixon v. Weinberger* that psychiatric patients have a right not only to treatment but to treatment in "the least restrictive setting." The effect was to force states to move still more patients from hospitals to community living facilities.

Civil liberties lawyers also initiated court cases in many states making it increasingly difficult to involuntarily commit individuals to hospitals without their consent. A landmark decision was the 1972 *Lessard v. Schmidt* case in Wisconsin in which a judge ruled that the only grounds justifying involuntary hospitalization were dangerousness of the person to self or to others. Bruce J. Ennis, a leading ACLU lawyer and subsequent chairman of the American Bar Association's Commission on the Mentally Disabled, wrote at the time that "the goal [of legal efforts] should be nothing less than the abolition of involuntary hospitalization."

A third legal thrust led to court rulings allowing seriously mentally ill individuals to refuse treatment. A harbinger of things to come was seen as early as 1973 when the City Council in Long Beach, New York, alarmed by the rapidly increasing number of discharged mental patients living in hotels there, passed an ordinance stating that anyone "requiring medication for a mental illness or requiring outpatient medical or psychiatric care shall not continue to be registered in the hotels if, without said medication, the resident may be a danger to himself or others or may not know the nature or quality of his acts." The "acts" the city fathers had in mind included those in a local Catholic Church "where discharged patients reportedly have urinated on the floor during Mass and eaten the altar flowers." The New York Civil Liberties Union immediately challenged the Long Beach ordinance as unconstitutional saying, in effect, that it is illegal to require discharged patients to take medication as a condition for continuing to live in the community. And Long Beach lost.

A psychiatric patient's right to refuse treatment became much more widely utilized after a judge affirmed that right in 1979 in the Massachusetts case of *Rogers v. Okin*. Two years later civil liberties lawyers again prevailed in a similar case, *Rennie v. Klein*, in New Jersey, and since that time the courts in several states have reaffirmed the right of seriously mentally ill individuals to refuse treatment except in extreme circumstances.

The net effect of these court decisions has been to increase the rate of deinstitutionalization and to permit mentally ill individuals, once released from a hospital, to remain free and psychotic in the community. The consequences of these decisions can be seen almost everywhere. In Texas, patients have been released from state hospitals to nonexistent community facilities in order to achieve a more favorable staff-to-patients ratio. In the District of Columbia, patients have been released from St. Elizabeths Hospital to "the least restrictive setting" of community living despite strong evidence that many nursing homes and boarding houses are more restrictive than the hospital. In New York City, Mayor Edward Koch has attempted to involuntarily hospitalize mentally ill homeless persons despite bitter opposition from attorneys representing the New York Civil Liberties Union. And in every state overtly psychotic individuals who had been deinstitutionalized from state mental hospitals are living on city sidewalks and in parks, steadfastly invoking their legal right to refuse treatment for their illness.

It should be added that most civil liberties lawyers who have worked to defend mentally ill individuals are well-intentioned. They quote Thomas Jefferson and are concerned about civil rights, the stigma of hospitalization, and the potential for abuse of involuntary hospitalization such as has occurred with political dissidents in the Soviet Union. Unfortunately these lawyers also have outmoded ideas about the nature of serious mental illnesses. They have read Freud and Szasz and believe that the mental illnesses are caused by faulty upbringing or by social injustices. They have seen *One Flew Over the Cuckoo's Nest* and *King of Hearts* and accept the thesis that opening hospital gates is the best remedy for problems of the hospitalized mentally ill. As one civil rights lawyer for the Mental Health Law Project said in 1974: "They [the patients] are better off outside of a hospital with no care than they are inside with no care. The hospitals are what really do damage to people." It would be difficult today to persuade mentally ill homeless persons foraging in dumpsters of the truth of that statement.

The central question regarding legal aspects of serious mental illnesses is: under what circumstances does the state have the right and obligation to protect individuals who appear unable to protect themselves? New York's Mayor Koch answered the question this way: "If they can't care for themselves, shouldn't we help them? We wouldn't let 5-year-old children live out on the streets and fend for themselves. Well, mentally ill homeless people may be 55 years old in body but acting like they're 5 years old and unable to take care of themselves . . . Both morally and legally we have an obligation to help those who can't or won't help themselves."

8

Where Did All the Psychiatrists Go?

An essential ingredient in good psychiatric care for the mentally ill is a sufficient number of competent psychiatrists, psychologists, and psychiatric social workers. From the earliest discussions of federal support to improve care for the mentally ill in the United States this fact was accepted as axiomatic, and for that reason federal support for the training of these professionals was included in the original proposed legislation to create a National Neuropsychiatric Institute.

During hearings on the legislation in 1945 and 1946 witnesses testified that there were approximately 3,000 trained psychiatrists in the entire country. Of the estimated 3,000 trained psychiatrists, it was said that 1,596 (53 percent) were employed by public mental hospitals and thus were providing care for seriously mentally ill patients. It was also estimated that there were approximately 4,200 fully trained psychologists in the United States and approximately 2,000 psychiatric social workers. Thus the total number of mental health professionals available in 1945 was approximately 9,200.

There was widespread agreement during the 1945–46 hearings that more professionals were needed. Estimates of the number of personnel needed to fully staff the nation's public institutions for the mentally ill were: 3,500 additional psychiatrists, 1,800 additional psychologists, and 6,000 additional psychiatric social workers. If fully implemented, that would have brought the total number of mental health professionals in the United States to 20,500.

Virtually no opposition was raised to the proposed use of federal funds to train more professionals, as everyone agreed that current services for the mentally ill, especially in state mental hospitals, were disgraceful. It was simply assumed during the hearings that the newly trained professionals would fill the gaps in the hospitals and would serve the seriously mentally ill. A question was raised by one congressman, mentioned in chapter 2, as to whether psychiatrists trained with public funds might go directly into private practice following their training, but Dr. Robert Felix reassured him that some kind of mandatory payback obligation would be attached to the program. Later in the hearings Dr. Edward A. Strecker, professor of psychiatry at the University of Pennsylvania and former president of the American Psychiatric Association, commented on the same issue:

> The other point is, and I think the bill provides for it, that fellows, men who have had the benefit of being educated in psychiatry as a result of the funds derived from the bill, it would be only fair to say they would owe a certain amount of service to psychiatry, and perhaps to the government and to the states, in return for the education they have received. At least, that would be the way I would interpret it, and the way I believe it would be interpreted.

When the bill passed, creating the National Institute of Mental Health, federal funds for training professionals were part of the bill. The first federal grants to medical schools and universities to carry out this training were awarded in 1948 and totaled $1.4 million; in subsequent years the amounts were as follows:

FEDERAL NIMH GRANTS FOR TRAINING
MENTAL HEALTH PROFESSIONALS
(IN MILLIONS)

1948	$1.4	1967	104.9
1949	1.7	1968	109.5
1950	4.0	1969	118.7
1951	2.0	1970	116.8
1952	3.8	1971	114.2
1953	4.0	1972	114.1
1954	4.5	1973	77.3
1955	4.6	1974	100.0
1956	6.6	1975	94.1
1957	12.3	1976	87.7
1958	14.2	1977	85.4
1959	20.0	1978	84.4
1960	28.9	1979	90.4
1961	42.6	1980	90.4
1962	43.7	1981	81.4
1963	57.2	1982	57.5
1964	76.9	1983	35.9
1965	83.2	1984	36.1
1966	96.7	Total 1948–84:	$2,107.1

The total amount awarded through 1984 was over $2 billion; at the height of the program between 1967 and 1974 the grants averaged over $100 million per year.

On the average, approximately 40 percent of the total training funds went for the training of psychiatrists; the remainder went for the training of psychologists, psychiatric social workers, psychiatric nurses, and to other smaller programs such as that for teaching psychiatry to medical students. By 1972 it was estimated that the federal government was supporting three-fourths of all trainees in psychiatry in the United States; the other fourth was being subsidized by the states in state mental hospital training programs. It should be noted that, except for a small federal training program for anesthesiologists, which lasted only a few years, psychiatrists have been the only medical specialists whose residency training programs have been supported by a special federal training program.

A MOST EXCLUSIVE PROFESSION

Federal funds for training psychiatrists, psychologists, and psychiatric social workers have now been given out for forty years. The increase in the number of these professionals has been impressive, as shown in the following table and chart:

NUMBER OF TRAINED MENTAL HEALTH PROFESSIONALS

	1945	1985	Increase
Psychiatrists	3,000	32,255	10-fold
Psychologists	4,200	44,580*	10-fold
Psychiatric social workers	2,000	54,883*	27-fold
Total	9,200	131,718	14-fold

*1983 number

Altogether the number of trained mental health professionals has increased from approximately 9,200 to 131,718, an increase of 14-fold. During this same forty-year period the population of the United States increased from 133.4 million to 239.3 million, an increase of 1.8-fold. Data from the National Institute of Mental Health show that at least three-quarters of psychiatrists trained during the forty year period were beneficiaries of federal training funds, and it is likely that this is also true for psychologists and psychiatric social workers.

From the earliest days of the training programs, however, doubts were expressed as to whether the professionals who were being trained were really providing services for the seriously mentally ill. Despite Dr. Felix's assurances to Congress, no public service obligation was tied to federal training funds until 1981. Until then, the psychiatrists, psychologists, and psychiatric social workers were free to go directly into private practice following completion of their subsidized training, and that was what the vast majority of them did. Directors of the training programs were aware of this trend from the beginning, but to raise the issue publicly would have jeopardized continuation of the federal funds.

By 1955 Mike Gorman, who had lobbied strongly for the NIMH training program and testified in favor of increased support for it during the congressional hearings that year, was

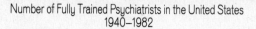

Number of Fully Trained Psychiatrists in the United States
1940–1982

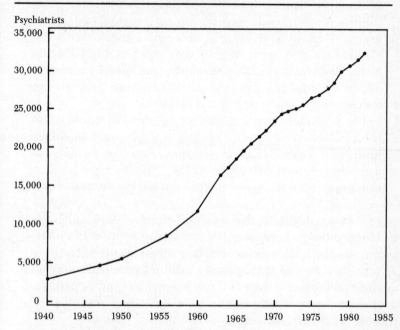

becoming publicly concerned. Almost without exception, he said, the best psychiatrists in the country were unwilling to accept jobs in state mental health programs or state mental hospitals. He wrote:

In the past few years, the people have become aroused about the need for better state mental hospitals. Since the end of World War II, they have supported bond issues aggregating close to $2 billion for the improvement of physical facilities. Even more important, they have supported a number of successful efforts to take the mental hospitals out of politics and place them in separate departments administered by medical men.

Heeding the insistent cry of the people, a number of governors have shaken off the shackles of the past and sought

165

out top psychiatrists to head up their state programs. In only a few cases have they succeeded. For the most part, the leading psychiatrists have turned down challenging opportunities to spearhead revolutionary state mental health programs. I know, and bitterly, whereof I speak. With the election of a new group of governors in November 1954, the National Mental Health Committee was asked to lend its efforts in obtaining top psychiatrists to head programs in several of the key states in the country.

The procedure was a disheartening one. We would comb through the same handful of people we thought might be interested. Even though the salaries offered were high—in a number of cases, $20,000 to $25,000, usually far more than the governor's salary—we were invariably turned down
. . .

In state after state, dynamic new programs are still in the blueprint stage because of the wall between private psychiatry and the state mental hospital systems. Many of the very psychiatrists who are the most caustic and condescending in their public discussions of the deficiencies of public psychiatry are the ones who cannot spare even one hour of their busy week for teaching in a state mental hospital.

Gorman went on to warn psychiatrists that if they did not accept the jobs they were needed for, then those jobs would eventually be given to psychologists, social workers, and nonpsychiatric administrators, which is exactly what happened.

In the decade between Gorman's expression of concern and the beginning of the community mental health center program, it became apparent that America's mental health professionals were not interested in working with the seriously mentally ill. At the time when federal funds began to be used for training the professionals, in 1948, it was estimated that approximately 52 percent of all psychiatrists were employed full time in public practice, that is, in state mental hospitals. By 1965 a survey of psychiatrists by the National Institute of Mental Health revealed that only 14 percent of them were employed full time in mental hospitals, which included private as well as public settings, and another 6 percent were employed full time in public and private psychiatric outpatient clinics. In other words, a decreasing percentage of psychiatrists was providing services to the seriously mentally ill. Six years later another survey of American psychiatrists reported that 14 percent of psychiatrists' time was spent working in state mental hospitals and another 7 percent was spent in community mental health centers. By this time over $1 billion had been spent by NIMH on training mental health professionals; the justification for the program had been to make more professionals available to treat the seriously mentally ill; yet the program appeared to be having the opposite effect.

There were, to be sure, many reasons why psychiatrists trained under the federally funded programs eschewed the seriously mentally ill and opted instead for the private practice of counseling and psychotherapy. Money was part of it; with increasingly liberal insurance benefits to cover much of the cost of psychotherapy it was easy for psychiatrists to find private patients and to make more money than they could earn in the public sector.

Money, however, was only part of the answer. Probably more important than money in determining the career path of psychiatrists was the prestige of psychotherapy, especially insight-oriented or psychoanalytic psychotherapy. Gorman had noted in 1955 that it was virtually impossible to recruit respected psychiatrists into state positions. If the leaders of the profession found public sector psychiatry beneath their dignity, then how could one expect young psychiatrists to select that career pathway? In the years between 1950 and 1980 a psychiatrist who opted to work in a state mental hospital would have been selecting the lowest-status job in the entire psychiatric hierarchy and would have been considered professionally aberrant. Furthermore, clinical psychologists and psychiatric social workers are influenced by psychiatrists; insofar as the psychiatrists defined working with the seriously mentally ill as a low-status activity, psychologists and psychiatric social workers did likewise.

Another aspect of the mental health profession that had become apparent by the mid-1960s was its progressive concentration in economically affluent areas. In the 1965 survey of psychiatrists carried out by the National Institute of Mental Health, for example, it was found that affluent Westport, Connecticut, had 30 practicing psychiatrists for its population of 10,000 people, while the blue-collar suburban area of Gary-Hammond-East Chicago had only 7 practicing psychiatrists for its population of 600,000. New York City, Boston, Washington, and San Francisco together had 28 percent of the nation's psychiatrists but only 10 percent of the population. Another survey found that two adjacent buildings on New York's 96th Street alone contained the offices of sixty-five psychiatrists, more than could be found in any one of sixteen states. In the years since the 1965 survey, the selective migration of psychiatrists to areas of affluence has been verified many times. Not to be left behind, psychologists and psychiatric social workers migrated with the psychiatrists, and by 1980 all three groups of professionals were concentrated in areas of the United States with "higher income, higher education, more urbanization, [and] more insurance availability."

As might be expected, individuals receiving the services of these professionals were not seriously mentally ill. For example, when private psychiatrists in Boston were surveyed in 1969 it was found that only 20 percent of their patients were sick enough to be labeled psychotic or borderline. Their patients were typically young, college-educated people with relatively minor problems. In fact, one-quarter of all private psychiatric patients in Boston were young women in their 20s and early 30s who lived within an area of less than a hundred blocks. Psychiatry, it appeared, had become a very exclusive profession.

By the time community mental health centers started to open in the late 1960s and early 1970s, then, it was apparent that psychiatrists, psychologists, and psychiatric social workers were selectively avoiding patients with serious mental illnesses. Even as leaders of American psychiatry, such as Dr. Jack Ewalt, were assuring Congress that "I have no worry at all about our ability to staff these mental health centers," data were accumulating at the National Institute of Mental Health suggesting that somebody should have had such worries. If CMHCs were supposed to take over the function of state mental hospitals, but psychiatrists, psychologists, and psychiatric social workers were not interested in working with patients from the state hospitals, then logic suggested that the program was not going to work.

A few professionals did note these trends and tried to warn their colleagues. Foremost among them were psychologists M. Brewster Smith and Nicholas Hobbs, both of whom had been members of the Joint Commission on Mental Illness and Health. They published in 1966 an assessment of professional staffing problems in CMHCs that would turn out to be remarkably prophetic:

> The more advanced mental health services have tended to be a middle-class luxury; chronic mental hospital custody a lower-class horror. The relationship between the mental health helper and the helped has been governed by an affinity of the clean for the clean, the educated for the educated, the affluent for the affluent. Most of our therapeutic talent, often trained at public expense, has been invested not in solving our hard-core mental health problem—the psychotic of marginal competence and social status—but in treating the relatively well-to-do educated neurotic, usually in an urban center . . . This disturbing state of affairs exists whether the patient is treated privately or in a community facility, or by a psychiatrist, psychologist, or other professional person. If the community representatives who take responsibility for policy in the new community mental health centers are indignant at this inequity, their indignation would seem to be justified on the reasonable assumption that mental health services provided at public expense ought to reach the people who most need help. Although regulations stipulate that people will not be barred from service because of inability to pay, the greatest threat to the integrity and usefulness of the proposed comprehensive centers is that they will nonetheless neglect the poor and disadvantaged, and that they will simply provide at public

expense services that are now privately available to people of means.

Among psychiatrists there were also expressions of concern, but these too were largely ignored. An example is this from 1972:

> But the problem is not just that the time [of American psychiatrists] is spent in private practice. The problem is that the private practice is grossly maldistributed geographically, unavailable to minority group members or the poor, and not aimed toward the high-risk groups who need the care most . . . The patients seen by private psychiatrists are white and affluent. One survey of private psychiatrists revealed that less than 1 percent of their patients were nonwhite. Another study showed that only 3 percent of the patients seen by private psychiatrists were on welfare . . . American psychiatrists offer their patients a two-class system that exceeds the limits which are acceptable in a democracy. If you have money and are lucky you will get treatment; if not, you will just have to do without . . . Do we really believe it is justified to spend public money to train psychiatrists who are only going to be readily available to the elite?

INCREASING USE OF FOREIGN MEDICAL GRADUATES

While increasing numbers of psychiatrists, psychologists, and psychiatric social workers were being trained with federal funds, state mental hospitals in the 1960s and '70s were finding it increasingly difficult to fill professional staff positions. And because of continuing media exposés about conditions in the institutions during these years, state officials were under tremendous pressure to increase the number of professional staff, especially psychiatrists, and to upgrade care.

The solution to this dilemma came from the United States Immigration Service, which in 1962, 1965, and 1970 supported legislation liberalizing American immigration laws. The new laws made it easier for professionals from other countries to come to the United States, and doctors were high on the list of the most desirable immigrants. Some officials suggested that for the United States to import these professionals from poorer countries was not morally supportable—indeed, Senator Walter Mondale as early as 1966 labeled it "a national disgrace"—but the forces of pragmatism prevailed.

State mental hospitals in the United States immediately seized upon foreign medical graduates as a means of filling the positions that American medical graduates were refusing to take. Since the vast majority of foreign medical graduates had received little or no psychiatric training in their own countries, many state hospitals set up their own residency training programs for them. By 1970, 34 percent of all psychiatric residents (1,370 out of 4,040) in the United States were foreign medical graduates. By 1973, there were more Indian psychiatrists working in state mental hospitals in the United States than psychiatrists in all of India; the five Pakistani psychiatrists at a single state hospital in Missouri were more than existed for the fifteen million Pakistanis living in the Punjab. By 1986 in the United States, there were 1,331 Indian practicing psychiatrists, compared with 511 in India; 157 Pakistani practicing psychiatrists, compared with 63 in Pakistan; and 113 Egyptian practicing psychiatrists, compared with 50 in Egypt.

Many of the foreign medical graduates were unable to pass state licensing examinations because of language problems, poor training, or lack of competency. To fill vacant positions in the hospitals, therefore, all except seven states amended their medical licensing laws by 1971 so that foreign medical graduates could practice in state mental hospitals on special state permits. In states like New York and Ohio, 40 percent of the physicians in state mental hospitals were unlicensed, while in West Virginia it was 90 percent. By 1972 a spokesman for the American Medical Association estimated that 7,500 unlicensed foreign medical graduates were at work in public mental hospitals in the United States.

The use of unlicensed physicians to care for the seriously mentally ill in public hospitals has been, without question, the nadir of American psychiatry. One obvious problem is language, since many foreign medical graduates speak poor English. Some states set up special language courses for them, but meanwhile hospital patients, many of whom have difficulty communicating with anyone because of their illness, were confronted with physicians who could neither understand nor be understood.

Much more serious than language problems was increasing evidence that some of the unlicensed foreign medical graduates were incompetent. A highly publicized case in 1972 was a physician at Elgin State Hospital in Illinois who was investigated in connection with the deaths of eighteen hospital patients. This unlicensed doctor had been employed in the state mental hospital under a special state permit as the hospital pathologist. According to a report in the *Chicago Tribune,* the physician had "demonstrated total medical incompetence in working with corpses, so mental health officials demoted him by transferring him to the hospital wards where he treated live patients." Another disturbing aspect of the case was the fact that the physician who had been in charge of approving the first physician's credentials had himself failed the state licensing exam ten times.

There were and are many foreign medical graduates who are as competent, or more competent, than most American medical graduates. In fact most of the significant advances in psychiatry up until recent years have come from physicians who graduated from foreign medical schools. Despite this fact, throughout the 1970s evidence continued to accumulate that the licensed foreign medical graduates being employed in state mental hospitals—to say nothing of the unlicensed ones—were as a group considerably less competent than American medical graduates. The evidence consisted of their pass rate on the examination of the Education Council for Foreign Medical Graduates (ECFMG), their pass rate on state licensing examinations, and the relatively low percentage who were able to obtain specialty certification by the American Board of Psychiatry and Neurology.

The moral aspect to the situation has two facets. First, the foreign medical graduates are there because American medical graduates, despite having received their specialty training in publicly subsidized programs, have refused to take the jobs. This fact has been virtually ignored by the American Psychiatric Association and by psychiatrists generally. Second, it has been estimated that the annual dollar value of foreign medical graduates who come to the United States "approximately equals the total cost of all our medical aid, private and public, to foreign nations," as the wealthiest nation in the world continues to take valuable resources from poorer nations.

A TWO-CLASS SYSTEM

Throughout the 1970s the use of foreign medical graduates to staff state mental hospitals increased. A survey by the NIMH in 1975 found that foreign medical graduates constituted 50 percent of the psychiatric staff of state mental hospitals. In some states the percentage was much higher, such as Rhode Island (87 percent), West Virginia (84 percent), South Dakota (80 percent), Montana (77 percent), Florida (77 percent), Virginia (74 percent), and Maryland (74 percent). A variable number of the foreign medical graduates were unlicensed; overall the number unlicensed was 42 percent, but in West Virginia, for example, 82 percent of the state hospital psychiatrists were unlicensed.

Another NIMH survey, in 1980, found that foreign medical graduates had continued to increase and comprised 54 percent of state hospital psychiatric staff positions. The number who were unlicensed, however, had decreased to 21 percent. This decrease was not due to states becoming more selective in their employment policies, but rather to 1976 amendments to the Immigration and Nationality Act, which made it more difficult for foreign medical graduates to come to the United States. The unlicensed doctors were most frequently newly arrived; the longer physicians remain in the United States the more likely they are to be able to take remedial courses and eventually pass the licensing examinations.

The most recent year for which data are available on the use of foreign medical graduates in state mental hospitals is 1982, when it was found that *63 percent* of all psychiatrists in these hospitals were foreign medical graduates. There is no reason to believe that the percentage has decreased since that time; if anything it has probably increased. The employment of these doctors in public psychiatric institutions has become so much a part of American culture that when Barbra Streisand was examined by two psychiatrists in the 1987 film *Nuts,* both were portrayed as foreign medical graduates, one incompetent, the other unable to speak comprehensible English.

In the 1970s and '80s the widespread use of foreign medical graduate psychiatrists in state mental hospitals spilled over to community mental health centers. American psychiatrists were attracted to CMHCs in the earliest years of the program, when CMHCs were being promoted as the wave of the psychiatric future. The attraction wore off quickly, however, when the psychiatrists were assigned responsibility for seriously mentally ill patients, most of whom needed medication and some of whom needed hospitalization. Psychologists and psychiatric social workers in the CMHCs appropriated for themselves the status role of psychotherapist, and psychiatrists complained that they were only needed to write prescriptions. American psychiatrists exited CMHCs in large numbers to return to private practice.

Since CMHCs, like state mental hospitals, had to fill their psychiatric positions to meet minimal standards for operating, they filled the jobs with the only psychiatrists who were available—foreign medical graduates. Although there has been no systematic survey, an estimate as early as 1972 suggested that "perhaps half of all CMHC psychiatrists are foreign-born." An observer in 1982 noted that "supervisory and other mental health professionals in community mental health centers frequently comment that only a 'substandard' psychiatrist would practice there." American-trained psychiatrists also left positions as directors of the CMHCs; in 1971 55 percent of CMHC directors were psychiatrists, but by 1980 only 16 percent of them were.

In 1981 the NIMH, concerned about the continuing exodus from public facilities of psychiatrists generally and American-trained psychiatrists specifically, published a report subtitled

"Where Have All the Psychiatrists Gone?" The report documented the number of psychiatrists who had left state mental hospitals, community mental health centers, and public psychiatric outpatient clinics to work instead in private psychiatric hospitals and private practice. The answer to the question was obvious: American psychiatrists had left positions in public psychiatry for positions in private psychiatry.

It is instructive to compare the present situation with the one that existed in 1945 when federal training funds were first proposed to increase the number of professionals. In 1945 there were only 3,000 psychiatrists in the United States but 1,596 of them (53 percent) worked in the public sector in state mental hospitals. By 1985 the number of psychiatrists had increased to 32,255. A 1984 survey identified 7,622 psychiatrists in public sector jobs (state and county mental hospitals, outpatient clinics, and community mental health centers). Of these at least 60 percent were foreign medical graduates. The number of American-trained psychiatrists in public sector jobs in 1984, therefore, was approximately 3,053, slightly less than twice the number that had been in public sector jobs in 1945. Since the population of the United States has almost doubled during those forty years, the number of American-trained psychiatrists in public sector jobs is virtually unchanged despite forty years of federally supported training programs.

Nor are prospects any brighter for the future. A 1980 survey of psychiatric trainees found that only 15 percent of them "planned to enter public service," while observations of psychology trainees and social work students have reported that a very small percentage of them are interested in public practice of any kind. State mental hospitals and community mental health centers will have to continue recruiting any warm body with the proper professional degree attached. This is true not only in states traditionally hard-pressed to recruit successfully, like West Virginia and Mississippi, but also in states that should be able to attract good professionals. For example in early 1988 it was revealed that Springfield State Hospital in Maryland was employing two psychiatrists who had been investigated by the State

175

Commission on Medical Discipline. One had "served jail time for Medicaid fraud and drug distribution," and the other "had taken hallucinogenic drugs with his patients and had sex with one of them." The Commission allowed both men to keep their medical licenses only if they agreed to practice in a state mental hospital. The superintendent of the hospital said "he was glad to be able to recruit" them.

9

The Politics of Perdition: 1968–1988

T he lack of housing for released mental health patients, the
failure of community mental health centers to provide aftercare, increasingly rigid commitment laws, and the mental
health professionals' abdication of responsibility for the seriously
mentally ill—all were becoming apparent in the early 1970s.
Deinstitutionalization was a disaster looking for a place to happen; the question was not whether it would happen but simply
when.

At another time in American history, professionals and officials
in charge of programs for the mentally ill might have acknowledged the failures of their programs and instituted mid-course
corrections. That possibility was precluded on November 6,
1968, by the election of Richard M. Nixon as president. Both
Martin Luther King and Robert F. Kennedy had been assas-
sinated in the months leading up to the election, and over
541,000 American troops were bogged down in the jungles of
Vietnam in a war that was being lost. The optimism of the Great
Society years seemed like a memory from the distant past.

Nixon's election was anathema to most psychiatrists, especially to those active in the community mental health center movement. Psychiatrists as a group are strongly Democratic by persuasion; in the 1964 election 71 percent of psychiatrists and 95 percent of psychoanalysts voted for President Johnson. In 1968 a poll published one month before the election showed that whereas 66 percent of all physicians intended to vote for Nixon only 41 percent of psychiatrists intended to do so. Not only did psychiatrists vote against Nixon, but approximately half of them regularly contributed money to candidates of their choice.

The dislike between President Nixon and America's psychiatrists was mutual. Almost 2,000 psychiatrists answered a 1964 poll by *Fact* magazine asking about the mental status of Barry Goldwater and his psychiatric fitness to be president. The blatant misuse of their responses to discredit a Republican candidate was widely commented on by the media. Psychiatrists, according to Nixon supporters, were virtually synonymous with liberals. On the other side, most psychiatrists disliked Nixon not only because of his conservative domestic policies and authoritarian position on law-and-order issues but because of his formal, humorless demeanor and his secretive, some even said paranoid, personality traits. Nixon seemed to American psychiatrists the very antithesis of their hero, John F. Kennedy, whose visible legacy to psychiatry continued to be the CMHC program.

It was clear to mental health professionals, then, that a Nixon presidency was not going to be good for them. A prelude to the expected clash occurred six months after Nixon took office; the Community Mental Health Centers Act was due to expire, and congressional hearings to extend the legislation were scheduled for July 1969. Earlier that year the National Institute of Mental Health had weakened its political bargaining position by leaving the protective aegis of the National Institutes of Health (NIH). The NIH is a research entity and, as such, relatively sheltered from the partisan political winds that regularly sweep down the Potomac. NIMH left NIH because it no longer considered itself a research institute but rather as the overseer of a vast service organization, which then numbered more than 200 operating CMHCs but which was projected to grow to 2,000 centers. NIMH saw itself not only as too big to be part of NIH but as an equal to it.

President Nixon had inherited a major problem from Presidents Kennedy and Johnson in the war in Vietnam, and it was to this problem which he directed his attention during his early months in office. In June 1969, Nixon met with South Vietnam's President Thieu on Midway Island and then announced that 25,000 Americans would be withdrawn from Vietnam in the first stage of de-escalation. The following month Nixon visited Vietnam and other Asian nations and made clear that they should not count on the United States indefinitely to fight their battles for them.

Hearings on the bill entitled "Community Mental Health Centers Amendments of 1969" opened before the Senate Subcommittee on Health on July 28, 1969, while President Nixon was on his trip to Southeast Asia. The new administration was so involved with getting the Vietnam problem under control that it had not had time to look at its domestic programs. Most of the hierarchy of the Department of Health, Education and Welfare were still holdovers from the Kennedy-Johnson years; for example, one of the officials representing the Nixon administration at the 1969 CMHC hearings was Dr. Joseph English, who had been a Kennedy confidant and one of the architects of the Great Society programs.

The chairman of the Senate Subcommittee on Health was Democrat Ralph Yarborough of Texas, and he made it clear from his opening statement that he thought the CMHC program should be extended and enlarged. The CMHCs, Yarborough said, had "heralded a new era in the compassionate treatment of the mentally ill—an era focusing on the concept of providing care to the mentally ill in the community where they live." The primary purpose of CMHCs, added Yarborough, was:

> to overcome prolonged treatment in an overcrowded, overburdened, and less effective state hospital, which often has offered little hope of recovery for their patients and in too many instances were primarily institutions for quarantining

179

the mentally ill, not for treating them. We became committed, at the inception of the Community Mental Health Centers Act, to an important struggle to develop a broad range of services for promptly diagnosing mental disorders and treating them effectively; for rehabilitation of those suffering from mental illness; and for preventing the occurrence of mental diseases whenever possible.

The specter of brutality in state mental hospitals was raised several times during the hearings as it had been in 1945, 1955, and again in 1963. Mike Gorman, with echoes of Vietnam, added a contemporary note when he compared state mental hospitals with a Prisoner of War (POW) camp he had been in during World War II: "I saw conditions worse [in state mental hospitals] than I saw in POW camps, having been an inhabitant of one for eleven months. I would rather have been a POW in a camp than be in 95 percent of the state hospitals in the United States."

According to several witnesses, the continuing decline in the population of state hospitals could by implication be attributable to CMHCs. For example:

We have seen a steady decline in population of state and county mental hospitals and a progressive reduction in new admissions to those same hospitals.

With the development of the community mental health centers program—an entirely new system for the delivery of comprehensive mental health care to all Americans—we have seen a definite trend toward better utilization and a more equitable distribution of scarce professional manpower.

The 1969 hearings made it clear, however, that CMHCs had become politicized. When President Nixon's representative from the Department of Health, Education and Welfare testified that the CMHC program should be phased out, Senator Yarborough countered by comparing the cost of CMHCs with the cost of waging war in Vietnam ("$21,663 and $2/3$ cents for ammunition for the coming year to shoot at each Vietcong and North Vietnamese"). It was pointed out that community mental health centers symbolized services to people, as opposed to Vietnam, which meant killing people, and that continued support of the war was at the expense of human services. One witness at the hearings even invoked the image of President Kennedy who had "shaken and reshaped . . . our national priorities for the conservation of human resources by a new mental health and mental retardation program." The Nixon administration needed no reminding that CMHCs had been a Kennedy program.

Despite the political overtones of the 1969 hearings, the attention of Nixon loyalists was on Vietnam, and the CMHC legislation passed Congress without difficulty. Construction grants for CMHCs were liberalized and staffing grants extended from four to eight years. During the hearings several witnesses acknowledged that some states were not enthusiastically supporting the development of community mental health centers, but nobody inquired why this might be so. If CMHCs were in fact allowing states to empty their hospitals, one might have expected the states to be strong supporters of the centers. Instead, witnesses for the CMHC extension asked for more federal support and for a longer period of time. As Mike Gorman phrased it: "We are just beginning to learn to walk. Let us walk for ten years and then we will begin to run, but we don't have the capability yet." In fact, the CMHC program, severely crippled from birth, would never crawl let alone walk.

NIXON SELF-DESTRUCTS

By early 1970 President Nixon's staff had trained its sights on domestic programs, and the National Institute of Mental Health was being asked hard questions. Why should the federal government continue to support the creation of new CMHCs when the program had been started merely as a demonstration project? If the centers were working as well as NIMH claimed, why were states not assuming the federal share of the costs? And why was the federal government supporting the training of psychiatrists who, it appeared, were not then taking jobs in state mental hospitals or CMHCs but rather going directly into private practice?

They were valid questions, but in the atmosphere of the time they would not be addressed. On November 15, 1969, the largest antiwar rally in the history of the United States took place in Washington. Shortly thereafter the My Lai massacre in Vietnam was brought to public attention, and on April 30, 1970, Nixon announced he had ordered American troops into Cambodia to attack Vietnamese bases. Antiwar sentiment became synonymous with anti-Nixon sentiment. It became unnecessary for the mental health establishment to answer the questions being asked; all they had to do was point out that Nixon, the incarnation of evil, had been asking them. Community mental health centers and other NIMH programs became banners behind which the liberals of the psychiatric community could assemble and march.

The atmosphere at the National Institute of Mental Health by late 1970 was one of siege. The Republicans were cleaning house and had ousted NIMH Director Yolles as well as his immediate superior, Dr. Joseph English. As Yolles later recalled:

Who would have thought, in those heady months of growth that by 1970 a president and "his men" would actively seek to terminate federal support—of both the community mental health centers program and the training of psychiatric manpower? But these things happened: and to use a verb of the times, the White House "stonewalled" development of these programs and tried, actively, to reverse that progress by "phasing out" support that would have made it possible at least to maintain the status quo.

Dr. Saul Feldman, another NIMH official, described the Nixon era at NIMH as follows:

During the early '70s, a common enemy in the form of the Nixon administration caused many in the community mental health movement to become even more strident and perhaps defensive in their advocacy of the program. As the efforts to discontinue federal support for the centers increased, so did the claims for them, and the interest in critical self-examination seemed to diminish substantially. In the struggle for survival the virtues of the community mental health centers were magnified, the defects were overlooked, and there was a tendency to perceive the environment in two simple dimensions—the "good guys" who supported them and the "bad guys" who opposed them.

Mike Gorman bluntly characterized Nixon's efforts as a "policy of trying to wipe out the mental health centers" which was "vicious and unwise."

There were at the time individuals both outside and inside NIMH who had grave doubts about the efficacy of both the CMHC program and federal support of psychiatric training. Not only was it clear that CMHCs were not treating the mentally ill being discharged from state hospitals, but some CMHCs were known to be building swimming pools with federal construction funds, while others were being utilized primarily as federally funded private hospitals by private psychiatrists. A book published in 1971 by Dr. Anthony Panzetta, a strong supporter of CMHCs, listed in painful detail a multitude of conceptual and operational defects in the CMHC program and predicted that the program would fail. Throughout the professional literature, an increasing number of articles cast doubt on the outcome of deinstitutionalization—articles with titles such as "The Chronic Mentally Ill Shuffle to Oblivion" and "Discharged Mental Patients—Are They Really in the Community?" Similarly, the psychiatric training programs were widely known to be producing mostly private psychiatrists who had no interest in the mentally ill, and a few officials within NIMH wondered whether this was a justifiable use of public funds. Most people at NIMH, however, were not interested in such questions; if CMHCs and training programs were not doing what they had agreed to do, NIMH did not want to know. This was, as was said at the time, "the heart of the problem—the slow, sad steps which lead to a minuet of mutual deception."

Between 1970 and 1972 the Nixon administration increased pressure on the NIMH, attempting each year to reduce its funds and cut its programs. Each year NIMH relied on a sympathetic Democratic Congress to come to its rescue, which it invariably did. Federal training funds for psychiatrists, psychologists, and psychiatric social workers continued to be given at a rate of $110–120 million a year between 1968 and 1972. Federal funds for community mental health centers were reduced by the president from $110 million in 1968 to $71 million in 1970, but Democratic supporters in Congress had restored the program to $198 million by 1973. The Nixon administration thereupon impounded and refused to spend some of the CMHC appropriations and relented only when forced to do so by a federal court. New CMHCs continued to become operational, the numbers climbing from 165 in 1968 to 255 in 1970 to 400 by 1973. It was evident that Congress intended to continue the mental health programs of the Great Society in direct opposition to the wishes of the president.

On June 17, 1972, five men were arrested breaking into the Democratic National Headquarters in the Watergate office building in Washington. Over the next four weeks they would be linked to G. Gordon Liddy and E. Howard Hunt and the Republican Committee to Reelect the President run by former Attorney General John Mitchell. The following month Democrats selected George McGovern to oppose Nixon. The legislation authorizing community mental health centers was due to expire and hearings on the program had been scheduled. NIMH and its supporters, fervidly hoping for a McGovern victory in November, arranged with Congress to extend the CMHC legislation for a year and put off the expected confrontation with the White House. This was successfully done in perfunctory hearings on September 18, 1972, during the brief course of which it was again stated to be "readily apparent that the community mental health centers programs have played an important role in decreasing the utilization of state mental hospitals."

Nixon's overwhelming victory over McGovern in the November 1972 elections could have spelled disaster for the mental health establishment. But the president had troubles. On February 7, 1973, the Senate established a Select Committee on Presidential Campaign Activities to investigate Watergate. In March, James W. McCord, one of the Watergate burglars, named John Mitchell as the "overall boss" of the operation, and the following month FBI Director Patrick E. Gray resigned after admitting that he had destroyed evidence in the Watergate case at the request of Nixon aides. Ten days later two of Nixon's closest aides, H.R. Haldeman and John Ehrlichman, resigned along with other officials. It was apparent that the Nixon presidency was unraveling.

THE 1973 HEARINGS

It was in this political climate, in March 1973, that hearings on the CMHCs began before both Senate and House subcommittees. Caspar W. Weinberger, Secretary of Health, Education and Welfare, was responsible for arguing the Nixon administration's position that:

[the CMHC] program has proven itself and should now be absorbed by the regular health service delivery system. . . . These centers should now face the test of operating on their own without special federal assistance. Moreover, those that cannot meet this test should not be perpetuated by extending the period of federal assistance beyond the eight years which they are entitled to under the current law. In addition, the success of the individual centers which do prove viable should be adequate incentive for other localities to undertake to bring these services to its people. The need for federally funded demonstrations, however, has been met.

Weinberger noted that seventy-five community mental health centers had started without any federal funds and argued strongly that the federal government had no business providing mental health services other than as demonstration projects: "I have told you as completely and candidly as I can that I think it a very wrong and inappropriate and improper role for the federal government to be in, to provide permanent delivery and treatment and care in this or other fields."

With Nixon's popularity declining dramatically, virtually nobody in Congress was prepared to defend the administration's position. Nixon was staunchly opposed to CMHCs and other federal mental health programs. To oppose such programs was to agree with Nixon, and that, given the continuing evolution of the Watergate revelations, was not politically wise. To support CMHCs, then, was not only to support humanistic concepts of government associated with presidents Kennedy and Johnson but also to oppose Richard Nixon.

The shape of the CMHC hearings became immediately apparent when *Republican* Senator Richard S. Schweiker of Pennsylvania opened by criticizing Secretary Weinberger, claiming that CMHCs had not been intended merely as demonstration program: "The point you are missing and overlooking, Mr. Secretary, is the purpose for which the act was passed. You are overlooking the program's concept. Now you are totally gutting the program." Senator Harold E. Hughes of Iowa also disagreed strongly with Weinberger and accused the Nixon administration of accepting mediocrity as the standard for mental health services:

I disagree so thoroughly with what the Secretary is saying that to continue the questioning would only emphasize the differences, and I doubt if it would serve much purpose as far as the hearing is concerned.

It seems to me that they have adopted a policy of addressing inequality by reducing the services to the lowest possible level at all points.

But it was Senator Edward M. Kennedy of Massachusetts who attacked Weinberger most persistently. Kennedy referred to studies done under NIMH contracts showing that many community mental health centers would close without federal funds.

Weinberger dismissed the studies and implicitly attacked NIMH, part of his own department, as having "a lot of ordered studies" designed to produce prearranged results "that many times the people [at NIMH] ordered and requested initially." Kennedy raised the possibility that Congress would pass the CMHC legislation even over a veto by President Nixon and told Weinberger: "It appears quite clear that you have made up your mind, and the Congress be damned." Weinberger replied shortly thereafter: "If you wish to misquote me continually, of course you are free to do so."

The political nature of the CMHC debate was also evident in hearings on the bill before the House Subcommittee on Public Health and Environment. Congressman Paul G. Rogers of Florida, a staunch defender of NIMH programs, pointedly asked Dr. John S. Zapp, representing Secretary Weinberger, what role White House aides Ehrlichman and Haldeman had had in decision-making at the Department of Health, Education and Welfare regarding community mental health centers:

> MR. ROGERS: That was Mr. Ehrlichman. Did he have any input in the decision as to whether this program continues or not?
>
> DR. ZAPP: I can state he has not been on my call sheet, Mr. Chairman. I don't—
>
> MR. ROGERS: Yes, but did he call you? I am not talking about the sheet now. I wasn't thinking of his calling you but I am thinking of his input into the decision-making. Did either Mr. Haldeman or Mr. Ehrlichman provide any input?

Later, Congressman William R. Roy of Kansas sarcastically drew Mr. Zapp's attention to the resignation of the White House aides: "Somebody in OMB, or whoever is left in the White House, is making absolutely totally absurd decisions that you, out of conviction or for other reasons, are coming up here trying to impose upon us."

In such a milieu it was not surprising that substantive issues about the effectiveness of CMHCs were not raised. Instead there were ritual assertions that CMHCs were effective because the state mental hospital population was dropping. Despite the fact that NIMH had accumulated much data by 1973 indicating that CMHCs were playing little role in emptying the hospitals, the NIMH briefing book prepared for the congressional hearings in 1973 declared definitively that "the community mental health center has had a major impact on the utilization of the state mental hospital."

When Congressman Rogers asked NIMH Director Bertram S. Brown for documentation on CMHC effectiveness, Brown replied that "where a center has been operational three years or longer, the possibility of a person being a mental patient in that area is reduced by a third." This claim was contradicted by other studies NIMH had carried out up to that time. When an NIMH official who had helped compile that data was recently asked where the one-third figure had come from he acknowledged with a smile that it had been a product of "a special analysis." "You know," he added with a note of regret, "we were all good soldiers then."

As the CMHC legislation was being debated by Congress, the continuing revelations of Watergate brought the scandal ever closer to the White House. In October 1973, Vice-President Spiro Agnew resigned after being charged with income tax evasion. Ten days later the "Saturday night massacre" took place with the firing of Special Prosecutor Archibald Cox and the resignations of Attorney General Elliot Richardson and his assistant, William D. Ruckelshaus. In March of 1974 seven former White House aides, including Haldeman, Ehrlichman, and Mitchell, were indicated for obstructing the Watergate investigation. In July the Supreme Court ruled against President Nixon and ordered him to turn over tape recordings of White House conversations. The House Judiciary Committee then approved two articles of impeachment against the president, and on August 8, 1974, President Nixon resigned. The joy in the mental health community was unrestrained.

The CMHC legislation was not passed by Congress until 1975, nearly two years after the hearings were held. The bill faced a certain veto in the White House, and that honor fell to Nixon's successor, President Gerald R. Ford. Following Ford's veto, both Senate and House overrode it four days later. President Kennedy's memory was invoked and it was said that the CMHC program would live on as a symbol of his concern for the mentally ill.

The actual CMHC legislation that emerged in 1975, however, was quite different from the bill passed in 1963. In the original legislation, CMHCs had to deliver five "essential services": inpatient, partial hospitalization, outpatient, emergency services, and consultation and education. The evidence available to NIMH by 1975 suggested that CMHCs were not providing services for the seriously mentally ill and that outpatient services were the dominant essential service. The mental health community lobbied hard to get the 1975 CMHC legislation passed by Congress and then to override President Ford's veto. The price of such lobbying, however, was that more essential services were added to the CMHC mandate so that when the bill finally emerged they had increased to twelve—the original five plus (6) screening of patients prior to admission to state hospitals, (7) follow-up care for those released from mental hospitals, (8) developing transitional living facilities for the mentally ill, and providing specialized services for (9) children, (10) the elderly, (11) drug abusers, and (12) alcohol abusers. The logic behind adding seven more essential services for CMHCs that had been unable to provide the first five was, to say the least, difficult to follow.

ROSALYN CARTER'S COMMISSION

The psychiatric community greeted the election of Jimmy Carter to the White House in November 1976 with great enthusiasm. Carter's wife, Rosalyn, had been actively involved in promoting community mental health centers in Georgia. In addition, Dr. Peter Bourne, who had worked as Carter's deputy campaign director, had been the director of a CMHC in Atlanta. After eight lean years under Nixon and Ford, the mental health table would again be set and there would be a feast for all.

One of the first acts Carter carried out as president was to create a Commission on Mental Health with his wife as honorary Chairwoman. Significantly, this commission's title included mental *health* alone; the other half of the name of the earlier 1955 Joint Commission on Mental *Illness* and Health had fallen by the wayside in the intervening twenty-two years. The charge of the Carter Commission was "to review the mental health needs of the nation and to make recommendations to the president as to how the nation might best meet these needs." Thirty-five task panels were assembled under the direction of Dr. Thomas E. Bryant, and the Commission proceeded to hold public hearings and collect information.

The product of the year's deliberations was a 2,139-page preliminary report, which was submitted to President Carter in April 1978. It contained 117 recommendations and, like its Joint Commission predecessor, contained something for everyone. It offered advice about everything from guidance for parents to the role of women in the military to the mental health of the physically handicapped. It was, in short, a true mental health document.

Included in the Carter Commission report were several sections sharply critical of care for the seriously mentally ill:

Time and again we have learned—from testimony, from inquiries, and from the reports of special task panels—of people with chronic mental disabilities who have been released from hospitals but who do not have the basic necessities of life. They lack adequate food, clothing, or shelter. We have heard of woefully inadequate follow-up mental health and general medical care. And we have seen evidence that half the people released from large mental hospitals are being readmitted within a year of discharge. While not every individual can be treated within the community, many of the readmissions to state hospitals could have been avoided if comprehensive assistance had existed within their communities.

Two of the thirty-five task panels were primarily concerned with this problem and their reports illustrate why the Carter Commission will be among the least remembered commissions in American history. First was a panel on "Community Mental Health Centers Assessment," the majority of whose members were running CMHCs or had been involved in originally setting up the program. The panel sharply criticized CMHCs for offering "a distressing lack of services for previously institutionalized patients returning to the community," noting that as of 1975 only 10 percent of CMHC admissions were diagnosed with schizophrenia, while 21 percent had "neuroses and personality disorders" and another 22 percent had "social maladjustment" or "no mental disorder." The report added: "It does appear from CMHC admissions data that the total [CMHC] program is moving from caring for the most severely mentally disabled, the type most likely to spend time in a state hospital."

After acknowledging the serious shortcomings of CMHCs the task panel declared that the Nixon and Ford administrations had been primarily responsible for these shortcomings:

> Over the past years there has been a failure of federal oversight, technical assistance, evaluation, and leadership that is at the heart of the current matter. It is important to note that over these same years previous administrations had sought to end the program, arguing that a successful demonstration project no longer needed to be demonstrated. In the face of this erosion of support (manifested most strikingly by the administration's impoundment of congressional authorized funds) and diminishing resources for program support, there has been an increasing need for such services and leadership. In many ways, to criticize the centers themselves for many (but not all) of their failings is to "blame the victim."

Despite the stated shortcomings, the Carter Commission declared that the CMHC program was an unqualified success: "In community after community around America, the CMHC program has created important, useful mental health services that would not be in existence if the program had not produced them." The task panel then concluded its exercise in Byzantine logic by arriving at a highly predictable conclusion: CMHCs deserved more federal funds.

The task panel report on "Deinstitutionalization, Rehabilitation, and Long-term Care" was, if anything, an even more remarkable document. It described in great detail the lack of services for the seriously mentally ill and pointedly noted:

> Ironically although [the seriously mentally ill] are the primary reason for the existence of many mental health services, they have too frequently been excluded from the service delivery system. The President's Commission on Mental Health has at this time a unique, and extremely important, responsibility to recommend that this history of neglect be stopped.

In describing the lack of services for the seriously mentally ill, the task force *never once* mentioned community mental health centers. It was as if they did not exist. Instead the task panel recommended that states "designate an agency in each geographic area to assume responsibility for ensuring that every chronically mentally disabled person's needs are adequately met." The designated agency would further "ensure that every chronically mentally disabled individual receives quality mental health care and supportive services." In short, the panel was describing the primary function originally envisioned for community mental health centers and, without mentioning the fact that six hundred of them had already been set up with federal funds, recommending that such a program be begun.

The evidence that CMHCs were not doing the job they were intended to do was continuing to accumulate even as the task panels were deliberating. On January 7, 1977, the Comptroller General of the General Accounting Office issued a report to Congress detailing how "many mentally disabled persons have been released from institutions before sufficient community facilities and services were available and without adequate planning and follow-up." Later in 1977 the Secretary of the Department of Health, Education and Welfare established a Task Force on Deinstitutionalization of the Mentally Disabled to address the issues raised by the GAO Report. The Task Force noted the low priority given to services for the seriously mentally ill, the "deep-seated attitudes of fear and loathing held by the lay community and many services providers," and also the "conflicting policies between federal and state program partners," a situation that "wastes resources and creates opportunities to avoid responsibility."

Meanwhile a consensus was emerging at NIMH that deinstitutionalization was a well-intentioned plan that had gone astray. The few research projects on deinstitutionalization that had been funded by NIMH all indicated that patients being released by state mental hospitals were receiving minimal services. For example, a 1974 study by the Stanford Research Institute in California had found that most patients placed in board and care homes were not receiving psychiatric care from CMHCs (or anywhere else), often lived in clusters of these homes that amounted to impersonal psychiatric ghettos, and in many cases "lead even more isolated existences in the community than they did in the hospital." The patients had merely been transinstitutionalized, not deinstitutionalized, and the rhetoric of President Kennedy's 1963 special message to Congress acquired an increasingly hollow ring: "When carried out, reliance on the cold mercy of custodial isolation will be supplanted by the open warmth of community concern and capability. Emphasis on prevention, treatment, and rehabilitation will be substituted for a desultory interest in confining patients in an institution to wither away."

Even more alarming than the research on deinstitutionalization that NIMH had funded was the research that NIMH had not funded. By 1981 there had been just *five* studies done in the United States on alternatives to long-term hospitalization despite the fact that during the previous two decades more than *400,000* beds had been closed in state and county mental hospitals. Braun *et al.* summarized this state of affairs:

193

The failure to have evaluated adequately the effect of discharging hundreds of thousands of chronically ill patients from large public mental hospitals has been a major defect in the conduct of public policy . . . Given the magnitude of the social policy change entailed by deinstitutionalization and the two decades that have elapsed since it was put into motion, it is astonishing that so little productive effort has been put into evaluating the effects of the policy.

Even without additional research, however, by 1977 it was clear that something had to be done to improve services for the discharged mental patients beginning to accumulate in public shelters and on the streets. The answer proposed by NIMH was the Community Support Program (CSP), initiated with $3.5 million in 1977, which grew ten years later into a $15-million-a-year program. The money is given to states to help coordinate services "for one particularly vulnerable population—adult psychiatric patients whose disabilities are severe and persistent."

The kinds of services offered to the seriously mentally ill under the CSP program guidelines include the following:

- Medical and mental health care
- Crisis stabilization in the least restrictive setting possible, with hospitalization available when other options are insufficient
- Psychosocial rehabilitation services
- Backup support to families, friends, and community members
- Involvement of concerned community members in planning and offering housing or work opportunities
- Supportive services of indefinite duration, including supportive living and working arrangements and other such services for as long as they are needed

These are remarkably similar to the services supposed to be provided to the seriously mentally ill by CMHCs.

The Community Support Program has in fact been a good program, enabling states to make modest progress in planning services for the seriously mentally ill. This success, however, should not obscure the fact that it is a program whose purpose is to correct the deficiencies of the $3 billion CMHC program, which has failed in its primary mission. Rather than try and correct the CMHC program, the NIMH simply gave up and started another program instead. One may argue with the wisdom of replacing a Mercedes that is not working with a Hyundai rather than repairing the Mercedes. The logic becomes more strained when one continues to make payments on both cars.

FROM CARTER TO REAGAN

Despite the muddle of President Carter's Commission on Mental Health and its inability to confront the failure of CMHCs its final report did lead to two useful products. One was the Mental Health Systems Act, proposed to Congress on May 15, 1979, and finally signed into law on October 7, 1980. The legislation was passed largely by the efforts of Rosalyn Carter who worked hard to stir enthusiasm for it and became the first president's wife since Eleanor Roosevelt to testify before a congressional committee. If carried out, the Mental Health Systems Act would have prioritized psychiatric services for the seriously mentally ill, improved aftercare and rehabilitation services for patients released from mental hospitals, and required states to draw up detailed plans for providing services for these patients. But the act was signed into law less than one month before President Carter was overwhelmingly defeated in November 1980 by Ronald Reagan, and none of these things came to pass.

The other useful product of the Carter Commission was a mandated "national plan for the chronically mentally ill." In 1979 the Secretary of the Department of Health and Human Services directed Surgeon General Julius B. Richmond to prepare such a plan, and this was done over the following eighteen months. Altogether 245 participants and consultants divided into eleven committees took part in the exercise.

The National Plan, as described in its final report, was "designed to provide a national blueprint for action, to provide federal policies in view of past experiences . . . and to provide clear, consistent directions for federal, state, and local government action." Its forty-five recommendations were targeted at the seriously mentally ill, "these highly dependent and vulnerable people [who] live on the margin of society, shuffled into uncertain shelter arrangements, ignored by service providers, and rejected by neighbors." Many of those recommendations were logical and long overdue and if carried out would have substantially improved services for the seriously mentally ill.

The weakness of the National Plan was that it failed to address two of the most important causes of the problem—the failure of community mental health centers to assume responsibility for the seriously mentally ill, and the failure of psychiatrists, psychologists, and psychiatric social workers to work with these patients despite the fact that the training of these professionals had been supported with public funds. The National Plan could also be faulted in recommending something for everyone without establishing priorities about what should be done first. Finally, the National Plan assumed that the federal government should accept an increasing share of responsibility from the states for the problems of the seriously mentally ill, a debatable issue that will be discussed further in chapter 10. Despite such shortcomings, however, the National Plan was an important document. It officially proclaimed for the first time that deinstitutionalization, though well intentioned, had gone terribly wrong; and it contained both useful analysis and creative recommendations. Public discussion of these would have increased the chances of finding solutions to the problems of the seriously mentally ill.

Toward a National Plan for the Chronically Mentally Ill was released one month after Ronald Reagan's election. Since the National Plan called for increased federal involvement in services for the seriously mentally ill, its reception by the new administration was predictably frigid. The National Plan was, for all intents and purposes, dead on arrival on Capitol Hill, and bound volumes were transferred from in-boxes to obscure shelves with little more than a glance.

President Reagan's approach to the seriously mentally ill was predictable. As governor of California he had presided over a massive exodus of patients from state mental hospitals and shift of fiscal responsibility from the state to the counties. For the reasons previously outlined, deinstitutionalization failed in California as it failed elsewhere. This failure was obvious by early 1981 when Reagan assumed control of the White House. There was to be no acknowledgment of the failure, however, and no alternative solutions proposed for the problems of the seriously mentally ill. It was the kind of domestic problem that President Reagan was not very good at solving—if it could not be solved with an axe, then it could not be solved at all.

Some of President Reagan's domestic policies during his two terms in office exacerbated the problems of the seriously mentally ill. The Department of Housing and Urban Development, for example, sharply reduced incentives for builders to put up low-income housing, and the number of available units dwindled with each passing year. The administration also attempted to reduce federal SSI payments to the disabled by reviewing cases and applying stricter criteria for eligibility. Many seriously mentally ill individuals living in the community had their SSI benefits rescinded until Reagan's policy was reversed through court action and public outcry. In early 1987 the Reagan administration proposed reducing SSI payments to the disabled by subtracting the value of food, clothing, and housing received from charities, churches, and public shelters. After members of Congress labeled the policy "an absolute outrage" and "terminal sleaze," this policy was also reversed.

The Reagan administration action that received most attention from the psychiatric community, however, was the block granting of federal funds for CMHCs to states under the 1981 Omnibus Budget Reconciliation Act. This was done as part of a philosophy of transferring federal responsibility to states, but in fact it had little significance. The federal funds transferred to states comprised less than 5 percent of the total federal funds going to programs for the seriously mentally ill; most such funds are under the Medicaid, Medicare, SSI, and SSDI programs. The transfer was merely a tinkering with the status quo.

It was during the Reagan presidency, however, that the problem of the homeless mentally ill became an important public issue, discussed prominently by the media. Advocate for the homeless Mitch Snyder went on periodic fasts to force the administration to improve public shelters in the District of Columbia. Hollywood stars took to the grates within sight of the White House to publicize the plight of the homeless. The net effect was to increase public awareness of the problem, so that by January 1989, when Reagan left office, a national poll showed that 51 percent of Americans claimed to "personally see homeless people around [their] community." No leadership had emerged from the Reagan administration on the problem of homelessness in general or the homeless mentally ill in particular. The debacle of deinstitutionalization, however, rose above politics. Three Democratic and three Republican presidents had presided over the process; Reagan had the misfortune to be in office when its consequences finally came to public notice.

In January 1989, George Bush inherited the homeless problem as one of the major domestic issues facing his administration. In his inaugural address Bush mentioned the problem, and at a news conference the following month he was more specific:

> We must care about those in "the shadows of life," and I, like many Americans, am deeply troubled by the plight of homelessness. The causes of homelessness are many, the history is long, but the moral imperative to act is clear.
>
> Thanks to the deep well of generosity in this great land, many organizations already contribute. But we in government cannot stand on the sidelines. In my budget, I ask for greater support for emergency food and shelter, for health services, and measures to prevent substance abuse, and for clinics for the mentally ill—and I propose a new initiative involving the full range of government agencies. We must confront this national shame.

Incoming Secretary of Housing and Urban Development Jack Kemp seconded this concern and vowed to get America's low-income housing programs back on track. Whether such rhetoric would or could be translated into action, however, was another question; Washington is after all the K mart of the spoken word.

10

Cicero's Conclusion

Any man can make mistakes, but only an idiot persists in his error.
—CICERO, *PHILIPPICS* 6

The care of the seriously mentally ill in twentieth century America has been a public disgrace. Over fifty years of warehousing patients in inhumane state hospitals has been followed by almost forty years of dumping them into bleak boarding homes or onto the streets. It has been an era of remarkably poor planning and inept policy formulation. Professional self-interest has been confused with altruism, official inaction with benevolence, ideology with science, and ignorance with omniscience.

The benefits to seriously mentally ill individuals from federal programs have been remarkably meager given the amount of money that has been spent. In research, for example, over $2.8 billion was spent by NIMH between 1948 and 1985. A shockingly small percentage of it was specifically targeted toward serious mental illnesses such as schizophrenia. Much of it funded research on normal behavior ("Problem-Solving Behavior of Family Groups," "Human Territoriality in Home and Neighborhood") and social problems ("Earned Family Income and the Urban Crisis," "Effects of Metropolitan Open Space on Community Life"). In 1985 only 9.5 percent of the NIMH research budget went for research on schizophrenia despite the fact that patients with this disease occupied more than half the psychiatric hospital beds in the country and constituted the vast majority of the homeless mentally ill. After 1985 the percentage of NIMH research funds going to schizophrenia research increased under the more enlightened directorships of Dr. Shervert Frazier and Dr. Lewis Judd; this represented a step in the right direction but was still of marginal significance given the magnitude of the problem.

WHERE DOES ALL THE MONEY GO?

In 1963 approximately $1 billion in public funds was spent on services for the seriously mentally ill. By 1985 the figure had increased to approximately $17 billion. How many individuals with serious mental illnesses were significantly better off in 1985 than they were in 1963? How can a system that costs so much money be so mediocre? Where did that $17 billion go?

Part of the $17 billion went to support discharged patients living in nursing homes, boarding houses, and other community facilities. These funds, predominantly SSI, SSDI, and Medicaid, have spawned a burgeoning nursing home and boarding house industry for the benefit of private entrepreneurs. Some individuals with serious mental illnesses have been able to use these funds to live in situations better than they would have had in hospitals. For many others it is questionable whether or not they are better off; many have been transinstitutionalized rather than deinstitutionalized, with their location changed more than the quality of their lives.

Another portion of the $17 billion supported the disjointed psychiatric system that fails so many of the seriously mentally ill. Services in state mental hospitals, psychiatric units of general hospitals, and emergency rooms are utilized over and over again by the same patients caught in an endless revolving door. Such disjointed and overlapping care is very expensive: a single difficult patient can use up to $100,000 per year in psychiatric services. It is much less expensive to keep such patients well, but the system of care is not organized to accomplish that goal in most cases.

Still another part of the $17 billion went to support the mental health industry. This includes psychiatrists, psychologists, psychiatric social workers, nurses, and other professionals and non-professionals who provide direct services. It also includes federal, state, and local bureaucracies, which supervise, coordinate, consult, contract, pass paperwork, and generate additional tasks for the individuals actually doing the work. The magnitude of the bureaucracies in states such as New York and Massachusetts is notorious; it has been said that public psychiatric services in such states could be improved dramatically simply by assigning clinical responsibilities to all the officials.

Finally, a portion of the $17 billion went to support counseling and psychotherapy services for individuals with problems of living. Insofar as funds that were originally intended for the seriously mentally ill are used for this purpose, then a kind of fraud has been perpetrated. A traditional function of government is to transfer resources from groups that are more competent and able to care for themselves to groups that are less competent and not able to care for themselves. The seriously mentally ill are a classic example of the latter group. Therefore when community mental health centers are set up for the seriously mentally ill but used for other groups, or when mental health professionals are trained to provide services to the seriously mentally ill but instead provide services to comparatively well individuals, then government resources have merely been redistributed within the more competent group.

It is also useful to ask how much the seriously mentally ill have benefited from the programs set up under the National Institute of Mental Health. Since 1948 the federal government has invested $2.8 billion in mental health research, $2 billion in training mental health professionals, and $3 billion in setting up community mental health centers. If that $7.8 billion had never been spent, would most seriously mentally ill individuals notice the difference? Would they be any worse off than they already are? If instead of 789 CMHCs, 789 sheltered workshops and job training centers had been built, or 789 psychosocial rehabilitation centers such as Fountain House in New York, or 789 community residences to house the seriously mentally ill, then the mentally ill would have received some tangible benefit from the program. If the federal money had been used to improve existing outpatient clinics and fund model programs in state mental hospitals, the mentally ill would have been much better off. A Great Society was promised, but only a grate society arrived.

HAVE WE LEARNED ANYTHING?

Perhaps the most disturbing aspect of the contemporary psychiatric scene in the United States is not merely the failure of services for the seriously mentally ill but that psychiatric professionals and public officials appear to have learned so little by that failure. Some of this can be attributed to true ignorance, but the rest represents the rationalization of officials intent on covering their posteriors. Some of the self-serving myths have been repeated so often that they have come to be believed.

One example is the myth that CMHCs were never intended to treat the seriously mentally ill but rather were set up to be counseling and psychotherapy centers. The director of a CMHC in Florida, for example, wrote an article in 1986 decrying efforts to force CMHCs to provide care for mentally ill patients being discharged from state hospitals. That was not intended to be the primary purpose of CMHCs, he wrote: "Now is the time to go back to the John F. Kennedy administration philosophy of a *balanced* mental health system which has as its focus PSYCHOTHERAPY."

Another widely circulated myth is that CMHCs have failed mainly because not enough of them were built. Many early planners envisioned covering the nation with a total of 2,000 centers although only 789 were eventually funded. The fact that the 789 centers have been failures from the point of view of the seriously mentally ill has not discouraged some officials from using intellectual alchemy and claiming that 2,000 centers would have been a success.

A variation on this myth, illustrated by a recent statement by Senator Daniel P. Moynihan, is that deinstitutionalization and CMHCs failed because not enough psychiatric professionals were trained:

> I also said [in 1962] we needed to train three times the existing number of doctors, nurses, social workers, and psychologists and psychiatrists by 1980 to staff the new centers. We didn't meet that goal, either. The number of psychiatrists—needed to prescribe and monitor medication for the severely mentally ill—did not even double. And over the years, psychiatrists as a percentage of center staffs declined as they pursued careers in other settings.

In fact the number of psychiatrists in the United States tripled between the time Moynihan helped plan the CMHC program and 1980, while the number of psychologists and psychiatric social workers more than tripled. In fact, between 1945 and 1985 the number of psychiatrists and psychologists increased tenfold and the number of psychiatric social workers increased by a factor of twenty-seven. The problem was not the *number* of professionals trained but that the professionals, once trained, refused to work with the seriously mentally ill.

Another myth, usually promoted by state officials, is that the problem of the homeless mentally ill today has not been caused by deinstitutionalization but is simply a product of housing shortages. The denial of an association between the homeless mentally ill and deinstitutionalization contravenes elementary principles of common sense; 433,707 beds were closed in state mental hospitals between 1955 and 1984. Perhaps the most creative attempt by state officials to shift blame was in Michigan where a study by the state Department of Mental Health suggested that many of the homeless mentally ill were individuals without homes who then *became* mentally ill *because* they were homeless. In late 1987 Michigan state officials were still insisting that " 'dumping' people out of psychiatric facilities is not the cause of homelessness . . . The root causes of homelessness are poverty, unemployment, and a scarcity of safe, affordable housing." Certainly these other factors have played a role in causing homelessness, but casual observation of the homeless mentally ill on the streets of Detroit will confirm for anyone the crucial role played by the state's program of deinstitutionalization.

The ultimate myth about services for the seriously mentally ill is that these services are a success. The promotion of this idea can be found in speeches and writings of professionals and officials who were responsible for the programs, and often have an Alice-in-Wonderland tone. In 1983, for example, two former NIMH officials proclaimed, "Mental health centers have been an important factor in reducing the use of state hospital facilities in many areas throughout the country by providing a range of alternatives, including community-based inpatient and day treatment." It is as if by saying these words over and over again they can magically make them true.

WHAT IS NEEDED

The problems of the seriously mentally ill in most areas of the United States have truly reached crisis proportion. The lack of hospital beds for those who need them regularly leads to situations such as in New York City, where seriously mentally ill individuals "were handcuffed to the armrests of wheelchairs Friday morning as they waited for beds . . . Sometimes patients have to sleep in shifts [in the waiting area] because there is not enough room." The director of one emergency room characterized the situation as "crazy—we are at a point where the [psychiatric] system is breaking down totally." As if to illustrate the point, in early 1989 New York City officials announced a new policy of discharging some patients from psychiatric wards of city hospitals and *placing them directly in shelters for the homeless.* Two of the shelters, they said, would be staffed with psychiatrists, nurses, social workers, and a recreation aide, thus being essentially like a hospital ward, in the middle of a homeless shelter. Mentally ill individuals can now therefore make a full circuit, from a state mental hospital to public shelters for the homeless to psychiatric wards of city hospitals to public shelters for the homeless that are set up like psychiatric hospital wards. This is the *planned* system—if a mentally ill person proposed such a system, we would count it as grounds for involuntarily committing him!

Many of the mentally ill who are not treated join the growing legion of the homeless; in a single February weekend in New York City in 1988 three homeless individuals froze to death. If the current crisis had been caused by a hurricane, tornado, or flood the governor would have declared an emergency and called in the National Guard. No such solutions have been proposed. Instead most psychiatric professionals and state officials continue to express concern through ceremonial hand-wringing and reflex finger-pointing, all anxious to establish the fact that the problem is not *their* responsibility. These are not going to solve the problems of the seriously mentally ill. Neither are symbolic tinkerings with the status quo—Band-Aid solutions for major hemorrhages.

What is *not* needed to solve the problem is more money except for research. The $17 billion per year in public funds spent on mental health services in 1985 is probably sufficient to provide excellent care of the seriously mentally ill *if* the money is used wisely. Studies have shown that good services for such individuals living in community facilities cost no more than mediocre services for them in state hospitals. Rehabilitative services for the seriously mentally ill can also be cost-effective by decreasing the need for rehospitalization and, for those able to work, decreasing utilization of support programs such as SSI.

Rather what is needed is a combination of the following:

1. The seriously mentally ill must get first priority for public psychiatric services.

2. Psychiatric professionals must be expected to treat individuals with serious mental illnesses.

3. Government responsibility for the seriously mentally ill must be fixed at the state or local level.

4. Housing for the seriously mentally ill must be improved in both quantity and quality.

5. Laws regarding the mentally ill must be amended to insure that those who need treatment can be treated.

6. Research on the causes, treatment and rehabilitation of serious mental illnesses must increase substantially.

1. *The seriously mentally ill must get first priority for public psychiatric services.*

The diversion of psychiatric resources intended for individuals with serious mental illness to individuals with less serious problems has been the shame of American psychiatry. Time and again over the years psychiatric professionals have gone before Congress citing the needs of the seriously mentally ill to justify their request for funds; time and again when the money was granted it was used primarily for counseling and psychotherapy services. It has been a psychiatric version of the bait-and-switch game so well known in shoddy merchandising.

Individuals with serious mental illnesses are remarkably treatable and rehabilitable, much more so than most laypersons realize. They need access to a well-run hospital for brief rehospitalizations or adjustment of their medication, decent housing, vocational training and opportunities, a social network, adequate income if unable to work, outpatient medication maintenance, medical care, and a supportive counselor or "case manager" to help them learn to live with their disease and coordinate rehabilitation. The vast majority of individuals deinstitutionalized from state mental hospitals *can* successfully live in the community *if* services are provided for them. The "if" remains, however, but a gateway to a hypothetical land.

If change is to take place, then it will be necessary to mandate by law that a publicly supported psychiatric facility must serve the seriously mentally ill as its first priority. Some states have taken timid steps in this direction; in order to be effective the state must actually withdraw public funds from CMHCs and outpatient clinics that do not comply.

Another step in this direction would be to change the name of all mental health facilities to mental illness facilities. Thus there would be community mental illness centers, mental illness professionals, State Departments of Mental Illness, and a National Institute of Mental Illness. Such semantic changes would go far toward reminding professionals what their first priority should be. The myth of mental health, carried like an icon through almost three-quarters of a century, would finally be put aside, a pernicious relic of the past.

2. *Psychiatric professionals must be expected to treat individuals with serious mental illnesses.*

There are an estimated two million seriously mentally ill patients in the United States. There are an estimated 132,000 psychiatrists, psychologists, and psychiatric social workers. If the patients were divided among the professionals, then each professional would treat fifteen patients, a reasonable number for which to take professional responsibility. Such a caseload could be managed in less than half of a professional's work week, thereby leaving time for other activities.

The problem is that most mental health professionals are not interested in treating seriously mentally ill patients. The solution is to train mental illness professionals rather than mental health professionals and to expect professionals trained with public funds to repay that investment with a specified period of public service. A payback obligation for publicly subsidized training was agreed upon by federal officials in congressional testimony as early as 1945 but was not finally implemented until 1981. Even today the payback obligation is only incurred by individuals who accept a stipend for their living expenses; most psychiatrists, psychologists, and psychiatric social workers continue to be trained in programs supported by federal and state funds yet have no payback obligation whatsoever. Every mental illness professional trained with public funds should have such an obligation.

Given the current deluge of untreated mentally ill individuals on the nation's streets, however, states are justified in taking emergency action to get help. This can be done in each state by requiring each psychiatrist, psychologist, and psychiatric social worker in the state to provide four hours a month of pro bono service to patients with serious mental illnesses. The requirement can be implemented by law as a condition of professional licensure to practice in the state and can remain in effect for a specified period of time, such as three years, until the emergency situation is under control. Those who argue that this is an infringement on professionals' liberties should weigh it against the disease-caused infringement of liberties with which untreated mentally ill individuals must live each day.

3. *Government responsibility for the seriously mentally ill must be fixed at the state or local level.*

Public funds that currently support the seriously mentally ill, come from a mixture of federal (Medicaid, Medicare, SSI, SSDI), state (several departments) and local sources (see Appendix B). As discussed in chapter 7, one of the consequences of this fiscal jumble is a shell game in which each level of government attempts to pass responsibility for the seriously mentally ill on to other levels of government. Thus in a city such as New York, Mayor Koch attempted to move homeless mentally ill individuals off the streets to a city hospital while simultaneously trying to persuade reluctant state officials to open more beds in state mental hospitals; the federal government at the same time announced a sharp reduction in federal payments for housing the homeless in the city. The homeless mentally ill get caught between the branches of government, squeezed into conditions of further degradation and dependency.

Improvement in the present situation is not likely to take place until responsibility for the seriously mentally ill is fixed at a single level. The state is the most logical level since it has traditionally had that responsibility. In larger states such as California, state officials may wish to delegate the responsibility to the counties or cities. The federal government is too far removed from the problem to take responsibility for services though it can play an important role in data collection; the setting of standards; demonstration projects; the funding of research, consultation, and education; and legal action against states that violate civil liberties (e.g., enforcement by the Department of Justice of the Civil Rights of Institutionalized Persons Act).

There can be no true responsibility without fiscal resources to implement it, however. That means that federal dollars intended to support programs for the seriously mentally ill should be block granted to states, including Medicaid, Medicare, SSI, and SSDI funds. This would require federal legislation and would be a significant diminution of federal authority. A formula would have to be utilized to insure that states with lower per capita incomes received proportionately more funds and that states would be monetarily penalized if they failed to meet minimum standards of care for the seriously mentally ill.

States should also be encouraged to let a thousand flowers bloom in their plans for organizing such services, including the use of health maintenance organizations, performance contracting, consumer vouchers, and private sector providers. Remarkably little is known about the best method of funding services for the seriously mentally ill, because the current multi-government fiscal hodge-podge discourages innovation or experimentation. With responsibility fixed at a single level of government and with careful evaluation studies of the different approaches, the best methods would become clear.

Having responsibility and fiscal resources fixed at a single level would have many advantages. Decisions regarding patient care could be made on the basis of the clinical needs of patients, not on the basis of shifting costs to another level of government. States would discover that keeping mentally ill individuals well is less expensive than rotating them through multiple hospitalizations and living situations with all the social chaos and expenses such moves entail. Rehabilitation of the seriously mentally ill would become a respectable profession because it would be found to be cost-effective. And those with serious mental illnesses might have an opportunity for the first time in this century to live their lives in dignity.

   4. *Housing for the seriously mentally ill must be improved in both quantity and quality.*

The dumping of over 400,000 seriously mentally ill individuals into communities that neither wanted them nor had adequate housing for them will be remembered as the hallmark of deinstitutionalization. As early as 1975 the *New York Times* noted editorially: "But what kind of crusade is it to condemn sick and fearful people to shift for themselves in an often hostile world; to drag out, all too commonly, a hungry and derelict existence in a broken-down hotel if they are lucky; victimized, if they are not, by greedy operators of so-called halfway houses that are sad travesties on a fine concept?"

Despite such public misgivings, deinstitutionalization continued, with low-income housing becoming scarcer with each passing year. By 1986 it was not uncommon to read stories such as the following:

> Joel Rabinowitz of Alexandria, Virginia, a magna cum laude college graduate, was hospitalized with schizophrenia. His elderly parents could not manage him at home so alternative housing was sought. In a single year he was placed in fourteen different living arrangements because no group home was available. These included a city hospital, a jail, the YMCA, an unsupervised apartment, and an alcohol detoxification center despite the fact he had no drinking problem. The City of Alexandria had "not a single long-term group home for the mentally ill." In fact, for Virginia "with an estimated 43,000 to 61,000 chronically mentally ill" there were "only seven licensed group homes" for the entire state.

The creation of housing usually involves federal, state, and local governments, yet nobody has taken responsibility for housing the seriously mentally ill. According to the report of the Carter Commission, the U.S. Department of Housing and Urban Development's "involvement in providing housing for people with various disabilities was almost nonexistent until the Department created the Office of Independent Living for the Disabled in 1977," yet by that time deinstitutionalization had been proceeding for almost twenty years. By 1980 an assessment of HUD's programs estimated that less than one-tenth of 1 percent of HUD-supported housing units had gone to "chronically mentally ill persons."

There can be no solution to the problems of the seriously mentally ill or the homeless in America until the quantity of low income housing is increased. Yet during President Reagan's two terms the federal government sharply *decreased* its already limited involvement in the creation of such housing. The Stewart B. McKinney Homeless Assistance Act, passed by Congress in 1987, provided $180 million in housing assistance for homeless individuals and was a modest step in the right direction, but much more is needed. The work of exceptional community mental health centers, such as the Weber County CMHC, which created a housing network for mentally ill individuals in Utah, has demonstrated that such housing can be created utilizing federal, state, and local resources. In most localities, however, virtually no efforts have been made to do so.

The quality of housing available for the seriously mentally ill and homeless should also be assessed. A belief is widespread among many public officials that because a person has been mentally ill *any* housing is sufficient; in many cities patients released from mental hospitals have been placed in housing that would be deemed unfit for anybody else. One can argue on humanitarian grounds that a person who has had the misfortune to be seriously mentally ill deserves *better* housing than other people, not worse housing. In order to guarantee the quality of such housing, therefore, there must be stringent state and local licensing laws and periodic unannounced inspections.

5. *Laws regarding the mentally ill must be amended to insure that those who need treatment can be treated.*

Good care for the seriously mentally ill is never likely to be achieved as long as courts continue ordering hospitals to discharge patients to grossly inadequate living facilities; as long as laws make it very difficult to rehospitalize individuals who need

211

to be rehospitalized for further treatment; and as long as seriously mentally ill individuals are routinely able to refuse treatment. The laws affecting each of these areas must be closely evaluated and, where necessary, changed.

The court decisions mandating minimum treatment standards for the seriously mentally ill in mental hospitals (e.g., *Wyatt v. Stickney* in Alabama, *O'Connor v. Donaldson* in Florida) were in many ways steps in the right direction. The harmful side effects of these decisions came because many states used them as justification for emptying their state mental hospitals as a means of shifting fiscal responsibility to the federal government. Future legal cases regarding standards of care for the seriously mentally ill should apply equally to patients both inside and outside the hospital. Furthermore, placing responsibility and funding for both inpatients and outpatients at the same point at the state or local level should make it more likely that the patients' needs are of primary concern rather than the funding source.

Laws governing the involuntary commitment of seriously mentally ill individuals need to be amended in most states. To be admitted now, according to one observer, a "person has to be either killing himself in front of the admitting doctor or trying to kill the admitting doctor." Similarly, laws that enable seriously mentally ill individuals to refuse treatment need to be amended. In both these areas the proposal is not to return to the past, when psychiatrists could unilaterally decide who got hospitalized, for how long, and how they were to be treated. A realistic system is one that would allow for legal representation of patients and their right to appeal. It would counterbalance these rights, however, with the rights of society to treat individuals who need treatment, and it would require continuing treatment where indicated as a condition for the patient to live outside the hospital.

6. *Research on the causes, treatment, and rehabilitation of serious mental illnesses must increase substantially.*

Remarkably little research has been done on the causes of serious mental illnesses, on treatments for these diseases, or on the rehabilitation of individuals affected. Given how expensive these disease are, this failure to do research has been foolish on economic grounds alone. Serious mental illnesses such as schizophrenia and manic-depressive psychosis are the most under-researched diseases in the developed world. For each patient with schizophrenia in the United States, for example, approximately $20 per year is spent on research; by contrast, for each patient with multiple sclerosis $161 is spent on research, for each patient with cancer $300 is spent on research, and for each patient with muscular dystrophy over $1,000 is spent on research.

Research on serious mental illnesses should be increased. For example, in 1988 $38 million was spent on schizophrenia research by the NIMH; that figure represents more than a doubling of funds since 1983 when lobbying groups began to exert political pressure. The amount should be $150 to $200 million a year to even begin to be comparable to research funds available for other major diseases. Part of this increase could come by reallocating present research funds away from research areas of lower priority, and part of the increase would require new allocations. In terms of cost-benefit considerations, research on serious mental illnesses is an excellent investment.

Research is one area in which the federal government can play a major role. Deciding which research has merit and deserves funding is an activity most efficiently done centrally, not separately by each of the fifty states. Therefore, although responsibility for services should be fixed at a state or local level, primary responsibility for research should continue to be fixed at the federal level as is currently the case.

WHO WILL PROVIDE LEADERSHIP?

Prescribing improvements in services for the seriously mentally ill is comparatively easy to do. Bringing about those improvements is another matter; the natural inertia that accrues to the status quo and the vested interests of psychiatrists, psychologists, and psychiatric social workers who wish to continue it are

213

major impediments to change. If change is going to come, then, the inertia and vested interests will have to be counterbalanced by other forces. Where will these forces come from?

Mental health professionals have professional organizations such as the American Psychiatric Association, the American Psychological Association, and the National Association of Social Workers. These professional organizations, although given to periodic hand-wringing and expressions of anguish about the plight of the seriously mentally ill, have rarely represented anyone's interests other than their own. The organizations are nothing more nor less than professional unions and function primarily to serve their members' economic interests. One should no more expect such organizations to provide leadership on care for the seriously mentally ill than one would expect the Teamsters or AFL-CIO to do so.

The National Mental Health Association has shown as much interest in "mental health" as in serious mental illness. This is not surprising since the organization is the successor of the National Committee for Mental Hygiene. Over the years it has championed counseling and psychotherapy and has consistently lobbied for the promotion of "mental health" despite the fact that nobody knows what it is or how to do it. The inability of the National Mental Health Association to comprehend what has gone wrong with care for the seriously mentally ill is illustrated by recommendations it made to state affiliates in 1985 on the problem of the homeless mentally ill: "[Local] Mental Health Associations should reaffirm their commitment to the policy of deinstitutionalization. Some people erroneously attribute the problem of homeless mentally ill people to the policy of deinstitutionalization." The National Mental Health Association promotes mental health through posters asking "Have you hugged your kid today?" This is very nice for children who need hugging, but for the seriously mentally ill it is about as relevant as the work of the American Dairy Association.

In the 1980s leadership for the mentally ill has emerged for the first time in the form of the National Alliance for the Mentally Ill. This organization, begun in 1979 with fewer than 300 members, has grown to over 80,000 members and 900 chapters; it consists of the families of mentally ill individuals, diagnosed primarily with schizophrenia, manic-depressive psychosis, and severe depression. Its focus is on severe mental illness, not mental health, and it has already become a powerful force for improved services in many states. It has set up inspection programs of state mental hospitals, brought pressure to bear on CMHCs to provide services for the seriously mentally ill, and lobbied state legislatures to focus "mental health" services on the mentally ill.

Another promising lobby for the seriously mentally ill, which also emerged in the 1980s, is the National Mental Health Consumers Association. This group consists of mental patients who demand improved services, better living conditions, and vocational opportunities. The group also fights stigmatization of the mentally ill. Although still in the early stages of development, this organization promises to complement the efforts of the National Alliance for the Mentally Ill.

For the first time, then, there is a potential coalition of forces that could lead to significant improvement in services for the seriously mentally ill. The patients themselves and families of these patients are the ones most directly affected by the failure of the present system. If they can enlist the assistance of mental illness professionals who also support change, members of the media (who have played a crucial role in exposing the deficiencies of the state mental hospital system in the past), members of the clergy and religious organizations who presently provide the majority of services for the homeless mentally ill, and a few influential public officials, then maybe—maybe—change will come about. A mental illness lobby, to be effective, would need the support of an informed public, which would make clear to public legislators that the deficiencies of the present non-system of care for the seriously mentally ill will no longer be tolerated.

215

TOWARD THE FUTURE

What if all the recommendations discussed above are carried out? What if seriously mentally ill individuals have adequate housing and good professional care? What if laws are amended so that sick individuals can be treated? What if research is increased? And what if both administrative and fiscal responsibility for the seriously mentally ill are clearly fixed at the state or local level? What will be different? How can improvement be measured?

One thing that would change would be that one-third of the homeless—the hallucinating, most visible third—would disappear. They would be living in halfway houses and other supervised living facilities, most of them taking medication regularly, and some of them working. A few would be back in the hospital, but most such individuals do not need long-term hospitalization. There would be a decrease in newspaper articles about homeless individuals being beaten or found frozen to death in the winter.

There would also be a perceptible decrease in the jail and prison population by at least 35,000 to 40,000 individuals (5 percent of the existing population). Given the current overcrowding of jails and prisons, such a reduction would be welcome. Mentally ill offenders arrested for minor crimes as a way of getting them off the streets would become uncommon. The police would spend less time picking up such individuals, taking them to emergency rooms, and testifying in court regarding them. More police time would therefore be available for other activities.

In mental hospitals, there would be an initial increase in admissions as many seriously mentally ill individuals living untreated in the community were returned for treatment. This would be followed by a decrease as those individuals were stabilized on medication and placed in supervised community living facilities. With good outpatient care and rehabilitation, the readmission rate of seriously mentally ill individuals would decrease sharply, the revolving door slowing until it would almost come to a stop. Furthermore, the total number of beds needed in public mental hospitals would decrease as the revolving door slowed. The programs at the Sacramento (California) CMHC in the 1970s and at the Dane County (Wisconsin) CMHC in the 1980s have shown that, with good outpatient psychiatric care and follow-up, remarkably few hospital beds are needed for seriously mentally ill patients. It is likely that the current number of psychiatric beds in public hospitals could be reduced by half, with the savings reinvested in further rehabilitation facilities for the seriously mentally ill. The primary focus of a State Department of Mental Illness would gradually shift from treatment to rehabilitation.

There would also be a noticeable decrease in violent acts committed by seriously mentally ill individuals. The media would less often append the phrase "former mental patient" to perpetrators of violent crimes. The population of forensic psychiatric facilities, for mentally ill individuals charged with crimes, would decrease sharply.

Finally, the quality of life for individuals with serious mental illnesses and their families would improve substantially. Most of these individuals would be living more normal lives, many able to work at least part time and to enjoy some social activities. Their families would be less frightened of them and therefore more supportive, and the occurrence of serious mental illness in a family would not be nearly as disruptive and all-pervasive as is presently the case.

Such a future is attainable if we wish to bring it about. The alternative is to continue the status quo, allowing seriously mentally ill individuals to drift along in the eddies of chance and occasionally wash up on urban shores. It is our choice.

APPENDIX A

Deinstitutionalization of Patients from Public Mental Hospitals by State

State	Number of Patients 1955[a]	1984[b]	Decrease in Patient Number	Percentage Decrease
Alabama	7,169	1,987	5,182	72
Alaska	0[c]	204	—	—
Arizona	1,755	571	1,184	68
Arkansas	5,017	223	4,794	96
California	36,482	5,326	31,156	85
Colorado	5,520	926	4,594	83
Connecticut	8,944	2,390	6,554	73
Delaware	1,414	534	880	62
D.C.	7,229	1,683	5,546	77
Florida	7,718	3,823	3,895	51
Georgia	11,468	3,875	7,593	66
Hawaii	1,232[d]	232[e]	1,000	81
Idaho	1,247	188	1,059	85
Illinois	38,001	4,141	33,860	89
Indiana	10,650	2,605	8,045	76
Iowa	5,394	919	4,475	83
Kansas	4,551	1,357	3,194	70
Kentucky	7,653	798	6,855	90
Louisiana	8,155	1,781	6,374	78
Maine	2,967	591	2,376	80
Maryland	9,180	2,724	6,456	70
Massachusetts	23,471	2,950[e]	20,521	87
Michigan	21,249	4,602[e]	16,647	78
Minnesota	11,448	2,334[e]	9,114	80
Mississippi	5,330	1,518	3,812	72
Missouri	12,124	2,255	9,869	81
Montana	1,958	335	1,623	83

State	Number of Patients 1955[a]	1984[b]	Decrease in Patient Number	Percentage Decrease
Nebraska	4,676	649	4,027	86
Nevada	416	115	301	72
New Hampshire	2,720	639[e]	2,081	77
New Jersey	22,124	5,600	16,524	75
New Mexico	1,059	212[e]	847	80
New York	94,175	23,109	71,066	76
North Carolina	9,863	3,037	6,826	69
North Dakota	2,077	516	1,561	75
Ohio	28,116	4,409	23,707	84
Oklahoma	7,901	1,239	6,662	84
Oregon	4,739	976	3,763	79
Pennsylvania	39,834	8,616	31,218	78
Rhode Island	3,416	371	3,045	89
South Carolina	5,929	2,411	3,518	59
South Dakota	1,595	417	1,178	74
Tennessee	7,555	1,896	5,659	75
Texas	16,553	5,017	11,536	70
Utah	1,359	307	1,052	77
Vermont	1,301	140	1,161	89
Virginia	10,856	3,566	7,290	67
Washington	7,604	1,208[e]	6,396	84
West Virginia	5,401	1,643[e]	3,758	70
Wisconsin	14,916	1,332[e]	13,584	91
Wyoming	639	350[e]	289	45
Total U.S.	552,150	118,647	433,707	79

[a] Figures are from *Patients in Mental Institutions* (Rockville, Md.: National Institute of Mental Health, 1955).

[b] Figures are from "Additions and Resident Patients at End of Year: State and County Mental Hospitals by Age and Diagnosis, by State, United States, 1984" (Rockville, Md.: National Institute of Mental Health, 1984).

[c] Sent to other states.

[d] 1958 data from Hawaii State Mental Health Division.

[e] 1982 number of patients in state and county hospitals, from *Mental Health, United States 1985* (Rockville, Md.: National Institute of Mental Health, 1985).

APPENDIX B

Who Paid for the Seriously Mentally Ill, 1963 and 1985: An Analysis of Government Fiscal Responsibility

The vast majority of costs for care of the seriously mentally ill have been paid from government funds—federal, state, or local—for over two hundred years in the United States. In the past two decades, however, there has been a dramatic shift in the distribution of this fiscal responsibility from state government to federal and local governments. The following is an attempt to quantify this shift.

Many of the numbers used are imprecise, as indicated in the footnotes. The lack of more precise numbers is itself indicative of the sprawling nonsystem of fiscal responsibility, which has grown haphazardly since the early 1960s. Given the enormous amount of money involved, it might be expected that public officials would have put in place a reporting system that would tell precisely where the money came from and where it went. Nothing of the kind has taken place. The situation is described in a recent review of Medicaid expenditures for the mentally ill: "In an era where funding patterns and sources are of primary concern to policy makers, advocates, and service providers, the lack of national data describing a billion-dollar funding system is remarkable. Without such information describing the nature of funding, comparisons between and among state Medicaid programs and their support for mental health services cannot be made."

The following numbers focus only on health care facilities that provide services for the seriously mentally ill as previously defined. No attempt is made to include the entire mental health industry. Specifically excluded are the 220 private psychiatric hospitals in the United States, the majority of whose patients do not qualify as seriously mentally ill; almost 70 percent of revenues in such hospitals come from medical insurance and patients' fees, while another 15 percent come from Medicare and Medicaid ($215.7 million in 1983). Also excluded are the many psychiatrists, psychologists, and psychiatric social workers who are in private practice doing counseling and psychotherapy; very few of their patients or clients qualify as seriously mentally ill and their services are irrelevant for the purposes of this analysis. Finally, the 139 Veterans Administration (VA) medical centers are not included. Many of their patients qualify as seriously mentally ill, and virtually 100 percent of VA funds come from the federal government, which has not changed over the past two decades.

WHO PAID IN 1963 (IN MILLIONS)

Where government funds went	Where government funds came from		
	Federal	State	Local
State mental hospitals and outpatient clinics	$9[a]	$960[b]	Rare states (e.g., Iowa) required counties to pay part of cost
Psychiatric units of general hospitals			Unknown amount; most fees paid by patients or by medical insurance
Living costs for seriously mentally ill individuals living in the community	$9[c]		Unknown amount for welfare, housing, police, jails, social services
Total: $1,000	$18	$960	Unknown; estimated at $20
Percentage of total government funds	2%	96%	2%

[a] Total grants for mental health services given by the National Institute of Mental Health.

[b] From *Compendium of State Government Finances in 1963,* Bureau of the Census (Washington, D.C.: Government Printing Office, 1964). This figure had increased from $560 million ten years earlier (M. Gorman, *Every Other Bed,* Cleveland: World Publishing Co., 1956; p. 25).

[c] In 1951 a study by the Social Security Administration of individuals who were "permanently and totally disabled" and receiving public assistance found that 2.6 percent of them were diagnosed with psychoses. By 1953 the number of individuals with psychoses receiving public assistance in the United States was estimated to be 4,500, and the total dollar value was approximately $3 million a year (Hearings on Mental Illness, Committee on Interstate and Foreign Commerce, House of Representatives, Oct. 8, 1953, p. 1088). Conservatively it will be assumed that this trebled between 1953 and 1963.

WHO PAID IN 1985 (IN MILLIONS)

Where government funds went	*Where government funds came from*		
	Federal	*State*	*Local*
State mental hospitals, outpatient clinics, and residential facilities directly under the state office of mental health	$ 710 Medicaid 181 Medicare 300 block grants 28 other federal 48 Medicaid & Medicare directly to state treasury ――― 1,267[a]	$6,549[a]	$262[a]
Psychiatric units of general hospitals	1,200 Medicare[b] 605 Medicaid[c]	495 state Medicaid matching funds	188[d]
Living costs for seriously mentally ill individuals living in the community	1,100 SSI[e] 1,300 SSDI[e] 40 HUD[f]	278 SSI supplement[g] 3 housing[f] 523 special education[h] 500 social services[i] 100 vocational rehabilitation[j]	Unknown amount for welfare, housing, shelters, police, jails, social services for seriously mentally ill; estimate $1,000 million
Ambulatory care, including day treatment programs and community mental health centers	220 Medicaid[k] Other federal funds included under federal funds to state office of mental health (above)	180 state Medicaid matching funds[k] Other state funds included under state office of mental health (above)	93[l]
Nursing homes (skilled nursing facilities and intermediate-care nursing facilities)	57 Medicare[m] 638 Medicaid[m]	522 state Medicaid matching funds	
Total: $17,120[n] Percentage of total government funds	6,427 38%	9,150 53%	1,543 9%

WHO PAID FOR THE MENTALLY ILL, 1963 AND 1985

a *Funding Sources and Expenditures of State Mental Health Agencies: Revenue/Expenditure Study Results Fiscal Year 1985.* (Washington, D.C.: National Association of State Mental Health Program Directors, July 1987).

b Federal Medicare funds to psychiatric units of general hospitals were $1,116 million for 1984 according to data compiled by Survey and Reports Branch, Division of Biometry and Applied Sciences, National Institute of Mental Health.

c Federal Medicaid to psychiatric units of general hospitals were estimated by the National Association of State Mental Health Program Directors to be $619 million for 1980. A study for 1983 reported $236 million for seventeen states for which data were available, but these did not include most of the large states. It seems reasonable, therefore, to estimate Medicaid payments to psychiatric units of general hospitals for 1985 as at least $1,100 million. This money would include federal Medicaid funds as well as state Medicaid matching funds, which are matched 50-50 in wealthier states but on a decreasing percentage (depending on state per capita income) to a low of 70-30 in Mississippi; overall a 55-45 federal-state match will be assumed. Thus, 55 percent of the $1,100 million ($605 million) were federal Medicaid funds and 45 percent ($495 million) were state Medicaid matching funds in 1985. In most states the Medicaid matching funds are not included in the budget of the mental health agency, but in a few states at least part of them are. For simplicity this analysis will assume that none are, which errs in the direction of assuming that states spent more on the seriously mentally ill than they actually spent.

d For 1980 it was reported that 7.5 percent of admissions to psychiatric units of general hospitals were "no payment" patients [C.A. Taube and S.A. Barrett, eds., *Mental Health, United States, 1985,* National Institute of Mental Health (Washington, D.C.: Government Printing Office, 1985) DHHS Pub. No. (ADM) 86-1378, p. 46]. It is assumed that reimbursement for such patients ultimately comes from the city and county government funds that support such hospitals. Total expenditures from all sources for psychiatric units in general hospitals was said to be $2,033 million in 1981 (*Mental Health, United States, 1985,* p. 68); if total expenditures for 1985 were $2,500 million, 7.5 percent of that would be $188 million.

e These numbers are based on "estimated national SSI payments on behalf of state residents with psychotic mental disabilities" for 1984: SSI $1,038 million and SSDI $1,280 million. *Selected State and Federal Government Agency Mental Health Expenditures Incurred on Behalf of Mentally Ill Persons* (Washington, D.C.: National Association of State Mental Health Program Directors, June 1985).

f U.S. Dept. of Housing and Urban Development (HUD) expenditures for Section 202 housing programs for the seriously mentally ill in 1983 totaled $18,067 million for seventeen states for which data were available (*Selected State and Federal . . .* , June, 1985). Since the 17 states included the majority of large states it will be assumed that the total of such federal expenses was $36 million in 1983, and that by 1985 this had increased to $40 million. Five states also had state-funded housing programs for the chronically mentally ill totaling $2.7 million, of which Rhode Island's program constituted half the total; it will be assumed that the $2.7 million increased to $3 million by 1985.

g In 1984, federal SSI payments for all disabilities totaled $8,281 million, and the state supplementation (both federally administered and state administered) totaled $2,091 million [*Social Security Bulletin, Annual Statistical Supplement 1984–85* (Baltimore: Social Security Administration, p. 241)]. Assuming the ratio was similar for 1985, then the $1,100 million federal SSI payments to individuals with "psychotic mental disabilities" would have been matched by $278 million of state SSI supplement.

[h] Special education expenditures on emotionally disturbed children by the states in 1983 totaled $394 million for twenty-six states (*Selected State and Federal* . . . , June, 1985). It is assumed that the fifty states therefore spent $758 million, and that this increased to $780 million by 1985. Of this total it will be assumed that two-thirds of the children qualified as seriously mentally ill, with state expenses thus totaling $523 million.

[i] State social service agency expenses for the seriously mentally ill totaled $162 million for the seventeen states for which data was available (*Selected State and Federal* . . . , June, 1985). For all fifty states this would be approximately $476 million for 1983 and an estimated $500 million for 1985.

[j] State vocational rehabilitation agency expenses for twenty-eight states in 1983 totaled $102 million (*Selected State and Federal* . . . , June, 1985). Thus for all fifty states it would have totaled approximately $182 million. However, these expenditures include patients with diagnoses of psychoneuroses and personality disorders as well as psychoses, so it will be assumed that only half the amount ($91 million) was spent on the seriously mentally ill. For 1985 it will be assumed that this had risen to approximately $100 million.

[k] Medicaid expenditures for ambulatory care programs were reported to be $290 million for forty-four states for 1983 and it was estimated the figure "may represent an underestimate by as much as 25 percent." Assuming that total Medicaid expenditures for ambulatory care programs in 1985 were $400 million, with an average federal-state match of 55-45, then federal Medicaid would have been $220 million and state Medicaid matching funds would have been $180 million.

[l] According to *Speciality Mental Health Organizations, United States, 1983–84, op. cit.,* there were 792 freestanding psychiatric outpatient clinics in the United States in 1984. Another 1,251 organizations were classified as multiservice mental health organizations. It is known that a minority of patients seen in these outpatient psychiatric clinics, probably under 20 percent, have serious mental illnesses. State funds for such clinics are included under the state office of mental health budget. Local government funds constitute 20 percent of the budgets of freestanding psychiatric outpatient clinics and 15 percent of multiservice mental health organizations. Based on the total budgets of these clinics and assuming that 20 percent of the funds support services to the seriously mentally ill, then local government would have spent $93 million in 1985.

[m] The percentage of nursing home residents who are seriously mentally ill is widely debated. A 1977 study found that 11 percent of such residents were "purely chronically mentally ill" and another 5 percent had a diagnosis of chronic mental illness with a physical disability (H.H. Goldman, J. Feder, and W. Scanlon, "Chronic Mental Patients in Nursing Homes: Re-examining Date from the National Nursing Home Survey," *Hospital and Community Psychiatry* 37 (1986): 269–272). A 1984 sample of nursing home residents in four states reported that 7.4 percent had been diagnosed with schizophrenia or other psychoses but 21.7 percent of the residents were receiving antipsychotic medication or lithium (B.J. Burns *et al.,* "Mental Disorder Among Nursing Home Patients: Preliminary Findings from the National Nursing Home Survey Pretest," *International Journal of Geriatric Psychiatry,* in press). In view of the above, a conservative 10 percent of nursing home residents will be assumed to be seriously mentally ill.

Medicare payments to nursing homes in 1985 were $574 million (data from the Office of the Actuary HCFA, Department of Health and Human Services); 10 percent of that is $57.4 million. Medicaid payments to nursing homes in 1985 included $5,073 million to skilled nursing facilities and $6,526 million to intermediate care facilities other than those housing individuals with mental retardation (Office of the Actuary, *op. cit.*); 10 percent of that total is $1,160 million, and this would be divided 55-45 between federal Medicaid and state Medicaid match.

[n] The $15,954 million total estimated government funds going to programs for the seriously mentally ill for 1985 is remarkably similar to an estimate made by different methods. Unpublished data by H. H. Goldman and R. G. Frank estimated that 43 percent of direct care annual costs of mental illness in the United States is for "the chronic mentally ill"; since total direct care mental health costs in 1983 were approximately $36,500 million, then the costs for "the chronic mentally ill" in 1983 would have been $15,700 million [J. A. Talbott and S. S. Sharfstein, "A Proposal for Future Funding of Chronic and Episodic Mental Illness," *Hospital and Community Psychiatry* 37 (1986): 1126–1130].

CONCLUSIONS

Between 1963 and 1985 a massive shift took place in government fiscal responsibility for the seriously mentally ill. Federal government increased its share of the fiscal burden from 2 to 38 percent, and local government increased its share from 2 to 9 percent. State government, on the other hand, decreased its fiscal burden from 96 to 53 percent. The federal government's present 38 percent share of the cost of programs for the seriously mentally ill stands in contrast to its 7 percent share of the cost of programs for education in the United States.

Total expenditures by all levels of government for the seriously mentally ill increased from approximately $1 billion in 1963 to $17.1 billion in 1985. In constant 1963 dollars, the $1 billion in 1963 would have been $3.4 billion in 1985. Population increases must also be considered. The United States population went from 189 million in 1963 to 239 million in 1985, a 26 percent increase. Allowing for both inflation and population increase, the true increase in government expenditures for the seriously mentally ill from 1963 to 1985 was four fold, from $4.3 to almost $17.1 billion.

Notes

Epigraphs
"The dead": W. Kennedy, *Ironweed* (New York: Viking, 1983), p. 223.
"Between the conception": T. S. Eliot, "The Hollow Men," *Collected Poems 1909–1962* (New York: Harcourt Brace Jovanovich, 1963).

Preface
"Those of us": Langsley quoted in A. F. Panzetta, "Whatever Happened to Community Mental Health: Portents for Corporate Medicine," *Hospital and Community Psychiatry* 36 (1985): 1174–79.

Chapter 1: Dimensions of a Disaster
"to degenerate into little": A. Q. Maisel, "Bedlam 1946: Most U.S. Mental Hospitals Are a Shame and a Disgrace," *Life,* May 6, 1946.
"hallucinating between fleeting": "Emptying the Madhouse: The Mentally Ill Have Become Our Cities' Lost Souls," *Life,* May 1981.
"the prevention of inappropriate": Bertram S. Brown, quoted in P. Braun, G. Kochansky, R. Shapiro, *et al.,* "Overview: Deinstitutionalization of Psychiatric Patients, A Critical Review of Outcome Studies," *American Journal of Psychiatry* 138 (1981): 736–49.
"the chronic mentally ill": J. A. Talbott, "Deinstitutionalization: Avoiding the Disasters of the Past," *Hospital and Community Psychiatry* 30 (1979): 621–24.
"The comprehensive mental": H. G. Whittington, Hearings on Community Mental Health Centers Amendments of 1969, Subcommittee on Health of the Committee on Labor and Public Welfare, United States Senate, July 30, 1969, p. 98.
"I was already": Whittington quoted in Panzetta.
"a cruel embarrassment": "Denying the Mentally Ill," *New York Times,* June 5, 1981, p. A-26.
"Ms. S., living": E. F. Torrey, E. Bargmann, and S. M. Wolfe, "Washington's Grate Society: Schizophrenics in the Shelters and on the Street" (Washington: Health Research Group, 1985).
In a 1986 survey of cities: "The Continued Growth of Hunger, Homeless-

ness, and Poverty in America's Cities: 1986" (Washington: United States Conference of Mayors, 1986).

studies in Washington, Boston, and Philadelphia: Torrey *et al.;* A. A. Arce *et al.,* "A Psychiatric Profile of Street People Admitted to an Emergency Shelter," *Hospital and Community Psychiatry* 34 (1983): 812–17; E. L. Bassuk, L. Rubin, and A. Lauriat, "Is Homelessness a Mental Health Problem?" *American Journal of Psychiatry* 141 (1984): 1546–50.

homeless individuals in Los Angeles: L. Gelberg, L. S. Linn, and B. D. Leake, "Mental Health, Alcohol and Drug Use, and Criminal History among Homeless Adults," *American Journal of Psychiatry* 145 (1988): 191–96.

"that 60 percent exhibit": N. L. Cohen, J. F. Putnam, and A. M. Sullivan, "The Mentally Ill Homeless: Isolation and Adaptation," *Hospital and Community Psychiatry* 35 (1984): 922–24.

"I first saw Ms. Z.": Clinical notes of author.

116,136 in 1984: "Additions and Resident Patients at End of Year: State and County Mental Hospitals, by Age and Diagnosis, by State, United States, 1984." Survey and Reports Branch, National Institute of Mental Health, 1987.

"When I saw Mr. A.": Clinical notes of author.

There is also evidence: J. R. Belcher, "Rights Versus Needs of Homeless Mentally Ill Persons," *Social Work* 33 (1988): 398–402; R. E. Drake, M. A. Wallach, and J. S. Hoffman, "Housing Instability and Homelessness Among Aftercare Patients of an Urban State Hospital," *Hospital and Community Psychiatry* 40 (1989): 46–51.

"The shame of the states": R. Peele, "Beyond Community Psychiatry,"

Psychiatric News, March 21, 1986, pp. 2 and 13.

"The man called himself": B. Eisenhuth, "Profiles of the Street People," *Hospital and Community Psychiatry* 34 (1983): 814.

"In 1987 a 29-year-old": "For Some Mentally Ill, Road to Treatment Begins in Jail," *Erie Alliance for the Mentally Ill Newsletter,* Buffalo, March 1987.

In Denver: H. R. Lamb and R. W. Grant, "The Mentally Ill in an Urban County Jail," *Archives of General Psychiatry* 39 (1982): 17–34.

in another study: P. Brown, *The Transfer of Care: Psychiatric Deinstitutionalization and its Aftermath* (London: Routledge and Kegan Paul, 1985), p. 138.

five county jails in California: Lamb and Grant.

a similar study: Ibid.

Another study: L. H. Roth and F. R. Ervin, "Psychiatric Care of Federal Prisoners," *American Journal of Psychiatry* 128 (1971): 56–62.

reported for New York State: H. J. Steadman, S. Fabisiak, J. Dvoskin, *et al.,* "A Survey of Mental Disability Among State Prison Inmates," *Hospital and Community Psychiatry* 38 (1987): 1086–90.

In Oklahoma: J. F. James, D. Gregory, R. K. Jones, *et al.,* "Psychiatric Morbidity in Prisons," *Hospital and Community Psychiatry* 11 (1980): 674–77.

study of inmates in Michigan: P. Luke, "67% of Inmates Need Some Mental Help, Survey Says," *Grand Rapids Press,* Sept. 4, 1987.

"Timothy Waldrop": Quotations and facts from M. Plott, "Man Who Blinded Self Is Moved from Prison," *Atlanta Constitution,* March 8, 1985.

In Fairfax County: "Northern Virginia Sheriffs Say Mentally Ill Are

Crowding the Jails," *Alliance of the Mentally Ill of Northern Virginia Newsletter,* Dec. 1986.

In neighboring Arlington County: Ibid.

Across the Potomac: *News from Threshold—D.C. Newsletter of the Alliance for the Mentally Ill,* March 1985.

"Wayne B.": Clinical notes of author.

In Erie County: G. Egri, L. Keitner, and T. B. Harwood, "Not Mad Enough, Not Bad Enough: Where Should They Go?" Buffalo: Erie County Dept. of Mental Health, mimeograph.

"George Wooten": Quotations and facts from L. Kilzer, "Jail as a 'Halfway House' or Long-term Commitment?" *Denver Post,* June 3, 1984.

one study in San Francisco's courts: G. E. Whitmer, "From Hospitals to Jails," *American Journal of Orthopsychiatry* 50 (1980): 65–75.

A 1982 survey of psychiatric inpatients: A. Karras and D. B. Otis, "A Comparison of Inpatients in an Urban State Hospital in 1975 and 1982," *Hospital and Community Psychiatry* 38 (1987): 963–67.

S. Sheehan: *Is There No Place on Earth for Me?* (Boston: Houghton Mifflin, 1982).

"Alan P.": Clinical notes of author.

A 1983 study in Los Angeles County: H. R. Lamb, "Incompetency to Stand Trial: Appropriateness and Outcome," *Archives of General Psychiatry* 44 (1987): 754–58.

"A 31-year-old": Ibid.

In 1961, the Joint Commission: *Action for Mental Health: Final Report of the Joint Commission on Mental Illness and Health, 1961* (New York: John Wiley and Sons, 1961), p. xix.

"Herbert Mullin": D. T. Lunde and J.

Morgan, *The Die Song* (New York: W. W. Norton, 1980), p. 313.

On December 31, 1987: "Suspect's Competence," "7 in Family Found Fatally Shot" and "Suspect Known as Recluse," *Washington Post,* p. A-8. See also "Suspect's Ills Are Described," *Washington Post,* Nov. 29, 1987, p. A-20.

"that mentally ill persons": P. Brown, p. 133.

Zitrin and his colleagues: A. Zitrin *et al.,* "Crime and Violence Among Mental Patients," *American Journal of Psychiatry* 133 (1976): 142–49.

"Sylvia Seegrist": R. S. Seegrist, "What Happened to Sylvia," *Philadelphia Inquirer Magazine,* Aug. 24, 1986.

Steadman *et al.:* H. J. Steadman, D. Vanderwyst, and S. Ribner, "Comparing Arrest Rates of Mental Patients and Criminal Offenders," *American Journal of Psychiatry* 135 (1978): 1218–20.

More recently, Karras and Otis: Karras and Otis.

"Where do you think": Lunde and Morgan, p. 313.

"Mary Ventura": "I'm Sick, I'm Sick, I Have No One," *New York Times,* Oct. 25, 1985, p. A-26.

"mentally disordered offenders": H. Hafner, "The Risk of Violence in Psychotics," *Integrative Psychiatry* 4 (1986): 138–42.

A review of studies: P. J. Taylor, "The Risk of Violence in Psychotics," *Integrative Psychiatry* 4 (1986): 12–24.

Another noteworthy aspect of the English: M. P. I. Weller, "Aspects of Violence," *Lancet* 2 (1987): 615–17.

"Lois E. Lang": S. Raab, "Deak Murder Suspect Had Been Found Paranoid," *New York Times,* Nov. 21, 1985, p. B-3.

"Juan Gonzalez": R. Sullivan, "City Inquiry in Ferry Slashing Criticizes

Hospital for Release," *New York Times,* July 12, 1986, p. A-1.

"may become violent": J. A. Yesavage, "Inpatient Violence and the Schizophrenic Patient: An Inverse Correlation Between Danger-Related Events and Neuroleptic Levels," *Biological Psychiatry* 17 (1982): 1331–37; see also K. A. Weaver, "Increasing the Dose of Antipsychotic Medication to Control Violence," *American Journal of Psychiatry* 140 (1983): 1274.

"In early 1986": Clinical notes of author.

In California in 1987: J. Cummings, "City of Future Splits Over Homeless," *New York Times,* Oct. 13, 1987, p. A-26.

"Good point": C. McFadden, "Homeless Are Going to the Dogs," *San Francisco Examiner,* Sept. 27, 1987, p. E-4.

"floating shelters for homeless": J. Barbanel, "H.R.A. Urges Using Ships as Shelters," *New York Times,* Oct. 10, 1987, p. 33.

Housing for mentally ill: 21 Ex-Mental Patients Taken from 4 Private Homes," *New York Times,* Aug. 5, 1979, p. A-33; "9 Ex-Patients Kept in Primitive Shed," *New York Times,* Oct. 21, 1982, p. A-21; "Fire Raises Questions about Mental Patients," *New York Times,* March 25, 1984, p. A-35.

Such individuals are sufficiently: R. T. Zera *et al.,* "Dumpster-Diving Injuries," *New England Journal of Medicine* 314 (1986): 319.

"It is not uncommon": "Man Crushed in Garbage Truck," *Miami Herald,* June 16, 1987.

The rehospitalization rate: P. Solomon, J. Davis, and B. Gordon, "Discharged State Hospital Patients' Characteristics and use of Aftercare: Effect on Community Tenure,"

American Journal of Psychiatry 141 (1984): 1566–70.

more psychiatrists and psychologists: E. F. Torrey and S. M. Wolfe, *Care of the Seriously Mentally Ill: A Rating of State Programs* (Washington: Health Research Group, 1988).

Furthermore, it claimed: J. M. Stubblebine and J. B. Decker, "Are Urban Mental Health Centers Worth It?" *American Journal of Psychiatry* 127 (1971): 908–14.

San Francisco was being cited: Hearings on Community Mental Health Centers Oversight, Subcommittee on Public Health and Environment, Committee on Interstate and Foreign Commerce, House of Representatives, May 9 and June 15, 1973, p. 21.

San Francisco vies with Los Angeles: Torrey and Wolfe, 1988.

"the city's police department": "Forcing the Mentally Ill to Get Help," *Newsweek,* Nov. 9, 1987, pp. 47–48.

As summarized in 1975: S. A. Kirk and M. E. Therrien, "Community Mental Health Myths and the Fate of Former Hospitalized Patients," *Psychiatry* 38 (1975): 209–17.

Hawaii was ranked last: E. F. Torrey and S. M. Wolfe, *Care of the Seriously Mentally Ill: A Rating of State Programs* (Washington: Health Research Group, 1986).

In Chambersburg, Pennsylvania: K. Simmons, "Center Faces Closing," *Chambersburg Public Opinion,* Oct. 1, 1987.

Another CMHC: Telephone conversation with Mr. Skronik of the Helen H. Stevens Community Mental Health Center, Carlisle, Penn., Dec. 1, 1987.

Dr. James L. McKee: R. French, "Big Bonus Prompts Park Center Trustee to Quit," *Fort Wayne News-Sentinel,* Oct. 17, 1987, and Editorial, "The

Straw That Broke Park Center's Back," *Fort Wayne Journal Gazette,* Oct. 30, 1987.

"would enable Park Center": *Directions,* newsletter of the Park Center, Fort Wayne, Indiana, Dec. 1983.

a 1986 national survey: Torrey and Wolfe, 1986.

"Mark X": B. Eisenhuth, p. 809.

"a man barricaded": C. Holden, "Broader Commitment Laws Sought," *Science* 230 (1985): 1253–55.

"In Washington, D.C.": E. F. Torrey, *Surviving Schizophrenia: A Family Manual,* revised edition, (New York: Harper and Row, 1988), p. 315.

"we are protecting": L. M. Siegal, "Feeling the Chill," *New York Times,* March 3, 1981, p. A-19.

"At a commitment hearing": D. A. Treffert, "The Obviously Ill Patient in Need of Treatment," *Hospital and Community Psychiatry* 36 (1985) 259–64.

a federal judge in Massachusetts: P. S. Applebaum and T. G. Gutheil, "The Boston State Hospital Case," *American Journal of Psychiatry* 137 (1980): 720–23.

"A large number of patients": H. R. Lamb and M. J. Mills, "Needed Changes in Law and Procedure for the Chronically Mentally Ill," *Hospital and Community Psychiatry* 37 (1986): 475–80.

"troll buster": "Take Mental Patients Off Streets, Back to Hospitals?" *U.S. News and World Report,* July 1, 1985, p. 55.

"a homeless man, attacked": "Homeless Man Is Assaulted," *New York Times,* Oct. 6, 1986, p. B-5.

In Quincy: "Quincy, Mass., Boys Charged in Slaying of Homeless Man," *New York Times,* July 14, 1985, p. 37.

"The attackers had pounded": "A Ferocious Crime Against the Helpless," *Cape Cod Times,* July 22, 1984.

"Phyllis Iannotta": W. Herbert, "Lost Lives of the Homeless," *Washington Post,* Oct. 19, 1985, p. G-4.

"they are lost in ravines": M. Starin, "What Mental Illness Doesn't Destroy, the System Does," *Poughkeepsie Journal,* Jan. 18, 1984, p. 5.

NIMH staff had prepared: Statement of Shervert H. Frazier, M.D., Director of the National Institute of Mental Health, before the Committee on Appropriations, United States Senate, Nov. 20, 1986.

In 1880: F. W. Wines, *Report on the Defective, Dependent, and Delinquent Classes of the Population of the United States* (Washington: Government Printing Office, 1888), p. ix–x.

"the result of society's": C. Krauthammer, "For the Homeless: Asylum," *Washington Post,* Jan. 4, 1985, p. A-15.

Chapter 2: The Making of the "Mental Health" Myth

In 1830 there were just four: Wines, p. 172.

"Instead of being a House": A. Deutsch, *The Mentally Ill in America* (New York: Columbia University Press, 1937), pp. 129–30.

"monasteries for the mad": B. Sicherman, *The Quest for Mental Health in America, 1880–1917* (Ann Arbor: University Microfilms, 1967), p. 251; also published by Arno Press, New York, 1980.

"the successive reports": W. J. Corbet, "On the Increase in Insanity," *American Journal of Insanity* 50 (1893): 224–35.

"The most striking": Wines, p. xxviii.

reaching 150,151 by 1904: Deutsch, *The Mentally Ill in America,* p. 232.

233

"The late nineteenth": Sicherman, p. 155.

"investigation into the mental": H. Eysenck, *Decline and Fall of the Freudian Empire* (New York: Pelican, 1986), p. 101.

"the etiological aspect": S. Fisher and R. P. Greenberg, *The Scientific Credibility of Freud's Theories and Therapy* (New York: Basic Books, 1977), pp. 134–164.

"The studies that have looked": Ibid., p. 164.

The evidence consists of: See, for example, H. A. Nasrallah and D. R. Weinberger, eds., *The Neurology of Schizophrenia* (New York: Elsevier, 1986).

"will remain forever": Eysenck, p. 208.

"The Freudian unconscious": Ibid., pp. 35 and 208.

"one of the most": G. N. Grob, *The State and the Mentally Ill* (Chapel Hill: University of North Carolina Press, 1966), p. 265.

"introduced psychoanalytic theory": Sicherman, p. 219.

"They all had in common": I. Hendrick quoted in J. Brand, "The United States: An Historical Perspective" in R. H. Williams and L. C. Ozarin, eds., *Community Mental Health: An International Perspective* (San Francisco: Jossey-Bass, 1968), p. 18.

"The future of psychology": E. Jones, *The Life and Work of Sigmund Freud* (New York: Basic Books, 1953), p. 57.

"In Europe I felt": Freud quoted in Brand.

C. Beers: *A Mind That Found Itself* (New York: Doubleday, Paget and Company, 1908).

"clearinghouse for the nation": Sicherman, p. 319.

"his doctor friends": *Action for Mental Health,* p. 69.

"Salmon was an individual": G. N. Grob, *Mental Illness and American Society, 1875–1940* (Princeton: Princeton University Press, 1983), p. 156.

"dependent very largely": Sicherman, p. 367.

"a field of mental hygiene": Ibid., p. 279.

"in the great movements": Grob, *Mental Illness,* p. 145.

"all forms of social": Sicherman, p. 333.

"Mental hygiene": Ibid., p. 332.

"May we by taking": Ibid., p. 335.

"educator, preacher": C. L. Dana, "The Future of Neurology," *Journal of Nervous and Mental Disease* 40 (1913): 753–57.

"children who are": Sicherman, p. 417.

"The basic question": F. Williams, "Is There a Mental Hygiene?" *Psychoanalytic Quarterly* 1 (1932): 113–20.

"such trite and bromidic": A. Deutsch, "The History of Mental Hygiene" in *One Hundred Years of American Psychiatry* (New York: Columbia University Press, 1944), p. 364.

"mental hygiene hides": K. Davis, "Mental Hygiene and the Class Structure," *Psychiatry* 1 (1938): 55–65.

Chapter 3: The "Conchies" and General Hershey Create NIMH

"a bill to provide": Hearings on the National Neuropsychiatric Institute Act, Subcommittee of the Committee on Interstate and Foreign Commerce, House of Representatives, Sept. 18–21, 1945, front cover.

"I might say": Ibid.

"miseries and": Deutsch, *The Mentally Ill in America,* p. 177.

"the whole field": H. A. Foley and S. S. Sharfstein, *Madness and Govern-*

ment (Washington: American Psychiatric Press, 1983), p. 7.

"nearly one-third": Maisel.

"alcoholics and psychotics": Ibid.

"a group of": Ibid.

"Day after day": Ibid.

"except the superintendent": Ibid.

"rats ate away": Ibid.

"the uncivilized social": Ibid.

"A United States congressman": F. L. Wright, *Out of Sight Out of Mind* (Philadelphia: National Mental Health Foundation, 1947), p. 124.

"He opened the door": Ibid., p. 55.

"from July 1, 1916": Hearings on the National Neuropsychiatric Institute Act, Subcommittee on Health and Education of the Committee on Education and Labor, United States Senate, March 6–8, 1946, pp. 167 and 169.

"Long ago they lowered": M. J. Ward, *The Snake Pit* (New York: Random House, 1946).

Hershey gave detailed testimony: House Hearings on the National Neuropsychiatric Institute Act, 1945, p. 36.

"were due to mental disease": Ibid., p. 122.

"Mental Illness": Ibid., p. 55.

"the war has not": Ibid., p. 59.

"where all phases": Senate Hearings on the National Neuropsychiatric Institute Act, 1946, p. 5.

"aid to the States": House Hearings, p. 11.

"This bill would do": Ibid., p. 10.

"An example of": Senate Hearings, p. 7.

"Half of All Hospital": *Washington Post*, Sept. 19, 1945, p. 1.

"Accurate statistics": H. S. Truman, "Compulsory Medical Insurance: the National Health Program." Message to the U.S. Congress, Nov. 19, 1945.

"60 percent of veterans'": Senate Hearings, p. 34.

"occupies half the population": House Hearings, p. 19.

"Deranged Mother Kills Son": Ibid., p. 106.

"the mental illness or mental": Ibid., p. 9.

"a maladapted way of life": A. P. Noyes, *Modern Clinical Psychiatry* (Philadelphia: W. B. Saunders, 1939), p. 434.

Although it was not widely known: Foley and Sharfstein, p. 18.

"Modern psychiatry": F. J. Braceland, "Psychiatry and the Science of Man," *American Journal of Psychiatry* 114 (1957): 1–9.

"It is not too much": Senate Hearings, p. 67.

"Up to now the job": House Hearings, p. 28.

"have some knowledge": W. C. Menninger, "Presidential Address," *American Journal of Psychiatry* 106 (1949): 1–12.

"Mental hygiene": R. H. Felix, "Mental Hygiene as a Public Health Practice," *American Journal of Orthopsychiatry* 21 (1951): 707–16.

"Prevention of mental illness": R. H. Felix, *Mental Health and Social Welfare* (New York: Columbia University Press, 1961), p. 8.

"education, social work, industry": Ibid., p. 21.

"consult their clergyman": Ibid, pp. 10–11.

"One evening, a man was trying": R. H. Felix, "Mental Hygiene and Public Health," *American Journal of Orthopsychiatry* 18 (1948): 679–84.

"The entire matter": House Hearings, p. 30.

"Mental Health Is Everybody's": N. A. Ridenour, *Mental Health in the United States: A Fifty-Year History* (Cambridge, Mass.: Harvard University Press, 1961), p. 115.

"problem in need of solution": House Hearings, p. 20.

"about juvenile delinquency": Ibid., p. 92.

"would like to see": Senate Hearings, p. 114.

"more stress on": Ibid., p. 137.

"the improvement of the mental health": Foley and Sharfstein, p. 19.

"I wouldn't want": House Hearings, p. 15.

"Under the provisions": Ibid., pp. 21–22.

"As I shall indicate": Ibid., pp. 83–89.

"one outpatient mental health clinic": R. H. Felix, "The Relation of the National Mental Health Act to State Health Authorities," *Public Health Reports* 62 (1947): 41–49.

"I feel sure, sir": Senate Hearings, p. 65.

"We have roughly calculated": House Hearings, p. 90.

28 percent of: Ibid., p. 18.

"I agree with everything": Ibid., pp. 77–78.

"That is . . . because": Ibid., p. 84.

"entire states, including": Ibid., p. 78.

"Rep. Brown: Let me ask you": Ibid., p. 96.

"I refer to the": Senate Hearings, p. 115.

"Men get strange ideas": House Hearings, p. 84.

Chapter 4: Freud and Buddha Join the Joint Commission

"Misery Rules in State Shadowland": Gorman's series in *The Daily Oklahoman* ran in September 1946. His book *Oklahoma Attacks Its Snake Pits* (Norman, Okla.: University of Oklahoma Press) was published in 1947 and then condensed in *Reader's Digest,* Sept. 1948, pp. 139–60.

"In some of the wards": A. Deutsch,

The Shame of the States (New York: Harcourt Brace, 1948), p. 28.

"less than 2 cents": Hearings on Mental Illness, Committee on Interstate and Foreign Commerce, United States House of Representatives, Oct. 8, 1953, p. 1035.

per patient under treatment: Ibid., p. 1050.

more than a billion dollars: Ibid., p. 1096.

"approximately from one-sixth": Ibid., p. 1035.

"Strengthening public health": Mental Health Program of the 48 States (Chicago: Council of State Governments, 1950), p. 222.

"If the whole nation": House Hearings, 1953, p. 1072.

"study current conditions": Hearings on Mental Health, Subcommittee on Health of the Committee on Labor and Public Welfare, United States Senate, March 30 and April 13, 1955, p. 55.

"I have never been able": Ibid., p. 70.

"single greatest problem": Ibid., p. 153.

"nip in the bud": Ibid., p. 73.

"There is a feeling": Ibid., p. 74.

"trying to get money": Ibid., pp. 82–83.

"for any other condition": Hearings on Mental Health Study Act of 1955, Subcommittee on Health and Science of the Committee on Interstate and Foreign Commerce, House of Representatives, March 8–11, 1955, p. 124.

"Approximately 750,000": Ibid., p. 1.

"unless something more": Ibid., p. 5.

"approximately one-half": Ibid., p. 13.

"have been in the hospital": Senate Hearings, 1955, p. 111.

"I remember, Mr. Priest": House Hearings, 1955, p. 51.

"were fed out of tin": Ibid., p. 46.
35 percent of the: Senate Hearings, 1955, p. 75.
"research being carried out": House Hearings, 1955, p. 43.
"They can go to work": Senate Hearings, 1955, p. 78.
"It is just like": House Hearings, 1955, p. 57.
"1 psychiatrist for 150": Ibid., p. 54.
"2 psychiatrists for approximately": Ibid., p. 45.
Dr. Felix described: Senate Hearings, 1955, p. 124.
"it would, in my opinion": House Hearings, 1955, p. 68.
"We need men with ideas": Ibid., pp. 132–33.
"to detect mental illness": Ibid., p. 10.
"brusqueness": F. J. Braceland, "Jack Richard Ewalt, 92nd President: A Biological Sketch," *American Journal of Psychiatry* 121 (1964): 9–16.
"known to be one": E. B. Drew, "The Health Syndicate: Washington's Noble Conspirators," *The Atlantic* 220 (1967): 75–82. Other information on Mary Lasker and Florence Mahoney is from this article.
"a warm relationship": Ibid.
M. Gorman: *Every Other Bed* (Cleveland: World Publishing Co., 1956).
"I was very happy": M. Gorman, "Community Absorption of the Mentally Ill: The New Challenge," *Community Mental Health Journal* 12 (1976): 119–27.
"a concentration camp": D. A. Felicetti, *Mental Health and Retardation Politics* (New York: Praeger, 1975), p. 106.
"Siberia, U.S.A.": D. Robinson, "Conspiracy USA: The Far Right Fights Against Mental Health," *Look,* Jan. 26, 1965, pp. 30–32.
Ezra Pound and John Kaspar: See E. F. Torrey, *The Roots of Treason: Ezra Pound and the Secret of St. Elizabeths* (New York: McGraw-Hill, 1984).
"Psychiatry is a foreign": J. Marmor, V. W. Bernard, and P. Ottenberg, "Psychodynamics of Group Opposition to Health Programs," *American Journal of Orthopsychiatry* 30 (1960): 330–345.
Across the country: Robinson.
"Mental health programs": A. Auerbach, "The Anti–Mental Health Movement," *American Journal of Psychiatry* 120 (1963): 105–112.
"It is amazing and appalling": Marmor *et al.*
Los Angeles City Council: Robinson.
"what is mental health": Marmor *et al.*
"the mental hygienist": K. Davis.
"A national mental health": *Action for Mental Health,* p. xiv.
"No further state hospitals": Ibid., p. xvi.
"hidden agenda was": Foley and Sharfstein, p. 23.
"operated as outpatient departments": *Action for Mental Health,* p. xiv.
"a main line of defense": Ibid.
"must concentrate on providing": Ibid., p. 120.
"Aftercare and rehabilitation": Ibid., p. xvii.
"It is self-evident": Ibid., p. xx.
"people who are emotionally disturbed": Ibid., p. xii.
"Nonmedical mental health": Ibid., p. x.
definition was published: M. Jahoda, *Current Concepts of Positive Mental Health* (New York: Basic Books, 1958). Joint Commission on Mental Illness and Health Monograph Series no. 1.
"I believe most patients": Ibid., p. 119.
although recent research: D. Gole-

man, "Trying to Face Reality? It May Be the Last Thing That the Doctor Orders," *New York Times,* Nov. 26, 1987.

"They feel comfortable": Ridenour, p. 139.

"a kind of resilience": Jahoda, p. 42.

"Mental health is the adjustment": W. Menninger, *Psychiatry in a Troubled World* (New York: Macmillan, 1948), p. 362, quoting K. Menninger, *The Human Mind* (New York: Knopf, 1946), p. 1.

Chapter 5: From the Suffering Sick to the Worried Well

E. Goffman: *Asylums: Essays on the Social Situation of Mental Patients and Other Inmates* (New York: Doubleday, 1961), p. ix.

T. Szasz: *The Myth of Mental Illness* (New York: Harper and Row, 1961).

G. Caplan: *An Approach to Community Mental Health* (New York: Grune and Stratton, 1961).

K. Kesey: *One Flew Over the Cuckoo's Nest* (New York: Viking, 1962).

"legal action against": T. Szasz, *Law, Liberty, and Psychiatry* (New York: Macmillan, 1963), p. 253.

"I do not see how": H. C. Solomon, "The American Psychiatric Association in Relation to American Psychiatry," *American Journal of Psychiatry* 115 (1958): 1–9.

"hospitalization as such is": Caplan, *An Approach,* p. 232.

"In other words": Ibid., p. 42.

schizophrenogenic mothers: G. Caplan, *Principles of Preventive Psychiatry* (New York: Basic Books, 1964), p. 78.

"not only a primer": R. H. Felix in Foreword to Caplan, *Principles.*

"This assumption": L. S. Kubie, "Pitfalls of Community Psychiatry," *Archives of General Psychiatry* 18 (1968): 257–66.

"mental health as a concept": Caplan, *Principles,* p. 37.

"the potential of a person": Caplan, *An Approach,* p. vii.

"the processes involved in": Ibid.

"A healthy family comes in": Ibid., p. 6.

"to join pressure groups": Caplan, *Principles,* pp. 62–63.

"Just as a modern police": M. B. Smith and N. Hobbs, "The Community and the Community Mental Health Center" in A. J. Bindman and A. D. Spiegel, eds., *Perspectives in Community Mental Health* (Chicago: Aldine, 1969); first published in *American Psychologist* 21 (1966): 299–309.

1918 influenza epidemic: See S. A. Mednick *et al.,* "The 1957 Helsinki Type A-2 Influenza Epidemic and Adult Schizophrenia," *Archives of General Psychiatry* 45 (1988): 189–92.

Rosemary was neither as bright: All descriptions of Rosemary Kennedy's behavior are taken from P. Collier and D. Horowitz, *The Kennedys: An American Drama* (New York: Warner Books, 1984) and D. K. Goodwin, *The Fitzgeralds and the Kennedys: An American Saga* (New York: Simon and Shuster, 1987).

classified as mild: Goodwin, p. 497.

"unnoticed" by the press: Ibid., p. 543.

"filled with eerie ellipses": Collier and Horowitz, p. 117.

"The basic skills": Ibid., p. 132.

"In the eighteen months": Goodwin, p. 640.

"wild moods" and "tantrums": Collier and Horowitz, p. 133.

"Pacing up and down": Goodwin, p. 640.

"In one traumatic incident": Collier and Horowitz, p. 133.

"quizzed rigorously": Ibid., pp. 133–34.

"schizophrenia represents": Noyes, op. cit., p. 434.

"chaotic sexuality": A. J. Rosanoff, *Manual of Psychiatry and Mental Hygiene* (New York: John Wiley and Sons, 1938), pp. 523–26.

"Disturbed patients often": W. Freeman, "Psychosurgery" in S. Arieti, ed., *American Handbook of Psychiatry*, vol. II (New York: Basic Books, 1959), p. 1528.

Joseph Kennedy Sr. had discussed: Goodwin, p. 641.

"She no longer realized": Goodwin, pp. 642–43.

"made her go from being": Collier and Horowitz, p. 134.

She specified that: Foley and Sharfstein, pp. 44 and 57.

The outcome of the Celebrezze: Ibid., pp. 46–49.

"a bold new approach": President Kennedy's 1963 special message to Congress is reprinted in Foley and Sharfstein.

"proposals are the outgrowth": Hearings on Mental Illness and Retardation, Subcommittee on Health of the Committee on Labor and Public Welfare, United States Senate, March 5–7, 1963, p. 17.

"report recommends planning": Ibid., p. 42.

"three-fourths of the state": Ibid., p. 16.

"our study shows us": Hearings on Community Mental Health Centers, Subcommittee on Public Health and Welfare, Committee on Interstate and Foreign Commerce, House of Representatives, March 26–28, 1963, p. 100.

"41 percent of the patients": Senate Hearings on Mental Illness and Retardation, 1963, p. 194.

"for making one of our": Ibid., p. 40.

"at long last": Ibid., p. 35.

"primarily institutions for quarantining": Ibid., p. 17.

"the basic purpose": Hearings on Mental Health, Subcommittee of the Committee on Interstate and Foreign Commerce, House of Representatives, July 10–11, 1963, p. 23.

"If you will do this": Senate Hearings on Mental Illness and Retardation, 1963, p. 191.

"Thirty years ago": Ibid., p. 36.

"I take it that you": House Hearings on Mental Health, 1963, p. 25.

"What you ultimately hope": Ibid., p. 101.

"As the president indicated": House Hearings on Community Mental Health Centers, 1963, p. 23.

"some of the psychiatrists": House Hearings on Mental Health, 1963, p. 21.

"I have no worry at all": Senate Hearings on Mental Illness and Retardation, 1963, p. 52.

2,900 psychiatrists would be needed: House Hearings on Mental Health, 1963, p. 71.

"since the development": Senate Hearings on Mental Illness and Retardation, 1963, p. 18.

"Mr. Roberts: So any way": House Hearings on Mental Health, 1963, p. 27.

"every state in the union": Ibid., p. 108.

"Mr. O'Brien: If by some miracle": Ibid.

"grubstake money": House Hearings on Mental Health Staffing, 1965, p. 250.

"I have never seen": House Hearings on Mental Health, 1963, p. 72.

many of the NIMH staff: Foley and Sharfstein, p. 72.

to project the total number: House

Hearings on Mental Health Staffing, Committee on Interstate and Foreign Commerce, House of Representatives, March 2–5, 1965, p. 57.

"Mr. Springer": Mr. Secretary, you are": Ibid., p. 51.

"the number of resident patients": Ibid., p. 56.

"that the public mental hospital": Ibid., p. 245.

"projects which I won't characterize": House Hearings on Mental Health, 1963, p. 66.

only one reported study: J. K. Wing, "Pilot Experiment in the Rehabilitation of Long-Hospitalized Male Schizophrenic Patients," *British Journal of Preventive and Social Medicine* 14 (1960): 173–80.

"when I was in Amsterdam": Senate Hearings on Mental Illness and Retardation, 1963, p. 49.

Chapter 6: Psychiatrists Who Would Be Kings

"Perhaps the most striking": F. D. Chu and S. Trotter, *The Madness Establishment* (New York: Grossman, 1974), p. 26.

"would require the active": Felix, "The Relation . . ."

"the next frontier": S. F. Yolles, "The Community Mental Health Center in National Perspective" in H. Grunebaum, ed., *The Practice of Community Mental Health* (Boston: Little, Brown and Co., 1970), p. 793.

"to improve the lives": S. F. Yolles, "Social Policy and the Mentally Ill," *Hospital and Community Psychiatry* 20 (1969): 21–42.

"in addition to treating": S. F. Yolles, "The Role of the Psychologist in Comprehensive Community Mental Health Centers: The National Institute of Mental Health View," *American Psychologist* 21 (1966): 37–41.

"the incidence of mental disorder": Caplan, *Principles*, p. 20.

"The psychiatrist is aware": S. F. Yolles, "Intervention Against Poverty: A Fielder's Choice for the Psychiatrist," *American Journal of Psychiatry* 122 (1965): 324–25.

"have not clearly supported": M. O. Wagenfeld, "The Primary Prevention of Mental Illness: A Sociological Perspective," *Journal of Health and Social Behavior* 13 (1972): 195–203.

"mental health education": B. S. Brown, "Philosophy and Scope of Extended Clinic Activities" in C. F. Mitchell, ed., *Extending Clinic Services into the Community* (Austin: Texas State Dept. of Health, 1961), p. 7.

"a socially defined condition": L. J. Duhl and R. J. Leopold, *Mental Health and Urban Social Policy* (San Francisco: Jossey-Bass, 1968), p. 3.

"Such a role": Ibid., pp. 4 and 14.

"The city . . . is in pain": L. J. Duhl, "The Shame of the Cities," *American Journal of Psychiatry* 124 (1968): 1184–89.

"as an organism": M. Dumont, *The Absurd Healer: Perspectives of a Community Psychiatrist* (New York: Science House, 1968), pp. 52–53.

"study after study": Ibid., p. 26.

"then it will be": Ibid.

"a dollar's worth": Duhl and Leopold, p. 15.

"To operate in the larger": Ibid.

"The community mental health center": S. F. Yolles, "Community Mental Health: Issues and Policies," *American Journal of Psychiatry* 122 (1966): 979–85.

"For some mental health": S. Feldman, "Ideas and Issues in Community Mental Health," *Hospital and Community Psychiatry* 22 (1971): 325–29.

"leading people": Williams and Ozarin, p. xiii.

"primary social systems": Ibid., pp. 511–12.

"who wants to be labeled": Wagenfeld.

"psychological and psychopathological": A. Rogow, *The Psychiatrists* (New York: G. P. Putnam, 1970), p. 147.

"If the race": G. B. Chisholm, "The Reestablishment of Peacetime Society: The Responsibility of Psychiatry," *Psychiatry* 9 (1946): 3–11.

"involved in housing": M. Gorman, "Community Mental Health: The Search for Identity," *Community Mental Health Journal* 6 (1970): 347–56.

"in many mental health association": Ridenour, p. 126.

"a victim of the Babel": H. C. Schulberg and F. Baker, "Varied Attitudes to Community Mental Health," *Archives of General Psychiatry* 17 (1967): 658–63.

"to resolve the underlying": A. F. Panzetta, *Community Mental Health: Myth and Reality* (Philadelphia: Lea and Febiger, 1971), p. 111.

"In planning services": H. Harris, "Planning Community Mental Health Services in an Urban Ghetto," in A. Beigel and A. I. Levenson, eds., *The Community Mental Health Center* (New York: Basic Books, 1972), p. 53.

"A community mental health center": J. R. Ewalt, Foreword in Grunebaum.

"The preventive psychiatrist": Panzetta, *Community Mental Health*, pp. 111 and 114.

"One way this approach": L. Bellak, "Toward Control of Today's Epidemic of Mental Disease," *Medical World News*, Feb. 6, 1970.

"community psychiatry is": L. Bellak, *Community Psychiatry and Community Mental Health* (New York: Grune and Stratton, 1964).

Nixon's former personal physician: C. McCabe, "On Looney Leaders," *San Francisco Chronicle*, Sept. 30, 1969.

"Some of my proposals": Bellak, "Toward Control . . ."

"enormous consequence that has": Panzetta, *Community Mental Health*, p. 124.

"to provide direct": S. Lehman, E. L. Struening, and M. E. Darling, "Lincoln Hospital Community Mental Health Center," in *Community Mental Health Center Data Systems* (Washington: Government Printing Office, 1969), p. 102.

"The conceptual models": S. R. Kaplan and M. Roman, *The Organization and Delivery of Mental Health Services in the Ghetto* (New York: Praeger, 1973), pp. 213–14.

"our centers and the aides": H. Peck, S. Kaplan, and M. Roman, "Prevention, Treatment, and Social Action: A Strategy of Intervention in a Disadvantaged Urban Area," *American Journal of Orthopsychiatry* 36 (1966): 57–69.

"the dispossessed how to use": Duhl and Leopold, p. 17.

"Community Takes Over Control": *New York Times*, March 6, 1969, p. 35.

two immediate precipitating: Chu and Trotter, p. 178.

Chapter 7: Signposts to a Grate Society

a 1971 NIMH survey: "The Discharged Chronic Mental Patient," *Medical World News*, April 12, 1974, pp. 47–58.

Long Beach, New York: Ibid.

In New York City: Ibid.

In San Jose: Ibid.

"nationwide in the period": K. Hopper and J. Hamberg, *The Making of*

America's Homeless: From Skid Row to New Poor (New York: Community Service Society of New York, 1984), p. 34.

One study of homeless women: C. Hartman, "The Housing Part of the Homelessness Problem" in *Homelessness: Critical Issues for Policy and Practice* (Boston: The Boston Foundation, 1987), p. 17.

Data available from the NIMH: "Provisional Data on Federally Funded Community Mental Health Centers," report compiled annually by the Division of Biometry and Epidemiology, National Institute of Mental Health.

"A basic finding": F. Baker, C. D. Isaacs, and H. C. Schulberg, *Study of the Relationship Between Community Mental Health Centers and State Mental Hospitals* (Boston: Socio-Technical Systems Associates, Inc., 1972); NIMH contract no. HSM-42-70-107; p. iii.

"A coordinated system": "Returning the Mentally Disabled to the Community: Government Needs to Do More" (Washington: General Accounting Office, 1977).

"The relationships between": "A Service Delivery Assessment on Community Mental Health Centers." Inspector General Report of the Dept. of Health, Education and Welfare, 1979.

"all identifiable characteristics": "Legislative and Administrative Changes Needed in Community Mental Health Centers Program." Washington: General Accounting Office, 1979.

A breakdown of patients seen at CMHCs in 1975: "Community Mental Health Centers: The Federal Investment" (Washington: Dept. of Health, Education and Welfare, 1978), DHEW publication no. (ADM) 78-677.

"the apparent decline": H. H. Goldman, D. A. Regier, and C. A. Taube, "Community Mental Health Centers and the Treatment of Severe Mental Disorder," *American Journal of Psychiatry* 137 (1980): 83–86.

Approximately half of all CMHCs: Baker *et al.*, p. 56.

"poorly staffed day programs": A. S. Bellack and K. T. Mueser, "A Comprehensive Treatment Program for Schizophrenia and Chronic Mental Illness," *Community Mental Health Journal* 22 (1986): 175–89.

"At one center the caller": "Survey Shows Many CMHCs Lack Emergency Services," *Psychiatric News,* Jan. 21, 1977.

In 1978, the last year: "Provisional Data on Federally Funded Community Mental Health Centers 1978–79." Division of Biometry and Epidemiology, National Institute of Mental Health, 1981.

when 175 CMHC directors: "Returning the Mentally Disabled . . ."

"there is no consistent": C. Windle and D. Scully, "Community Mental Health Centers and the Decreasing Use of State Mental Hospitals," *Community Mental Health Journal* 12 (1976): 239–43.

"the centers investigated": J. Spearly, "Evaluating the Impact of Community Mental Health Centers on Hospital Admissions," *American Journal of Community Psychology* 8 (1980): 229–41.

"statistics showed slightly less": Windle and Scully.

in Sacramento: D. G. Langsley, J. T. Barter, and R. M. Yarvis, "Deinstitutionalization: The Sacramento Story," *Comprehensive Psychiatry* 19 (1978): 479–90.

in Wyoming: J. R. Doidge and C. W. Rodgers, "Is NIMH's Dream Coming True? Wyoming Centers Reduce

State Hospital Admissions," *Community Mental Health Journal* 12 (1976): 399–404.

"William M., age 47": Quotations and facts from B. Eisenhuth, p. 818.

"These results do not support": W. Gronfein, "Incentives and Intentions in Mental Health Policy: A Comparison of the Medicaid and Community Mental Health Programs," *Journal of Health and Social Behavior* 26 (1985): 192–206.

"Clearly, then, Medicaid": Ibid.

In New York State: B. Pepper and H. Ryglewicz, "Testimony for the Neglected: the Mentally Ill in the Post-Deinstitutionalized Age," *American Journal of Orthopsychiatry* 52 (1982): 388–92.

total hospital expenditure in constant dollars: C. A. Taube and S. A. Barrett, eds., *Mental Health, United States 1985* (Rockville, Md.: National Institute of Mental Health, 1985); DHHS Publication No. (ADM) 86-1378; p. 69.

"They won't close Rusk": "Senator Says RSH Is Secure," *The Cherokeen,* Rusk, Texas, Dec. 12, 1985.

"we will reduce the number": Ibid.

"the goal should be nothing": B. J. Ennis, *Prisoners of Psychiatry* (New York: Harcourt Brace Jovanovich, 1972).

"requiring medication for a mental illness": "The Discharged Chronic Mental Patient," *Medical World News,* April 12, 1974.

"They are better off": Ibid.

"If they can't care": Editorial, *San Francisco Chronicle,* Nov. 8, 1987.

Chapter 8: Where Did All the Psychiatrists Go?

"The other point is": House Hearings on the National Neuropsychiatric Institute Act, 1945, p. 77.

Federal NIMH Grants for Training: Data is from the Division of Biometry and Epidemiology, National Institute of Mental Health.

By 1972 it was estimated: W. E. Barton, "Federal Support of Training of Psychiatrists," *Psychiatric Annals* 2 (1972): 42–59.

Number of Trained Mental Health Professionals: The number of psychiatrists in the United States in 1985 is taken from *Physician Characteristics and Distribution in the U.S.* (Chicago: American Medical Association, 1986), p. 19. The numbers of trained psychologists and psychiatric social workers are 1983 figures from D. J. Knesper and D. J. Pagnucco, "Estimated Distribution of Effort by Providers of Mental Health Services to U.S. Adults in 1982 and 1983," *American Journal of Psychiatry* 144 (1987): 883–88.

Data from the National Institute: Between 1948 and 1987 NIMH awarded 22,643 stipends for the training of psychiatrists (Telephone interview with Dr. Abe Abraham, NIMH, November 1987).

"In the past few": Gorman, *Every Other Bed,* pp. 146–47.

By 1965 a survey: *The Nation's Psychiatrists* (Chevy Chase, Md.: National Institute of Mental Health, 1969); PHS publication no. 1885.

Six years later another survey: "Census of U.S. Psychiatric Manpower, 1971" (Washington: American Psychiatric Association), mimeograph.

In the 1965 survey of: *The Nation's Psychiatrists.*

two adjacent buildings: J. Wykert, "World-wide Survey of Psychiatrists Reported at Congress," *Psychiatric News,* Sept. 15, 1971.

"higher income": D. J. Knesper, J. R. C. Wheeler, and D. J. Pagnucco,

"Mental Health Services Providers Distribution Across Counties in the United States," *American Psychologist* 39 (1984): 1424–34.

private psychiatrists in Boston: W. Ryan, *Distress in the City* (Cleveland: Press of Case Western Reserve University, 1969).

"I have no worry at all": J. Ewalt in Senate Hearings on Mental Illness and Retardation, 1963, p. 52.

"The more advanced": Smith and Hobbs.

"But the problem is not": E. F. Torrey, "Psychiatric Training: The SST of American Medicine," *Psychiatric Annals* 2 (1972): 60–72.

"a national disgrace": W. F. Mondale, "The Brain Drain from Developing Countries," *Congressional Record,* Aug. 31, 1966.

By 1970, 34 percent: "Distribution of Foreign-Trained and Domestic Medical School Graduates Among Psychiatric Residents" (Washington: American Psychiatric Association, 1970), mimeograph.

By 1973, there were more: E. F. Torrey and R. L. Taylor, "Cheap Labor from Poor Nations," *American Journal of Psychiatry* 130 (1973): 428–33.

By 1986 in the United States: Figures are from M. A. Eiler and J. D. Loft, *Foreign Medical Graduates* (Chicago: American Medical Association, 1986) and from membership lists of the World Psychiatric Association.

In states like New York: M. T. Malloy, "The Not-Quite Doctors, *The National Observer,* Dec. 2, 1972, p. 1.

7,500 unlicensed: Ibid.

"demonstrated total medical": G. Bliss and P. Zekman, "Orders State Medics Probe," *Chicago Tribune,* March 1, 1972.

Another disturbing aspect: Malloy.

The evidence consisted of: Torrey and Taylor.

"approximately equals the total": K. M. West quoted by E. F. Torrey, "American Medicine is Robbing Poor Nations," *Pharos of Alpha Omega Alpha* 31 (1968): 108–13.

A survey by the NIMH in 1975: J. Jenkins and M. J. Witkin, "Foreign Medical Graduates Employed in State and County Mental Hospitals" (Rockville, Md.: National Institute of Mental Health, 1976), Statistical Note no. 131.

Another NIMH survey in 1980: A. Checker and M. J. Witkin, "A Comparison of U.S. and Foreign Medical Graduates Employed by State and County Mental Hospitals, 1975 and 1980" (Rockville, Md.: National Institute of Mental Health, 1982), Statistical Note no. 161.

1982, when it was found: "State Policies on Hiring FMG's" (Washington: National Association of State Mental Health Program Directors, 1982), mimeograph.

American psychiatrists exited: G. H. Clark and J. V. Vaccaro, "Burnout Among CMHC Psychiatrists and the Struggle to Survive," *Hospital and Community Psychiatry* 38 (1987): 843–47; see also D. G. Langsley and J. T. Barter, "Psychiatric Roles in the Community Mental Health Center," *Hospital and Community Psychiatry* 34 (1983): 729–33.

"perhaps half of all CMHC": "Are Mental Health Centers Doing the Job?" *Medical World News,* April 28, 1972, pp. 13–14.

"supervisory and other mental health": G. B. Leong, "Psychiatrists and Community Mental Health Centers: Can Their Relationship Be Salvaged?" *Hospital and Community Psychiatry* 33 (1982): 309–10.

in 1971 55 percent: W. W. Winslow, "Changing Trends in CMHCs: Keys to Survival in the Eighties," *Hospital and Community Psychiatry* 33 (1982): 273–77.

"Where Have All the Psychiatrists Gone?": R. D. Bass, "Trends Among Core Professionals in Organized Mental Health Settings: Where Have All the Psychiatrists Gone?" (Rockville, Md.: National Institute of Mental Health, 1982), Statistical Note no. 160.

A 1984 survey: R. W. Redick, M. J. Witkin, J. E. Atay, *et al., Speciality Mental Health Organizations, 1983–84* (Rockville, Md.: National Institute of Mental Health, 1986); DHHS Pub. no. (ADM) 86-1490.

"planned to enter public service": W. Coryell, "The Organic-Dynamic Continuum in Psychiatry: Trends in Attitudes Among Third-Year Residents," *American Journal of Psychiatry* 139 (1982): 89–91.

observations of psychology trainees: Data from Schnitzer (1984), Alpert (1984), and Hogarty (1984) cited by S. A. Cole and D. S. Cole, "Professionals Who Work With Families of the Chronic Mentally Ill," in A. B. Hatfield and H. P. Lefley, eds., *Families of the Mentally Ill* (New York: Guilford, 1987), p. 295.

"served jail time": S. Schmidt, "Doctors Rarely Lose Licenses," *Washington Post,* Jan. 10, 1988, p. A-1.

"had taken hallucinogenic": S. Schmidt, "Rehabilitation at Work: Dr. Coombs," *Washington Post,* Jan. 11, 1988, p. A-1.

Chapter 9: The Politics of Perdition: 1968–1988

71 percent of psychiatrists: A. A. Rogow, *The Psychiatrists* (New York: G. P. Putnam's Sons, 1970), p. 126.

In 1968 a poll: Ibid., p. 125.

Almost 2,000 psychiatrists: M. L. Gross, *The Psychological Society* (New York: Random House, 1978), p. 62.

"heralded a new era": Senate Hearings on CMHC Amendments of 1969, p. 13.

"I saw conditions worse": Ibid., p. 53.

"We have seen": Ibid., p. 74.

Senator Yarborough: Ibid., p. 23.

"shaken and reshaped": Ibid., p. 103.

"We are just beginning": Ibid., p. 59.

"Who would have thought": S. F. Yolles, "The Future of Community Psychiatry" in W. E. Barton and C. J. Sanborn, eds., *An Assessment of the Community Mental Health Movement* (Lexington, Mass.: Lexington Books, 1977).

"During the early '70s": S. Feldman, "Promises, Promises on Community Mental Health Services and Training: Ships that Pass in the Night," *Community Mental Health Journal* 14 (1978): 83–91.

"policy of trying": Gorman, "Community Absorption . . ."

A book published in 1971: Panzetta, *Community Mental Health.*

throughout the professional literature: R. Reich and L. Siegel, "Psychiatry Under Siege: The Chronic Mentally Ill Shuffle to Oblivion," *Psychiatric Annals* 3 (1973): 35–55; H. Lamb and V. Goertzel, "Discharged Mental Patients—Are They Really in the Community?" *Archives of General Psychiatry* 24 (1971): 29–34.

a few officials: See, for example, E. F. Torrey, "Psychiatric Training: the SST of American Medicine," *Psychiatric Annals* 2 (1972): 60–71.

"the heart of the problem": E. F. Torrey and R. L. Taylor, "A Minuet of Mutual Deception: NIMH and the

Community Mental Health Centers,"
May 8, 1972, mimeo.

"readily apparent that the community": Hearings to Extend Community
Mental Health Centers Act, Subcommittee on Public Health and Environment, Committee on Interstate and
Foreign Commerce, House of Representatives, Sept. 18, 1972, p. 24.

"program has proven itself": Hearings
on Public Health Service Act Extension, Committee on Labor and Public
Welfare, United States Senate, March
22, 1973, p. 16.

"I have told you": Ibid., p. 41.

"The point you are missing": Ibid., p.
26.

"I disagree so thoroughly": Ibid., p.
39.

"a lot of ordered studies": Ibid., p. 29.

"It appears quite clear": Ibid., p. 41.

"If you wish to": Ibid.

"Mr. Rogers: That was Mr. Ehrlichman": House Hearings on CMHC
Oversight, May 9, 1973, p. 16.

"Somebody in OMB": Ibid., p. 27.

"the community mental health center
has had": Congressional briefing book
for House Hearings on CMHC Oversight, May 9, 1973, prepared by the
Support Branch, NIMH.

"where a center has been": House
Hearings on CMHC Oversight, May 9,
1973, p. 9.

"a special analysis": Interview with
NIMH official, August 1987.

"to review the mental health needs":
The President's Commission on Mental Health (Washington: Government
Printing Office, 1978), p. i.

"Time and again we have": Ibid., p. 5.

"a distressing lack of services": Ibid.,
p. 314.

"It does appear": Ibid., p. 324.

"Over the past years": Ibid., p. 315.

"In community after community":
Ibid., p. 314.

"Ironically although": Ibid., p. 371.

"designate an agency": Ibid., p. 367.

"many mentally disabled": "Summary of a Report—Returning the
Mentally Ill Disabled to the Community: Government Needs to Do
More." Report to the Congress,
Comptroller General of the United
States, General Accounting Office,
Jan. 7, 1977.

"deep-seated attitudes": Task Force
Report summarized in Toward a National Plan for the Chronically Mentally Ill (Washington: Department of
Health and Human Services, 1981);
DHHS Publication No. (ADM) 81-
1077.

"lead even more isolated existences":
M. Greenblatt and E. Glazier, "The
Phasing Out of Mental Hospitals in
the United States," American Journal
of Psychiatry 132 (1975): 135–40.

"When carried out": Reprinted in
Foley and Sharfstein, pp. 163–76.

"The failure to have evaluated": P.
Braun, G. Kochansky, R. Shapiro, et al.
"Overview: Deinstitutionalization of
Psychiatric Patients, A Critical Review of Outcome Studies," American
Journal of Psychiatry 138 (1981): 736–
49.

"for one particularly vulnerable": J. C.
Turner and W. J. Ten Hoor, "The
NIMH Community Support Program:
Pilot Approach to a Needed Social Reform," Schizophrenia Bulletin 4
(1978): 319–44.

"Medical and mental health care":
Ibid.

first president's wife: Foley and Sharfstein, p. 120.

"designed to provide": Toward a National Plan, pp. 1–10.

"these highly dependent": Ibid., p.
ES-1.

"an absolute outrage": "Welfare Cuts
Rescinded for Charity Takers," Wash-

NOTES TO PAGES 198–222

ington Post, Feb. 17, 1987, p. A-8.
"personally see homeless people": M. Oreskes and R. Toner, "The Homeless and the Heart of Poverty and Policy," *New York Times,* Jan. 29, 1989, p. C-5.
"We must care about those": report on President Bush's news conference, *New York Times,* Feb. 10, 1989.

Chapter 10: Cicero's Conclusion
"Now is the time to go back": W. C. Young, "Down the Tube with Outpatient Psychotherapy," *Psychiatric Outpatient Clinics of America Press* 17 (1986): 11–13.
"I also said we needed": D. P. Moynihan, "Help for the Homeless Mentally Ill," *Newsday,* April 7, 1987.
in Michigan where a study: The study, marked "not for quotation or citation," was done in 1985 by the Research and Evaluation Division of the Michigan Department of Mental Health.
" 'dumping' people out of psychiatric": T. D. Watkins, Director of Michigan Department of Mental Health, "Meeting the Needs of Our Homeless," *Detroit News,* Sept. 29, 1987.
"Mental health centers have been": Foley and Sharfstein, p. 103.
"were handcuffed to the armrests": J. Barbanel, "System to Treat Mental Patients Is Overburdened," *New York Times,* Feb. 22, 1988, p. A-1.
in early 1989 New York City officials: J. Barbanel, "New York Planning Transfers of Mental Patients to Shelters," *New York Times,* Feb. 25, 1989, p. A-1.
three homeless individuals: "3 Men Found Dead During the Weekend As Temperatures Dip," *New York Times,* Feb. 9, 1988, p. B-4.
Studies have shown that good services: See B. A. Weisbrod, M. A. Test, and L. I. Stein, "Alternative to Mental Hospi-

tal Treatment: Economic Benefit-Cost Analysis," *Archives of General Psychiatry* 37 (1980): 400–405; G. R. Bond, "An Economic Analysis of Psychosocial Rehabilitation," *Hospital and Community Psychiatry* 35 (1984): 356–62.
"But what kind": Editorial, *New York Times,* April 8, 1975.
Joel Rabinowitz: Quotations and facts from M. Jordan, "After 14 Moves, Alexandria Psychiatric Patient Still Has No Home," *Washington Post,* Jan. 2, 1986, p. C-1.
"involvement in providing housing": *Toward a National Plan,* p. A-2.
By 1980 an assessment: Ibid., p. A-4.
"person has to be either killing": R. Stengel, "At Issue: Freedom for the Irrational," *Time,* Sept. 14, 1987, p. 88.
"[Local] Mental Health Associations should": Task Force Recommendations for Mental Health Associations, National Mental Health Association, Alexandria, Virginia, Feb. 26–27, 1985.

Appendix B
"In an era where funding patterns": "Medicaid Expenditures for Mental Health Services: A Report of a Pilot National Data Base," *State Health Reports on Mental Health, Alcoholism and Drug Abuse* 34 (1987): 6–10. Washington: Intergovernmental Health Policy Project, George Washington University.
Specifically excluded are the 220: R. W. Redick *et al., Specialty Mental Health Organizations, United States, 1983–84,* Mental Health Service Systems Report Series CN no. 11, National Institute of Mental Health. (Washington: Government Printing Office, 1986); DHHS Pub. No. (ADM) 86-1490.

Index